S.C.

1
·G   3

Bizarre Beliefs

BIZARRE BELIEFS

by

SIMON HOGGART

and

MIKE HUTCHINSON

RICHARD COHEN BOOKS ● London

British Library Cataloguing in Publication Data:
A catalogue record for this book is available from the British Library.

ISBN 1 86066 022 3

First published in Great Britain by
Richard Cohen Books
7 Manchester Square
London W1M 5RE

1 3 5 7 9 8 6 4 2

Edited and designed by Delian Bower Publishing and NB Design
Picture Research by Anne-Marie Ehrlich

Cover photographs
Front: L to R, Images Picture Library, Images Picture Library, Mary Evans Picture Library
main picture, Mary Evans Picture Library
Back: L to R, Images Picture Library, Fortean Picture Library, Mary Evans Picture Library

Typeset in ITC Garamond

Printed in Great Britain by Butler & Tanner Ltd., Frome & London

To our parents
Mary and Richard Hoggart
and in memory of Edith and James Hutchinson

Acknowledgements

The authors would like to thank the following for their help and kindness:

Andrew Billen, whose idea for an *Observer* colour supplement article led to the writing of this book; Lewis Jones, for reading the draft and for many helpful suggestions; Dr Graham Wagstaff, for advice on the hypnosis chapter; Faye Burns, who has provided a cuttings' service and much support; James Randi, Paul Kurtz, Barry Karr and Gerald Flemming for backing over many years; Ray Hyman, Joe Nickell, Michael Coleman, Robin Allen, Chris Nash, Martin S Taylor, Ian Rowland, Richard Mather, Roger Busby, and Hilary Evans; Richard Cohen, Delian Bower, designer Nick Buzzard, (who postponed his honeymoon with Sharon to finish the book) Sharon Buzzard, and Anne-Marie Ehrlich.

Contents

Introduction

THE PARANORMAL REALLY DOES seem to be all around us. Hypnotists stalk the TV studios. In Britain, the land is awash with magical systems for winning the lottery. *The Sunday Times*, a newspaper proud of its rigid adherence to the facts, now prints a weekly horoscope, suggesting that heavenly bodies millions of miles away have a direct influence on our lives. Other papers and magazines boast of having 'the most authoritative astrologer', as if astrologers' skills could be measured, like pension fund managers.

Another paper, *The Observer*, implies that there is now so much evidence for telepathy that nobody can seriously doubt its existence. Innumerable television programmes describe paranormal events, and usually leave out evidence which might suggest a normal explanation. Stories about citizens being abducted by space aliens fill the newspapers, and are even taken seriously by at least one Harvard academic.

Nearly any tabloid paper will contain articles about hauntings and clairvoyants. The clock in Big Ben stops, the psychic Uri Geller declares that he did it by willpower and the papers print his claim as if it might be true. Learned 'experts' debate on TV whether crop circles are created by clever hoaxers or by beings from outer space, who, having flown for thousands of years across the galaxies, pause on Earth only to trample a few fields.

Every big bookshop has a 'New Age' section, often as large as the one on 'Current Affairs'. Otherwise sensible scientists and naturalists spend thousands of pounds and years of their lives searching for the Loch Ness Monster.

In short, the mysterious and the unexplained are everywhere. Indeed, few of us have not had some seemingly inexplicable experience at some time or other. The irrational certainty that something is about to happen – and it does! A series of curious happenings in an old house around dusk: the sound of furniture being moved around, or footsteps in an empty room. A visit to a fortune-teller who knew something about one's personal life which she could not possibly have found out by normal means, or who makes a firm prediction which promptly comes true.

And there are real coincidences. For no obvious reason you think of an old school friend you have not seen for years, who phones ten minutes later. In the morning you read about a village which you never knew existed; that afternoon you learn your parents plan to retire there. You dream that someone is ill, and dis-

Preceding page
This crop circle appeared in East Field, Alton Barnes, Wiltshire in early August 1994. It has been attributed to a circle-making team from London allegedly responsible for some of the most spectacular formations in 1994.

cover next day that they've died. You read in the paper about someone whose car broke down, causing them to miss a flight which later crashed.

Given that the world is such a complicated and confusing place, it is small wonder that we often think such events must be explained by the existence of strange, unknown forces. Nearly all of us, even the devout, find it hard to come to terms with the certainty of death; we seize on any shred of evidence which might imply there is an afterlife. Besides, mysteries are exciting and fun. It would be marvellous if there were a monster in Loch Ness; it's fascinating to consider whether space aliens arrived on earth to found ancient civilisations. Hypnotists and mind-readers can be very entertaining.

What we hope to do in this book is to show that there *is* an alternative explanation for almost everything in the paranormal world. Can we prove that strange events are, beyond any shadow of a doubt, the result of natural causes? Only very rarely, because generally you can't prove a negative. For instance, if you were confronted by someone who believed that many toys were made by elves in Santa's workshop, it would be no good telling him about your visit to the Fisher-Price factory. After all, the fact that many toys are made by people doesn't prove that the elves aren't hard at work as well.

Nor are we saying we're sure we're right. What we can do, though, is to offer an alternative explanation – one which may be more probable than the notion of vengeful spirits who smash crockery and throw telephones around the room.

Our favourite tool is Ockam's Razor. William of Ockam, a fourteenth-century English philosopher, said that 'Entities [by which he meant the assumptions used to explain things] should not be multiplied beyond what is needed'.

In other words, if there is an explanation which fits in with our existing knowledge of the world – for example, crop circles *could* be made by hoaxers – we don't need to posit the existence of little green aliens. Likewise spiritualist mediums: why believe they are acting as switchboards for the dear departed, when we know all about the tricks and delusions clairvoyants commonly use (and some can, if they wish, buy instruction books to learn)? Of course, the Razor does not invariably and certainly bring the correct answer. Rain might consist of condensed water vapour, and in most people's view, that is exactly what it always is. But that doesn't prove that it is never angels crying.

Or take the old philosophical conundrum: when you sit in a train and see Paddington Station start to move slowly past the window, how do you *know* that the train has set off, and that Paddington Station itself isn't heading east past your stationary carriage? The answer is that we cannot ever be entirely certain, but William of Ockam's handy device – it ought to come attached to a thinker's version of the Swiss Army knife – can give us a good working assumption that we are on our way towards Reading.

Not that it looks this way to enthusiasts of the paranormal. They argue, with some justice, that if just one single instance of – say – a man bending a key by mental ability alone were to be proved then all our laws of physics and all our understanding of the world would have to be rewritten.

A fortune-teller with tarot cards, a crystal ball, and joss sticks to create the right atmosphere.

Granted; but in that case very special standards of proof would be required, and they never seem to have the time or the patience for that. A single set of statistically significant guesses 'proves' telepathy to them, even if the same results cannot be obtained a second time. When scientists refuse to accept their findings, on the grounds that no one-off experiment can be said to *prove* anything at all, they accuse them of nit-picking.

The scientific approach is to say that, if one discovers by experiment that water boils at 100 °C, it should always boil at 100 °C. If it doesn't, for example on top of Mount Everest, then one works out the effect of air pressure on the boiling point, until finally one can predict the exact boiling temperature every single time under all circumstances.

On the whole, paranormalists can't be bothered with all that. They would rather gaze in awe at a single experiment that seems to confirm their views and not trouble with the wearisome business of trying to do it again. Some even go so far as to say that the wonders of which they speak cannot be proved by normal scientific means. Often these people are the angriest when scientists refuse to accept their findings. They want it both ways; they wish to be somehow 'beyond' dreary, earth-bound science, and yet they crave its imprimateur.

Now, no one in their right mind would argue that scientists don't make mistakes. They can be every bit as pig-headed and jealous as any other group of human beings, and just as blind to data which doesn't confirm what they already believe. But in the end, over the years – sometimes over the centuries – the scientific community tends to get it right. And scientists build on their work.

The experiments which, it is claimed, 'proved' the existence of telepathy led to little more than a few more unpromising experiments and silly newspaper columns. The discovery of electromagnetic waves, on the other hand, brought us radios, and radar, and X-rays and television and satellite phones and Voyager spacecraft and a thousand other useful devices. One result of all that real work is that the dead do walk and talk in my living-room, every time a Marilyn Monroe or Humphrey Bogart film comes on TV – a more impressive feat than any spiritualist has managed.

Followers of the paranormal find that kind of thing simply too boring. If you meet them you'll find them quite easy to wind up with anecdotes. You can excite them by telling them a story like this:

'I was lying in bed at night. Suddenly I heard a noise and I was wide awake.
I could hear my brother, who I knew was in America, asking me to help him.
His voice sounded distant but I was certain it was him. I was so convinced
I had heard him and that he did need my help that I found it hard to get
back to sleep.

'Next morning my mother told me that my brother had fallen seriously
ill in America and desperately needed money for an operation.'

By this time the paranormalist will be in a state of almost uncontrollable excitement, pulling out notebooks, etc. So it will be a difficult moment when you tell him or her that it was the phone which woke you, and your brother was on the line. The extraordinary fact that somebody can stand in a booth in the United States and, within seconds, be talking to someone else 5,000 miles away is of only marginal interest to such people. They prefer to concern themselves with ghostly tambourines, rattling chains and bent cutlery.

People often experience something which seems paranormal and come away saying: 'There must be something in it; I can't think of any explanation.' Well, whatever

"And we've just opened our brand new Gold Futures department."

it was may be inexplicable, at least in the sense that we don't know the answer; but just as often it is all too clear what happened. When the United States Air Force analysed 887 different sightings of Unidentified Flying Objects in 1965 they found explanations for all but 16. That doesn't prove that the remaining 16 were all flying saucers – it merely means that, for the moment, they remain unidentified.

Often our own perceptions mislead us. If someone says to you that a spiritualist 'knew our car was blue, and knew my wife's name was Elizabeth', are you quite sure that the medium said that outright? More often they would produce a whole string of remarks, waiting to see which the client picks up: 'I see a blue car parked in front of your house' and 'I'm hearing the name Elizabeth' would be typical examples. Since blue is believed to be the most popular colour for cars in Britain, and since Elizabeth is a very common name, this could as easily translate to: 'She knew the colour of our next door neighbour's car, and that my goddaughter's name was Elizabeth.' (And how can you be sure that they didn't look you up in the phone book, or drive past your house? It would be a pretty incompetent fake medium who didn't do a bit of research beforehand on a client they were expecting.)

What about the guesses they got wrong, and which you both ignored and forgot? Does a line such as 'I sense a great grief in your childhood' prove she knew your mother died, or merely that she was fishing for the sadness which most of us experience at some time in our youth? In the end, what can look like a miraculous piece of knowledge is actually no more surprising than the fact that there is one pellet in a shotgun cartridge which actually brings down the pheasant.

In the topsy-turvy world of the paranormal, only successes count, and failures somehow disappear from view. The American psychic Jeane Dixon is invariably described as the woman who predicted the assassination of President Kennedy.

Which, up to a point, she did. Back in 1956, she said that she thought the 1960 presidential election would be won by a Democrat, 'who will be assassinated or die in office, though not necessarily in his first term'.

Not a bad guess, one might think, until one studies Mrs Dixon's other prophesies, which include the Russian invasion of Iran in 1953, Red China's use of germ warfare against the US, Russia's success in putting the first man on the moon and a host of other events which never happened. Oh, and she even changed her mind about 'a Democrat', prophesying in 1960 that Richard Nixon would win the election. In the purlieus of the paranormal you can be celebrated for a record which would get a racing tipster sacked in a week.

Often we are deceived by our judgements of other people. The late Doris Stokes, at one time Britain's most celebrated medium, used to cheat in many different ways. One of the simplest was giving back information she had previously obtained from people she knew would be in the audience because she had arranged for them to have free tickets. Nobody ever challenged her by saying: 'Excuse me, I mentioned that my Aunt Doris was poorly when I spoke to your husband, and he offered to send me free tickets to this show. Therefore you are a fraud.' Even when Mrs Stokes made the most howling errors her admirers forgave her – while seizing rapturously on her occasional apparent successes. In any event, few people could believe that such a sweet, sincere old lady could be guilty of cheating. This is one way in which the paranormal gains credence. We are happier to accept the wildest improbabilities – such as that some people can channel messages from the dead to the living – than to contradict own own general experience of life, which tells us that on the whole sweet old ladies don't defraud us.

Corn circles are an amiable hoax which costs nobody anything, except perhaps the dignity of the 'cereologists', some of whom believe the patterns are made by a race of people who live under the Earth's crust. However, in the same way many people, thinking it improbable that pranksters would go to so much trouble, preferred to believe that a supernatural explanation was actually more likely.

Others are more sinister. The so-called Amityville Horror, which was turned into a hugely successful book and a film, was invented wholesale, starting from nothing except that the suburban house concerned had been the scene of a murder. The scam was meant to make money and did. Plenty of people use other mysteries as a means of relieving the gullible of their money. Take those in both America and Britain who promise to give your mind dominance over your body – clearly a very useful knack to have. The proof is that, having handed over a substantial fee, you will – to give one example – be able to walk on a bed of burning embers. As it happens, however, under the right conditions anyone can go fire walking, with no preparation at all. Both of us have done it, and it didn't hurt at all. The paranormal in this case acts as a disguise for elementary physics.

There is also a thriving business in invented mysteries, of which the Bermuda Triangle is probably the best known – though there is also a market for Lost Civilisations, some of which were, we are told, established by aliens in distant millennia. Almost anyone can invent a mystery by ruthlessly selecting only those 'facts' which support their theory, and suppressing anything which doesn't.

We created the fanciful and nonsensical idea of a haunted TV programme – the Benny Hill Show. To write your best selling book about this 'Production of the Damned', you start by finding the names of people who died while watching the show; there must have been hundreds every year. In some cases, the cause of death would have been hard to ascertain for sure; these are your prime examples of the curse at work. Interview people who worked on the programme and ask what strange events happened on set: the occasional accident, or a mysterious figure appearing in a shot. Embroider these incidents, and omit anything which might point to a normal explanation.

Remind readers how the show was cancelled for no apparent reason, and how Hill himself died earlier than one might have expected. The more bits and pieces of 'information' you add, the more people will take up the theme. Other writers will pick up your 'facts' and will begin to swap tales with

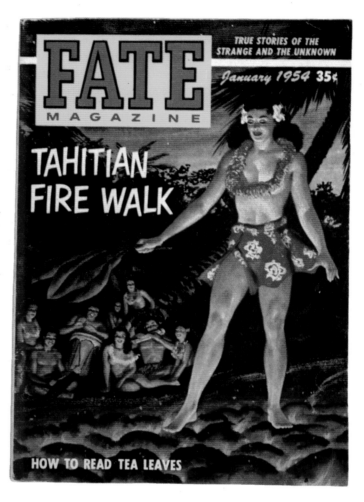

each other, never checking their provenance but adding a little bit more circumstantial detail every time.

The whole farrago is absurd, yet is no more ridiculous than the Bermuda Triangle legend, which was crafted using the same selectivity, exaggeration and remorseless lack of scholarship. We would not be at all surprised to find the spine-tingling story of a haunted TV show appear – as fact – in tabloid newspapers within the next few years; indeed, it has already happened, as we point out in the chapter on the Curse of Tutankhamun(see p191).

Apart from the work of obvious charlatans and those who prey on the foolish, does a belief in paranormal phenomena really matter? Up to a point, it doesn't. Nobody would begrudge anyone taking five minutes to read their newspaper horoscope over a cup of tea. Some people argue that a personal session with an astrologer or a clairvoyant can be more comforting and less expensive than fifty minutes with a psychotherapist; both offer undivided attention, and both suggest that their client's misfortunes and unhappiness are due to circumstances which

Fire walking has captured the imagination of people in many cultures around the world. It seems to be a case of mind over matter. Is there another more simple answer?

are not their fault. Yet we now know that the date and time of many of President Reagan's appointments were determined by the stars, via his wife, who consulted an astrologer in San Francisco. This seems more serious.

So, at another level, is such writing as *The Sun*'s column, 'Sextrology', which offers planetary advice on people's love lives. Here's a woman whose boyfriend is abroad and has only written to her once in nine months. 'Are all male Cancerians like this?' she asks, to be told that they are expert at hiding their feelings. So that's all right, then; it's not that he doesn't actually love her, merely that his stars are not propitious. The same column warns young women that Scorpios are 'superhuman' in bed. The newspaper would probably respond that this is all a 'bit of fun',

A UFO (or UFOs) photographed by schoolboy Stephen Pratt at Conisbrough, South Yorkshire on 28 March 1966. But can such fuzzy photographs ever prove the existence of UFOs?

yet people presumably read it hoping for guidance in their own lives.

For example, anyone who offered a miracle cream which cured cancer would end up in court. Yet Russell Grant, the popular British astrologer, published an astrological guide to health, telling Aries that they may suffer from anaemia and should pack extra vitamins and tonics. Leos were singled out to cut down on rich living which 'could lead to heart and circulatory hassles'. Virgos were accused of hypochondria, implying they should hesitate before seeking medical help. No one would dream of suing Grant for this nonsense.

Similarly, do books which suggest that there is a mysterious force sucking ships and planes into the Bermuda Triangle matter? Or those which say that astronauts from another planet used to visit us here? Or which allege that the runic writings of Nostradamus predict the future? (Notice that his work is always used to predict events, such as the Second World War, which have already taken place. When it comes to an earthquake on a particular day the writings are either silent, mistaken or, most commonly, incomprehensible.)

We believe that this kind of rubbish matters in that it is what TV people call 'noise'; a constant, distracting background interference with the truth. It's not uncommon for even the BBC, and other responsible broadcasting organisations, to adopt quite different standards when it comes to the paranormal. For example, in spring 1995 the BBC's Radio 4 carried an item about the Roswell incident (see our chapter on UFOs p19) in which three people who believed that the debris in Roswell was from an alien spaceship explained why. At the same time the programme ignored the official United States Air Force report which stated in 1994 that the crashed material came from a secret project designed to test the atmosphere for evidence of Soviet nuclear tests.

If someone alleged that a train crash had been caused by UFOs abducting the

driver, the BBC might have run an item – though it would hardly have ignored an official finding that the accident was due to signal failure. So why are the most elementary standards of journalism dropped when it comes to the paranormal? (To be fair, the BBC's 'Today' programme ran an item on the same incident a few weeks later, and gave a full hearing to the sceptical point of view.)

We certainly don't claim to have all the solutions to the myriad mysteries of the paranormal – and they crop up endlessly, like moles in a garden – but we would like to use this book to suggest a few answers.

What we also cannot do is explain away everything that's unexplained in people's lives. It could well be that a clairvoyant told you that you'd marry a man called Arbuthnot Pinkerton (of whom you'd never heard), and two years later you did. Or that truly weird occasion when, on a completely windless day, all the curtains in your bedroom began to billow out. Or the fact that your magazine horoscope promised financial fortune just before your uncle in Australia died leaving you £50,000. There may be explanations for all these things, and they might conceivably be genuine examples of the paranormal. But we can't tell without knowing *all* the facts – some of which your memory might just have decided to skip.

Nor can we possibly deal with *all* the evidence for ghosts, or telepathy, or the Bermuda Triangle, or anything else. There are millions of unexplained mysteries which we cannot cover here. What we can do is suggest a pattern, and a rational alternative. It is up to you to decide which to choose.

UFOs

YES, UFOs DO EXIST. There will always be unidentified flying objects – strange lights in the sky, balloon-shaped objects, inexplicable fires, weird bleepings and whirrings. But it takes quite a stretch of the imagination to believe that if we can't establish what they are, they must be alien spacecraft. Luckily the number of UFOs that cannot be accounted for by perfectly normal explanations is very low. We can even put a fairly precise figure on it as the US Air Force conducted its own investigations into UFOs back in the 1960s in a survey known as Project Blue Book. They analysed 887 sightings and got the following results:

Astronomical events	245 (27.6 per cent)
Aircraft	210 (23.7 per cent)
Satellites	152 (17.1 per cent)
Hoaxes, imagination etc	126 (14.2 per cent)
Insufficient data supplied	85 (9.6 per cent)
Weather balloons	36 (4.1 per cent)
Still being processed	17 (1.9 per cent)
Unidentified	16 (1.8 per cent)

Many UFO fans are tremendously excited by that last figure. But it's actually very small for a survey of this type; all it means is that sixteen events cannot be confidently popped into one of the other categories. If enough facts were available, they too would almost certainly turn out to be astronomical events, aircraft, satellites, and so forth.

But that won't stop the ufologists. For many of them it is axiomatic that governments cover up what's happening. In one of those circular arguments so beloved of paranormal believers, the fact that they won't admit to a cover-up just proves there must be a cover-up.

Like the Loch Ness Monster, UFOs are a fairly recent invention. In the Second World War, pilots occasionally returned to base reporting strange fuzzy lights in the sky. Sometimes these appeared to be flying alongside their planes, keeping pace, and USAF pilots called them 'foo-fighters'. A few even shot at them, thinking they must be enemy aircraft. After the war was over, it emerged that German and Japanese airmen had seen the similar phenomena. No one is yet quite sure what caused it, though ball lightning, static electricity and the planet Venus seen

through mist have all been suggested. As James Randi says drily in his book *Flim-Flam*, 'no doubt part of the explanation lies in the willingness of some pilots to share in the experience by perpetrating small mendacities'.

There was a curious pre-echo of the UFO excitement about a century ago with the Great Airship Craze which gripped the United States in the latter part of 1896 and the start of 1897. At this time the only steerable powered airships – as opposed to free-floating balloons – were in Europe. Yet around 100,000 people said they had sighted airships in American skies. Some even claimed to have spoken to the crew, who turned out to be normal Americans themselves. The more sightings there were, the more newspaper articles appeared, which led to more sightings.

No airship was ever found, which tended to convince some people that there was a government cover-up, possibly of a new secret weapon which was being tested. Even William Randolph Hearst, the model for Citizen Kane, felt it necessary to warn his readers against believing in the 'pure myth' that the sky was filled with airships.

An artist's impression of an airship seen at Oakland, California in November 1896 during the Great Airship Craze. Reproduced in the 'San Francisco Call', 19 November 1896.

Preceding page
A UFO photographed over São Paulo, Brazil on 9 May 1984 by Amilton Vieira who seems to have been the only witness to the event. It is odd that no one else in this city of over ten million people reported seeing this remarkable incident.

The real UFO craze did not begin until after the war. In 1947 a pilot called Kenneth Arnold said he'd seen a formation of saucer-shaped discs, 'flat, like a pie pan', flying above Mount Rainier in Washington State. The phrase 'flying saucer' caught the public's imagination immediately, and there were 122 sightings that year alone. As the excitement mounted – and the paranoia, since this was the height of the Cold War, and who knew what the Soviets might be up to? – the number of sightings grew and grew, climaxing with 1,501 reports in 1952. This was the *annus mirabilis* for flying saucers.

Of course, as the USAF found, it's impossible to offer a routine explanation for all of these sightings. The facts just aren't there all the time. People's memories are, as we know, too often at fault. Some are simple hoaxes, or a blend in which a genuine sighting of something is muddled or enhanced in the telling and re-telling. But ufologists have their own particular favourites, and we'll certainly be accused of ignoring the one which 'proves' the existence of alien space ships and the official government cover-up.

There are also plenty of hoaxes, often involving photographs, which makes them especially exciting. One case in the USA, still hotly disputed, is the Gulf Breeze sighting. A building contractor called Ed Walters, living in Gulf Breeze, Florida, took a number of Polaroid pictures which he sent anonymously to his local paper. When he later came forward to admit having taken the pictures, he was interviewed by investigators from a body called the Mutual UFO Network (MUFON). Their director, Walt Andrus, wrote 'This could develop into one of the most significant cases in UFO history. Even the sceptics may be overwhelmed with incontrovertible evidence.'

Walters received a $200,000 advance for a book called *The Gulf Breeze Sightings*, with talk of another quarter million or so for a television mini-series. But then the bubble burst. A model of a UFO which looked just like the one in the photographs was found under the insulation of a garage in the Walters' old home. It had been made in part out of a house plan which Walters himself had drawn. He said that the plan had been drawn *after* the UFO pictures were taken, but this was disputed by local officials, who said that it was two years older than Walters claimed.

Then a former schoolmate of the Walters' children came forward to say that he had known for two years that the photos were fakes. A local newspaper carried a story that Walters had been known to take double-exposure photographs of 'ghosts' with the same camera used for the UFO pictures. Walters meanwhile continues to say that the pictures are real, and that the model UFO had been put in his old house by debunkers. Why the debunkers should have hidden it in a place where it was only discovered when the new owner decided to modify a cooling system, he does not explain. MUFON still supports him.

Most UFO claims are made by ordinary people who aren't trying to fool anyone. They've seen something they can't explain and want to know what caused it. But even the most sincere and honest observer can have an unreliable memory, as anyone who's ever had to investigate a car accident or a bank robbery will tell you. This is made more difficult by the excitement anyone seeing a UFO is likely to feel. If you really suspect that a flying saucer is about to land in your backyard, you're hardly in the best mood for calmly noting exactly what is going on.

Sometimes UFO reports are given extra credibility because they were made by 'trained observers' such as policemen and pilots. But policemen and pilots are not trained to look for flying saucers or to distinguish between natural objects and alien spacecraft.

Take one of the most celebrated cases in UFO literature, when no fewer than three airplane crews independently reported what looked like a group of UFOs flying in formation. On the afternoon of 5 June 1969, an

An exaggerated version of Kenneth Arnold's UFO sighting of 1947 as seen by a magazine artist in 1948.

Said to have been taken by a pilot over Venezuela in 1963 and accepted as being a solid object because of its shadow, this photograph is one of at least two faked by Inake Oses. It was his way of retaliating against UFO enthusiasts who had ridiculed him for not being a believer.

American Airlines jet was en route from San Diego to Washington DC, flying at around 39,000 feet and approaching St Louis. The weather was clear and there were over two hours of daylight left. The captain had gone to the passenger cabin and his seat was occupied by a senior air traffic controller. Then the co-pilot drew his attention to what he later described as 'a flight of four – whatever they were – flying in formation'. One large UFO was being followed by three smaller ones. They appeared to be on a collision course with the airliner.

The longest of the UFOs seemed to be 18–20 feet long, and 7 or 8 feet high. The controller said that they were the colour of 'burnished aluminium' and seemed to be propelled by some sort of rocket, which emitted a tail of blue-green flame. Moments before the UFOs would have collided with the plane, they appeared to take evasive action. When the co-pilot reported the incident to the nearby St Louis airport tower, and asked if any unidentified targets had been seen on the radar, he was told that only two, not four, had been seen.

Flying eight miles behind and 2,000 feet below the American plane was a United Airlines jet. After monitoring the conversation with the tower, one of the United crew radioed down: 'We see it too.' An Air National Guard jet fighter was flying further behind, at an altitude of 41,000 feet. This pilot had also monitored the radio messages and shortly afterwards reported: 'Damn, they almost got me.' He explained that the UFOs had seemed to head directly towards him, but at the last moment had changed course to climb out of his path. This seemed like clear evidence that, whatever the strange objects were, they had to be under intelligent control.

The case baffled ufologists for three years. Then in 1972 one of them approached Phil Klass, a senior editor of *Aviation Week and Space Technology*, to ask whether he knew of any secret aircraft being developed in the area at the time. Klass said he didn't know of one, and in any case it would be tested in a remote area, not over somewhere as crowded as St Louis.

Klass guessed that it might be a meteor. A phone call to the Smithsonian turned up the fact that a meteor which had broken into pieces had been seen by a large number of people at the right time, and been photographed by some. A confusion over timing (it seemed to have turned up two hours too late) was resolved when it turned out that the crew had left their watches on Pacific time, two hours behind Central. The main problem was that the path of the meteor was fully 125 miles to the *north* of the three planes.

This puzzle was solved in a striking fashion. Another pilot and his friend were standing outside an airport near Cedar Rapids, Iowa, a *further* 100 miles north of the meteor. They reported seeing a group of UFOs to the Federal Aviation Authority at the airport immediately after the sighting. The pilot estimated the 'circular shaped and iridescent' objects to be just 1,000 feet above the ground, basing this figure on the altitude of a light aircraft which was about to land at the airport. The two men also reckoned that the objects had flown directly over the runway. Other ground observers, spread over two States, reckoned that the UFOs were at heights varying between 1,000 and 1,500 feet. Compare this with the flight crews who all said that the UFOs were close to their own altitudes of between 37,000 and 41,000 feet. All were clearly seeing the shattered meteor, its segments burning brightly as it shot through the earth's atmosphere, clearly visible over a diameter of at least 225 miles.

As for the two objects seen on the St Louis radar, the most likely answer is that they were the United Airlines and Air National Guard planes. If not, they could have been other aircraft in the vicinity.

There are two important lessons here: first, even 'trained observers' such as pilots and air traffic controllers can easily be deceived when they see something as rare and unfamiliar as a meteor entry; second, it is almost impossible to judge the height, distance and size of an object when there is nothing to compare it to. When those three factors are unknown it's also impossible to judge speed. (It is hard enough with familiar, expected objects. If you have ever looked out of a plane and seen another flying past you some way below, it's generally impossible to work out whether it's an executive jet quite close, or a 747 miles away. With a massive, speeding ball of flame it's pretty well impossible.)

Phil Klass's expertise in radar and aviation technology has enabled him to solve a number of UFO sightings which have baffled other investigators. The trouble is that any one specialist is unlikely to know all the possible prosaic explanations. Some UFO reports might need detailed knowledge of astronomy, meteorology, aeronautics, psychology, physics and other areas.

Kenneth Arnold's sighting of saucer-shaped discs - 'flat like a pie pan' - might have been a mirage like the one seen here. (Photograph by Donald Menzel in 1967.)

Another of the leading and best respected investigators is Allan Hendry, who became involved through his friendship with an astronomer and UFO buff called J Allen Hynek. In 1976 Hendry started a newsletter for Hynek's Center for UFO Studies. It was a full-time job and allowed him to spend all his working time following up UFO reports. In fifteen months he managed to investigate 1,300 cases.

Some were very simple, others took more time, and a total of 113 (8.6 per cent) stayed unsolved. But Hendry argues that if he had more time and facts he would have solved many of these. 'How can I be sure if my remaining "UFOs" aren't simply IFOs (Identified Flying Objects) misperceived, sincerely, to the point of fantasy?'

When UFO specialist Hilary Evans was shown the photograph above he was told by the photographer that it was taken in 1978 at Coromandel in New Zealand after he had learned about regular sightings of the craft. Evans later discovered that the photograph had already been published in the 'Official UFO Magazine' and taken in March 1968 near Kanab in Utah by Fritz van Nest.

For example, one of the minor cases he investigated was a UFO sighting by a woman who said she had seen something which looked like a star only much brighter. It had taken an hour to descend slowly to the horizon in a series of jerky movements. She had been convinced that she was looking at the illuminated window of a UFO through which she could see the round heads of the occupants inside, heads with silvery-coloured faces.

Hendry pointed out to her that Venus had been setting at exactly the right place at exactly the right time. She didn't accept this explanation, yet the jerky movement and the tiny head-shaped objects visible on the surface of a very bright but very distant object, are highly likely to be common tricks which our eyes play on us all the time.

Many people make similarly honest but mistaken claims. Often we misperceive what's in front of our eyes because it is so unusual. We try to fit everything we see (and hear) into our pre-existing knowledge of the world. When something comes along that we cannot pigeonhole easily, we are tempted to imagine that it must be paranormal, from outside anyone's experience.

Sometimes the explanation for a UFO is simple, straightforward and can be offered almost immediately. Take the great East Coast UFO of August 1986. This is thought to have had the biggest audience of any UFO seen in North America. There were sightings from Georgia and Lousiana in the south, as far west as Texas and Oklahoma, and as far north as Quebec. As the computer engineer and space expert James Oberg reported soon afterwards, descriptions varied enormously. It was seen as a pinpoint, a moving spiral, a glowing cloud and a big ball of fire. In Houston, a Mr Don Stockbauer spoke about an orangish nebulosity surrounded by an irregularly shaped white cloud elongated vertically, with a dim star-like nucleus. Brenda Newton of Rochester said: 'It started to get bigger and it had a tail. By the time we got out of the truck, it had begun to spiral. It lasted for a few minutes, then became like a dim star and floated towards the west.' Wayne Madea, an amateur astronomer in Maine, saw it emit 'a luminous, rapidly expanding, doughnut-like cloud'. At least one radio station in New York State carried live reports of the UFO's passage.

The following afternoon, Oberg was able to report that the UFO had been a rocket, launched by the Japanese from their own territory five hours before. The North American Aerospace Defense Command (NORAD), headquarters in Colorado, provided tracking data which matched perfectly. As Oberg puts it, the UFO was 'stuffed, boxed and buried' in the course of a week.

However, there were several lessons to be learned. One was the way that observers tended to conflate two separate events to create one vast mystery. For instance, one eyewitness, an air traffic controller in Syracuse, New York, said that he had seen three different coloured lights randomly moving and hovering for 45 minutes, after the UFO had passed by. They turned out to be B-52s landing at a nearby Air Force Base. In Clark County, Kentucky, some residents panicked when the UFO's arrival coincided with loud explosions. One local policeman said: 'The people said their homes shook and windows vibrated as if there had been an explosion or an earthquake...they said the whole sky lit up.' That particular mystery was solved when an anonymous caller phoned police to confess to setting of illegal fireworks at the same time as the UFO was visible.

Oberg reported another mystery. UFO groups tended to get different descriptions from the ones reported to the news media. For example, at the National UFO Reporting Center in Seattle, Robert Gribble received more than a hundred calls, consistently describing an object shooting straight up into the sky until it mushroomed at a certain altitude. The Center for UFO Studies in Illinois also received several calls: 'In each case witnesses said an object appeared to have exploded in the sky and then moved into a cloud.' Oberg comments: 'In these accounts, subconscious interpretations by the collectors had evidently coloured the straightforward, pure perceptions, and without other accounts the stories collected by the UFO groups could well have coagulated into a 'true UFO' if the solution had not been published so quickly.'

The most spectacular UFO event in Britain was the celebrated Woodbridge incident. A group of American airmen at the USAF base in Woodbridge, Suffolk, saw an alien spaceship just after Christmas of 1980. They saw it come down over the trees and land in a blaze of light. They tried to approach it, but as they did the UFO moved away, as if it were being controlled by an intelligence. Next day, landing marks were found on the ground, burns were seen on nearby trees and radiation traces were recorded in the area. Some seventeen days later, the event was described in careful detail in a memo by Lt-Col Charles Halt, the deputy base commander. When his account finally emerged in *The News of the World* in October 1983 it certainly seemed to merit the headline: 'UFO Lands In Suffolk. And That's Official.'

Here is most of Colonel Halt's memo, missing out some of the irrelevant detail:

1 Early in the morning (approximately 0300 local time) of 27 Dec, two USAF security police patrolmen saw unusual lights outside the back gate at RAF Woodbridge. Thinking an aircraft might have crashed or been forced down, they asked permission to go outside to investigate...the [by now three] individuals reported seeing a strange glowing object in the forest. The object was described as being metallic in appearance and triangular in shape, approximately 2 to 3 meters across the base and approximately two meters high. It illuminated the entire forest with a white light. The object itself had a pulsing red light on top and a bank(s) of blue lights underneath. The object was hovering on legs. As the patrolmen approached the object, it manoeuvred through the trees and disappeared. At this time the animals on a nearby farm went into a frenzy. The object was briefly sighted approximately an hour later near the back gate.

2 The next day, three depressions 10 inches deep and 7 inches in diameter were found where the object had been sighted on the ground. The following night (29 Dec 80) the area was checked for radiation. Beta/gamma

readings of 0.1 milliroentgens were recorded with peak readings in the three depressions and near the center of the triangle formed by the depressions...

3 Later in the night a red sun-like object was seen through the trees. It moved about and pulsed. At one point it appeared to throw off glowing particles and then broke into five separate white objects and then disappeared. Immediately thereafter three star-like objects were noticed in the sky, two objects to the north and one to the south, all of which were about 10 degrees off the horizon. The objects moved rapidly in sharp, angular movements and displayed red, green and blue lights. The objects to the north appeared to be elliptical through an 8–12 power lens. They then turned to full circles. The objects to the north remained in the sky for an hour or more. The object to the south was visible for two or three hours and beamed down a stream of light from time to time...

No wonder this cool, rational account, by a trained observer, of seemingly inexplicable events caused excitement. A book about the case, *Sky Crash*, called it an event 'unique in the annals of UFO history...the world's first officially observed, and officially confirmed, UFO landing and contact'.

Which merely goes to show that even American Air Force colonels can be deceived. The British writer Ian Ridpath went to the scene to investigate and discovered to his surprise that none of the locals were at all baffled. They knew exactly what the Americans had seen: a lighthouse.

This is at Orford Ness, five miles from the sighting in Rendlesham Forest, in exactly the direction where the airman had seen their UFO. Ridpath went with a BBC camera crew and discovered that the forest is higher than the coastline, making the lights from the lighthouse appear to hover just above the ground. It also looked close, just a few hundred yards away. The TV cameras captured it easily.

A local forester, Vince Thurkettle, told Ridpath that he had been to see the sinister depressions. He found they did not even make a symmetrical triangle and were clearly rabbit diggings, several months old, by now covered with fallen pine needles. The burn marks were axe cuts in the bark of trees indicating they were ready to be felled. Pine resin bubbles into the cut, making it look as if they have been scorched. The radiation readings were insignificant – very much what one would expect from the natural radiation which is always present.

But that still left the puzzle of the bright lights which looked like an air crash over the forest and which caused the patrolmen to go outside. Ridpath solved that when the local police told him that the date on Colonel Halt's memo was mistaken; they had been called to the scene by the USAF on 26 December, not the 27th. Shortly before 3 am on that date an exceptionally brilliant meteor had been seen over southern England and would have looked to someone at the base exactly like a flaming object crashing into the nearby forest.

The star-like objects were almost certainly just stars, and the one to the south was probably Sirius, the brightest star in the sky. The fascination of the story is the way that a series of quite separate items: a meteor, a lighthouse viewed from an unusual angle, stars, and rabbit diggings, were conflated in the minds of highly trained, observant men to create a tremendous mystery where none existed at all.

For ufologists, the greatest jewel in their crown is probably the Roswell Incident. This actually occurred in 1947, the same year that Kenneth Arnold saw

One of a number of photographs taken by Paul Villa in New Mexico. This UFO is said to have been 1 metre in diameter and to have hovered for three minutes. Another was 60 metres in diameter and hovered for ten minutes.

the original flying saucers. The story, as it first entered the annals of UFO lore, was that an alien spacecraft had crashed at Roswell, New Mexico. Not only had debris been recovered, but the bodies of the dead aliens had been taken away and secretly stored at the Wright-Patterson Air Force Base in Ohio.

Roswell simmered away in UFO lore for thirty years. Then in 1980 it was warmed up in a book called *The Roswell Incident*, by William L Moore and Charles Berlitz, the man who originally popularised the Bermuda Triangle. Eleven years later it was brought back to boiling point with the publication of *UFO Crash at Roswell*, by Kevin D Randle and Donald R Schmitt. From that moment on, the Roswell case has been regarded as one of the classic UFO events, perhaps the greatest of them all.

It seems a shame to have to explode the myth. It obviously pleases so many people and has led to so much innocent, if wasted, work. However, myth it most certainly is.

Contemporary reports about the debris described it as 'tinfoil, paper tape, and sticks', which hardly seems the likeliest material for intergalactic space travel. However, this debris was more than it seemed. It was said to have been unbendable, unbreakable, and to have strange hieroglyphics printed on it.

The Roswell story continued to bubble, and in 1993 Congressman Stephen Schiff, who had been contacted by constituents who claimed they were being harassed by government agents to suppress the facts, asked the Defence Secretary

Major Jesse Marcel, a US Army intelligence officer, posed with this wreckage which reporters were told was from a weather balloon which crashed at Roswell, New Mexico in 1947. Thirty-one years later in 1978, Marcel claimed that the crashed debris was different and had been changed for the photograph. This is probably true as it is now known that the actual debris was from a secret balloon project.

to investigate the incident. Finally the Air Force launched its own inquiry, the results of which appeared in September 1994.

The Air Force concluded that the debris was from a balloon which formed part of a once secret military operation, code-named Project Mogul. This used high-altitude balloons which carried instruments designed to detect Soviet nuclear tests.

This finding was then confirmed by one of the scientists who had worked on the project at the time. Charles B Moore said that he had not realised the connection between Roswell and Mogul until 1994, when he was shown a clipping from *The Roswell Daily Record* describing the debris: 'The tinfoil, paper tape and sticks made a bundle 3 feet long and 7 or 8 inches thick' and the rubber strips 'made a bundle about 18 or 20 inches thick', weighing around 5 pounds. Moore recognised the materials which had been used to make the balloon. The mysterious hieroglyphics were just symbols on tape which was used in the manufacture of the balloons by a toy or novelty company.

Naturally, no self-respecting ufologist could accept anything as obviously tainted as an official report. They even claim that film exists showing an autopsy on one of the aliens, attended, some add, by President Harry Truman. As recently as April 1995, the BBC's Radio 4 ran an item in which the alien landing at Roswell was discussed – without reference to the official report. It's as if the BBC were to suggest that a train crash had been caused by the driver being abducted in a flying saucer without mentioning the inquiry finding that it was due to signal failure. But with the paranormal, perfectly responsible broadcasters seem to feel that all the rules can be merrily broken.

And that's the trouble with official reports, always pouring cold water on the most exciting speculation. As the USAF Project Blue Book concluded back in 1965:

1 No unidentified flying object reported, investigated and evaluated by the Air Force has ever given any indication of threat to our national security.

2 There has been no evidence submitted to or discovered by the Air Force that sightings categorized as UNIDENTIFIED represent technological developments or principles beyond the range of present-day scientific knowledge; and

3 There has been no evidence indicating that sightings categorized as UNIDENTIFIED are extraterrestrial vehicles.

And so the cover-up continues, and no doubt will as long as people mistake weather balloons, landing lights, meteors, the planet Venus, and a distant lighthouse as proof that the little green aliens are on their way.

Alien Abductions

AN EERIE 'BLEEP BLEEP BLEEP' SOUNDS as the Mother Ship, ablaze with light, descends to earth in front of a group of awe-struck people. In moments they are whisked on board. Inside, weird creatures, reminiscent of humans but at the same time utterly different, examine their terrified victims, sending probes into their most intimate parts...

How exciting the experience has been for so many people! How convincing their detailed, gripping accounts have been, at least to tabloid editors and TV schedulers! Yet many puzzles remain. Why are so many of these abductions in the United States? Why does space alien interest seem to stop at the Mexican border?

And why are the aliens so different from each other? Some of them have 'cone-shaped eyes and ears', were 5 feet tall and had 'elephant-like grey wrinkled skin'. They floated, according to a 1973 account. In 1975 they were $4\frac{1}{2}$ feet tall, wearing flowing black robes, and had heads which were mushroom-shaped with white eyes and small flat noses, but no visible mouths or ears. Their hands had three webbed fingers and a thumb. In 1976 they were 'like humans, $4\frac{1}{2}$ feet tall, fingers that looked like the edges of birds' wings, complete with feathers'. By 1978 one was described as 'human, except his ears and mouth were slightly smaller, and he was fluorescent-looking...he spoke in English and appeared to have a slight German or Danish accent'.

Some of the details, such as size, are fairly consistent and close to the first – allegedly real – aliens shown on TV. Other points of physiognomy, e.g. webbed versus feathered fingers, are bewilderingly different. How many different planetary civilisations are sending astronauts to kidnap our people? (Possibly this judgement is a trifle harsh. Whitley Strieber, who may well be the most financially successful of all abductees, was grabbed by no fewer than four different types all at once.) And how is it that all these various visitors have created the right technology to glide their spacecraft in under some of the most sophisticated radar defences in the world?

The alien abduction scare is a particularly interesting example of a paranormal hysteria. The usual pattern is there: a single incident is reported, rather later in human history than one might expect for something of universal significance (the Loch Ness Monster in 1933; the first flying saucers in 1947. If so many different types of alien from so many parts of the galaxy are coming here, why did they all start in the 1960s?)

Preceding page
A scene from Hollywood's version of Travis Walton's abduction in the film 'Fire in the Sky' (1993) with D B Sweeney as Walton and Robert Patrick as Mike Rogers.

The original event leads to massive publicity in newspapers and, in later years, on television. After that dozens of people come forward claiming to have had the same experience. Believers in the new phenomenon eagerly embrace each incident. As, one by one, the stories are investigated and discredited, believers fall back on the familiar argument that – however dubious some details are – the sheer weight of numbers is enough to prove their case. Never mind the quality, they say, feel the width.

The saga of alien abductions also has much to teach us about 'hypnotic regression'. Many of the 'victims' found they could not remember all or anything of what had happened to them until they were placed in a hypnotic 'trance' [q.v.]. The fact that the stories they tell are wildly improbable, and in some cases quite impossible, suggests that hypnosis does not dredge the truth out of the subconscious. Indeed, as with 'past-life regression', it appears certain that the hypnotic state, whatever it is, allows people to produce ill-digested fantasy jumbled up with reality, none of which is of any use to someone who wants to find out accurately about past events. This has serious implications for the many cases of 'recovered memories' of abuse. There are people suffering long terms of imprisonment because of unsupported 'memories' called up by hypnosis, and many more families have been destroyed by the corrosive effect of this unproved and unreliable technique.

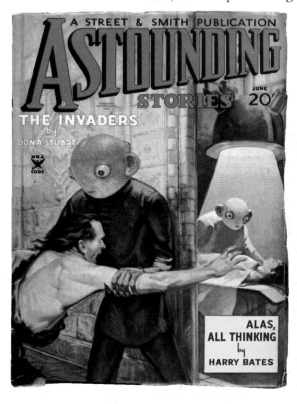

The idea of aliens abducting and examining humans dates back at least to this fantasy magazine published in 1935.

The modern era of alien abductions began in September 1961, when a couple from Portsmouth, New Hampshire, Betty and Barney Hill, were driving home from Montreal in the middle of the night. During the trip they 'sighted' a UFO, which they came to believe was chasing them. More worrying still, they arrived home two hours later than expected, causing them to feel that they had mysteriously 'lost' two hours.

Betty Hill was already a believer in flying saucers. When they saw this particular one, in the White Mountains of New Hampshire, Barney jumped out of the car to get a better view. Worried that they might be kidnapped, he quickly got back in. They left the main highway they'd been driving on, and took a series of more obscure roads – at which point a sceptic might suggest that, if they were following small, unfamiliar country roads in the middle of the night, they were lucky to arrive home only two hours late.

Next day Betty contacted her sister to tell her about their ordeal. She then took out a flying saucer book from the library and read it at one sitting. One week later she wrote to the director of the National Investigative Committee of Aerial

Phenomena (NICAP), describing how they had been followed by a UFO – but not, significantly, saying anything about being abducted.

Some days after that Betty had a frightening dream in which she and her husband had been taken on board a flying saucer. She had the same nightmare for the next four nights as well. At the time she thought it was only a dream, until colleagues suggested that it could be something more. When the NICAP investigators arrived to interview the Hills, she told them about the nightmares. They suggested that, since they had arrived home two hours late, this could be the explanation: they had been kidnapped for two hours, but the experience had been completely blotted out of their minds. Betty's nightmares might be the mind recovering its memories.

We can pause here, because this story is what set the template for subsequent alien abductions. An individual or group are pursued by the alien craft, taken on

Betty and Barney Hill from Portsmouth, New Hampshire were the first abductees thought to have been kidnapped by aliens in 1961. Their story received massive publicity.

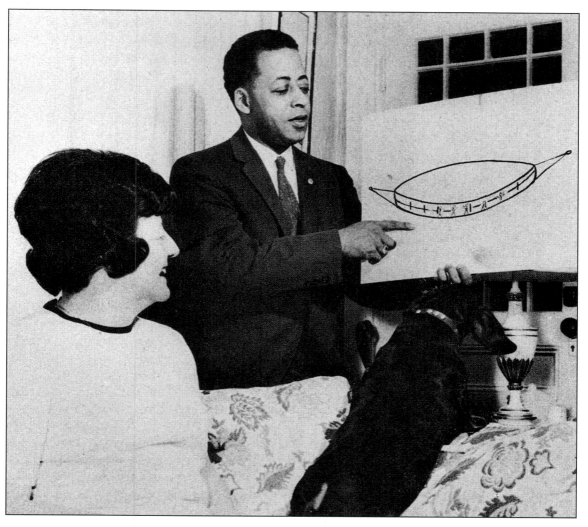

board, examined, and then released. Often all memory of the incident has gone, but can be recovered under hypnosis. The Hills' story matters because it was the first abduction story to be given massive publicity. It was featured in two best-selling issues of *Look* magazine in 1966, and in 1975 was told in a two-hour prime time NBC television programme. This in turn triggered numerous other stories of the same type.

Yet all the tale boiled down to was that a woman who believed in UFOs thought she had seen one. Later she had a recurring dream in which she was taken on board a flying saucer. That is all that happened. Everything else was a combination of supposition, self-delusion, exaggeration and exploitation.

Barney Hill was black and his wife white, which was highly uncommon in the US at that time. He was suffering from ulcers and high blood pressure; a psychiatrist thought this might be connected with feelings of guilt about leaving his black family to marry a white woman. He was sent to see Dr Ben Simon, a Boston psychiatrist who used regressive-hypnosis. Betty accompanied him, and Dr Simon soon realised that she needed treatment too. Both of them spoke to him under hypnosis.

In the later publicity Dr Simon was quoted as saying that the Hills had 'both consciously and under hypnosis told what they believe to be absolute truth'. No doubt they did; but that didn't mean that the doctor thought the event had actually happened. On the contrary, he was convinced that it hadn't. There were too many oddities and contradictions for the tale to be an account of a real event.

For instance, Betty said that the aliens had spoken to them in accented English, while Barney claimed that they had no mouths. They had had no trouble with the zip on Betty's dress, but were baffled by Barney's removable teeth. She explained that people needed false teeth as they grew older, but the spacemen could not comprehend the passage of time. Yet one of them later told her to 'wait a minute'. Telling the doctor how he had stopped the car to look at the UFO, Barney had screamed for help. His wife, by contrast, had shown no fear at all while describing being taken on board the flying saucer where, to quote the UFO investigator Philip Klass who has examined this case with immense care, 'she and Barney might be dissected like frogs' – or from which they might never return.

Most puzzling of all to Dr Simon was the fact that while both man and wife recalled their drive down from Montreal in much the same way, Betty could remember far more of the abduction than Barney. Having firmly concluded that the whole tale was a fantasy, Dr Simon wondered why Barney could recollect any of it. However, he learned that he had frequently heard his wife describing her story and the dream to friends and neighbours, and some of it had clearly stuck in his mind.

It also emerged that they both gave quite different descriptions of the aliens. Betty depicted them as men with bulbous 'Jimmy Durante' noses, dark hair and eyes, looking fairly human. Barney described them as having 'no ears, no hair, no nose, and a cranium shaped like a bullet tilted backwards 45 degrees'. They also had long eyes, which appeared to be wrapped round the side of the head.

A UFO researcher called Martin Kottmeyer, watching a repeat of the TV science fiction show 'The Outer Limits', recognised Barney's description. It looked remarkably like the space aliens who had appeared in an episode first broadcast on 10 February, 1964 – just twelve days before the hypnosis session at which Barney first mentioned the wraparound eyes.

Even some of the dialogue was similar to Barney's recollection. On TV one of the aliens says: '...in all the unities beyond all the universes, all who have eyes have eyes that speak. I learn each word just before I speak it. Your eyes teach me.' In his hypnosis session Barney quoted one of his abductors: 'They won't talk to me. Only the eyes are talking to me. I-I-I-I don't understand that. Oh, the eyes don't have a body. They are just eyes.'

Kottmeyer attributes this to a pseudo-memory as Barney's subconscious was called upon to imagine how an alien might look and talk. We would be inclined to say that this is not probable; if, as seems likely, Barney did watch the

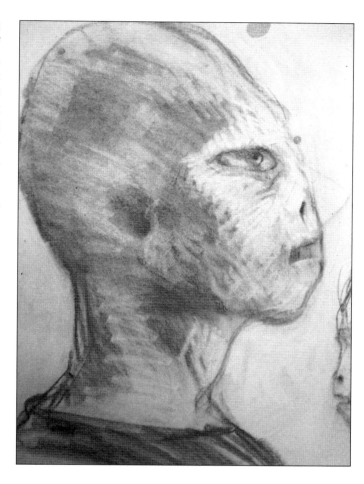

An artist's impression of the alien described by Barney Hill under 'hypnosis'.

programme it must have made a great impact on him and he could hardly have forgotten the alien in less than two weeks. It's more likely that he spent the time convincing himself that that was how aliens did look and speak. During the hypnosis, it would have been his conscious mind telling the story.

What killed off the last chance that there might be something in the Hills' story was work by another UFO investigator, Robert Sheaffer. Under hypnosis, Betty had described watching the almost full moon and

'a star down below the moon, on the lower left side of the moon. And then right after we left Lancaster [New Hampshire], I noticed that there was a star, a bigger star up over this one. And it hadn't been there before. And I showed Barney, and we kept watching it. It seemed to keep getting brighter and bigger looking.'

This was the UFO whose appearance had frightened them so much.

Sheaffer checked how the sky had looked that night, and found that Betty's memory was right. Just below and to the left of the moon, there *was* a star-like

Travis **Walton** (centre) and Mike Rogers (right) in 1985, ten years after they had recounted their experience of alien abduction in a forest in Arizona.

object, the planet Saturn. Just above it was Jupiter, which was exceptionally bright that night. Since she only mentioned a single star, plus the UFO, it seems virtually certain that the alien spacecraft was indeed Jupiter, converted into a flying saucer by a trick of the light, tiredness, and a viewer who already believed that some UFOs were piloted by intelligent beings.

This was glossed over in the accounts of the case, and in the 1975 TV movie – which also misrepresented Dr Simon's sceptical views. In the film, Betty encounters pale, bald aliens, around 4–4½ feet tall, with dark, almond-shaped eyes. This image became the stereotype for many later sightings, though as we have seen above, with highly significant differences.

Barely two weeks after the film was shown, there came an even more celebrated UFO abduction. What made this one especially convincing was that the event had been witnessed by no fewer than six people, and the kidnap was reported to the authorities at the time while the victim was still missing. At first sight it looked as close to proof as anyone could hope for.

Seven young woodcutters had been working in an Arizona forest. A UFO had descended, and 'zapped' one of them, Travis Walton, in a blinding beam of light. The other six had driven off in terror. When they plucked up the courage to return, the UFO, and young Walton, were gone.

Curiously, none of his family seemed particularly disturbed about this incident, or showed any fear about what might be happening to him. This was less surprising than it might seem; a while before, Travis had told his mother that if he ever were abducted by a UFO, she should not worry. Big brother Duane said he had often seen UFOs, and that he and Travis had discussed how they hoped to get on board a flying saucer one day. The whole family were UFO fans. Clearly they were all living on a different planet, though in a metaphorical sense.

The abductee turned up alive and well five days later, with no signs of mental or corporeal suffering. He claimed to have undergone a physical examination by the aliens.

The story was treated sceptically at first, even by ufologists. However, it attracted some credence when it emerged that both Travis and Duane had passed polygraph lie detector tests. The other six woodcutters had also taken similar tests while Travis was missing, to find out whether they had murdered him and hidden his body. Not surprisingly, five of the six passed. (Which makes you wonder what might have happened to the sixth, if Walton hadn't turned up safe.) At this point, the national tabloids began to take an interest.

When Klass investigated, however, he found a number of damaging facts. For one thing, Travis had taken an earlier polygraph test, with a senior and highly experienced operator called Jack McCarthy, who had found his whole story a 'gross deception'. Walton was using crude tricks to fool the machine, such as holding his breath. It emerged that Travis was a frequent practical joker, and had a criminal record for burglary and forgery.

Which left the question of why the other men had gone along with the story. Klass discovered that their crew-chief, Mike Rogers, had fallen a long way behind in his contract with the Forest Service, having bid much too low in order to get the job. He was facing substantial financial penalties, and his only hope lay in the Act of God provision in his contract. Presumably a UFO would count in this way, saving him from further losses. As it is, *The National Enquirer*, the racy supermarket tabloid which printed Travis's story, gave him $5,000 for the most impressive UFO case of the year.

Klass's investigation exposing the stunt was published later, and attracted far less attention than the original claims. But there was a happy ending for Travis Walton. In 1993, Paramount Pictures released a film about his experience, called *Fire In The Sky*, 'based on a true story'. To put it bluntly, there is nothing in the Travis Walton story to suggest anything more than a hoax by a bunch of cunning but not exactly brainy rednecks. No wonder it is so highly regarded by fans of alien abductions.

Between 200 and 300 Americans now claim to have been abducted by UFOs, and it would be tedious to go into all their cases. One of the best known was that of a fantasy writer called Whitley Strieber – the man who found four types of alien at the same time. Strieber's book *Communion* was the account of his 'abduction' in Christmas 1985, as recovered through hypnosis. He was paid $1 million for this, and it was a huge seller.

Strieber had already written two novels about invasions of the earth by alien powers. Perhaps that's why they decided to feel his collar: here was someone who could pass their message on. Or maybe they wanted to stifle his warnings. Who can say? It would be unkind to say too much about Strieber's book or his motives – he variously declares himself to be a mystic, a Zen Buddhist, and 'a worshipper of the earth as a Goddess/Mother.' He has also admitted to inventing many events in his life. Once he claimed in print to have been almost killed by a mad sniper who climbed a tower at the University of Texas in 1966. In *Communion* he admitted that he hadn't even been present; a year later he changed his mind yet again.

UFO fans, of course, will claim that the implosion of each story under the weight of reality proves nothing about the rest. Even suspicious, second-rate cases, have their value. As the ufologist J Allen Hynek (see the chapter on UFOs p19) said of the Walton case: 'It fits a pattern, see. If this were the only case on record then I would have to say, well, I couldn't possibly believe it. But at the Center for UFO Studies now we have some two dozen similar abduction cases currently being studied. Something is going on!'

A scene from the film 'Communion' (1989) based on Whitley Strieber's book. Christopher Walken played the part of Strieber.

Hypnosis is at the heart of a furious argument now raging over repressed memory, often described as false memory. In the United States (of course) 'therapists' using hypnosis have been calling forth from their clients a flood of memories of child abuse, sometimes occurring twenty or thirty years before. The majority of these have been firmly denied by the alleged perpetrators – commonly, though by no means always, the patient's father. In most cases there is not a shred of evidence to back up the claim, and the rest of the family has denied noticing anything wrong at the time. Doctors have said they saw no sign of physical mistreatment. In spite of this, several people have been convicted on the basis of 'recovered memory' alone. So sharp and clear are the memories that they have sometimes even convinced the people accused; they assume that they too must

have blanked out such terrible events for which they have been responsible.

So far the dispute about the existence of false memory has not been settled, though courts are increasingly unwilling to accept it unsupported by any other evidence. There have been several landmark acquittals in both the US and Britain. In 1994, Gary Ramona, an executive with a California wine company, was awarded half a million dollars compensation after his daughter had accused him of rape while undergoing regression therapy.

In 1995, a North Yorkshire shopworker was acquitted of having assaulted his daughter from the age of seven. (She was twenty-two at the time of the trial.) The prosecution had to admit finally that her memories of being assaulted were fictions which had emerged from 'therapy'. Poignantly, the father said of his daughter: 'I love her and desperately want her to get better. What she did is a manifestation of illness, not wickedness.'

The argument is exacerbated by the suspicion among some that the idea of false memory has been seized upon by child molesters as a way of avoiding exposure and punishment. It's often hinted that people who believe in false memory are complacent about child abuse, which is nonsense. Child abuse is a terrible and widespread problem, one which scars many children for the rest of their lives. Often the victims go on to become abusers themselves in a vicious circle which blights several generations. But that does not mean that recovered memories are real; there are too many indications that most are not.

Sigmund Freud believed in repressed memory for some time. He found disturbed young women who, under what was thought to be hypnosis, described suffering incestuous abuse from their fathers. Freud was startled that so many of the most respectable burghers of Vienna were behaving in this appalling fashion. Later he concluded that the women were producing not real memories, but Oedipal fantasies.

That lesson has not been fully learned, and there have been some worrying cases on both sides of the Atlantic. For example, in 1990 a fifty-one-year-old man called George Franklin was convicted of the murder of an eight-year-old girl twenty years before. He had been charged by his daughter who had 'recovered' her memory after her own daughter had looked up at her in a way reminiscent of the victim. The daughter's story changed in many important ways at different times: her sister had been present, or she hadn't; the murder had happened on the way to school in the morning, or on the way back after lunch; later, it had happened in the late afternoon (this last 'memory' coming after she had learned that the victim had not gone missing until after school). In short, she had numerous different recovered memories – yet the jury convicted her father on evidence which would have been laughed out of court if it hadn't had the mystique of recovered memory.

One of the most notorious cases was that of Paul Ingram, a deputy sheriff in the town of Olympia, Washington. He was accused of systematic rape of his own daughters and of allowing his friends to rape his wife. At first he denied doing any of this, though as questioning continued over the months he not only admitted committing many odious acts but recalled them in great detail. Richard Ofshe, a social psychologist from the University of California, and an expert on cults and mind control, was brought in to test him. Ofshe learned that Ingram had been using a meditation technique which involved going into a 'warm white fog'. Ingram, a devout Christian, believed that while he was in this state, God would bring him the truth.

Ofshe suspected that daydreams were being re-coded as memories, and decided to see if he could plant an invented story in Ingram's mind. He told him he knew he had made his sons and daughters have sex with each other in front of him. Ingram first denied this, then under pressure, recalled some details of the events. Next day, having been told to pray in his cell, he remembered more. At the third interview, he produced a three-page report, including the days of the week the incidents had occurred, conversations he had had with the children, and their ages at the time. All this wealth of detail had been conjured up by the implanting of an entirely fictitious event. Ingram was convicted of the other charges, and is now serving a twenty-year sentence. The case made a lengthy series of articles in *The New Yorker* magazine, and helped spark the present debate over false memory.

There are parallels with the abduction scares. Allegations of child abuse reached a climax in the 1980s, reminiscent of the McCarthy era and the Salem Witch Trials. Some of the most spectacular happened without anyone apparently noticing at the time. For instance, in 1988 Margaret Michaels was sentenced to forty-seven years in prison in New Jersey for having, allegedly, sexually assaulted children every day for 150 days in a preschool. She is supposed to have raped them, assaulted them with knives, forks, spoons, Lego® blocks, and even played the piano in the nude. All this went on for all that time without a single teacher, administrator or visitor noticing. She spent six years in jail before all 115 ridiculous counts of sexual and physical ritual abuse were overturned.

The biggest case of all, the McMartin Preschool Trial in California, ended in acquittals. The accused, Ray Buckey and his mother Peggy McMartin, were comparatively fortunate, though they had spent several years in jail. It emerged that some of the children who accused Buckey did not even attend the school when he was there. Some said they had been taken into tunnels under the school for devil worshipping rituals; no tunnels were ever found.

So why do children produce this evidence? As the child-abuse scare mounted (with some justification; in both Britain and the US the amount of real child abuse was for a long time hidden), social workers, investigators and the courts shifted the balance of credibility to the children. They deserved to be believed; why should they make it up? Various techniques were invented to elicit the truth from frightened and unwilling small witnesses.

Many had the opposite effect. As Professor J S Fontaine reported in a 1994 British survey (which also ruled out the existence of organised Satanic ritual abuse): 'In the thirty-eight case studies in detail there are some excellent interviews, but poorly conducted interviews, repeated at short intervals and over many weeks, are not uncommon. Leading questions, refusal to accept a child's denials, pressure by repeating questions and revealing information that other children have supplied, are all to be found in transcripts.'

In many of these cases, as with the alien abductions, it is the recovered memory – through interviews or hypnosis – which has given the story an imprimateur it does not deserve. None of the hundreds of abductees has produced a scrap of evidence beyond their own accounts – not a single alien artifact made of a material hitherto unknown to science, no alien skin or hair, no independent eyewitnesses – nothing at all except their own accounts, which are both similar yet curiously different on important points.

Almost anyone who stood up and told these exotic, unsupported yarns, would be scoffed at by the rest of the world. Yet because they have the cachet of hypnosis, their tales are taken seriously and turned into 'factual' films. The UFO tales are, at least, enjoyable as science fiction. The people in jail because of false charges recovered from deep inside their children's psyches are not quite so diverted.

The Bermuda Triangle

ONE OF THE MAIN SUBDIVISIONS of paranormal folderol is the invented mystery. It's easy to produce your own, and it can pay big money. Start by deciding what your mystery is, drag in every piece of information which seems to support it, ignore anything that doesn't, toss in some more data which does not support your case but can be made to look as if it does, and serve. The wonderful thing is that your readers, far from laughing scornfully, may be deeply impressed and provide you with yet more dubious facts and improbable material to make the mystery even greater.

The classic of the invented mystery genre is the Bermuda Triangle. If this mess of hokum and fraud can be said to have a starting date, it came on 5 December 1945, when five US Navy Avenger aircraft flew into the area and disappeared. The reasons for this tragedy have never been determined with absolute certainty, though there is a perfectly reasonable and non-supernatural explanation which fits all the known facts. That didn't prevent the legend from forming. Soon it began to be said that the planes had been sucked down by some mysterious and terrifying force.

As more accidents, crashes and calamities were added to the brew, the unknown force seemed to become yet more powerful. It not only dragged ships below the waves, but fetched down aircraft with the deadly accuracy of a SAM missile. It could even affect meteorological satellites hundreds of miles above the surface of the earth. Down at sea-level, mariners have experienced weird phenomena: the ocean going deathly quiet, strange lights appearing, fogs descending suddenly, the stars disappearing from view, sea creatures swimming desperately away. Christopher Columbus was even invoked as a victim of the sea's malign powers.

The search for the centre of the wonders soon narrowed to the fateful Triangle itself. This apparently quite arbitrary area has equilateral sides, each around 1,000 miles long, connecting Bermuda in the north-east with Miami in the west and Puerto Rico to the south. Quite why the force should exist inside a triangle, rather than a circle, a square or a shapeless splodge is never explained. Since adherents to the theory merrily add events which have happened hundreds, and sometimes thousands, of miles away from the Triangle, it's all the more difficult to understand.

And of course many unexplained events have occurred in that area – though far fewer than Triangle fans would have us believe. And in many cases, they are

Preceding page
Five Grumman Avenger
bombers similar to those
of Flight 19 which were
lost in the Bermuda
Triangle.

unexplained only because investigators are not 100 per cent certain of what happened; in almost every case, there is a perfectly plausible and usually probable reason for the incident. Triangle buffs find it convenient to ignore these, even when they are blindingly obvious, such as the existence of atrocious weather conditions.

Lovers of the paranormal tend to favour either quality or quantity – or, sometimes, a combination of the two. If their favourite phenomenon is manifested rarely (such as Alien Abductions see p33), then it is said to be of high quality: a single instance is enough to prove the case. If the examples are highly dubious, as with the Triangle, they go for quantity. So many events occurred, there *must* be something in it. And as with our imaginary haunted television show described in the Introduction (see p15), any event will do, however marginal. Take a typical example, the disappearance of a British plane in February 1953. This is said by Triangle lovers to have happened 'north' of the Triangle while the plane was en route to Jamaica, which itself is south of the Triangle. In fact, the plane was flying north-west from the Azores to Newfoundland, *away* from the dreaded area. It was due to fly on to Jamaica, which would have certainly obliged it to cross the Triangle, but hours or even days later. The crash occurred 700 miles north of the fatal zone, and of course 'researchers' make no mention of the weather, which consisted of gales, torrential rain, and winds up to 75 mph. If an event like that can be pressed into service, it's only surprising that Triangle fans haven't included the loss of the *Titanic* and the disappearance of the dinosaurs.

Some perfectly intelligent people are taken in by the nonsense. Take the normally excellent science programme 'Equinox' which is shown on Channel 4 in Britain. In 1992 they produced a programme which featured experts pointing out how ridiculous the Triangle theory was. Astonishingly, they then went on to suggest a 'scientific' explanation for the non-existent mystery.

Among the experts who had good financial reasons for needing to know the truth was Norman Hooke of Lloyd's Marine Information Services:

'Statistically we can tell you that information received from our worldwide sources proves that there are just as many losses in other wide expanses of ocean, such as the Atlantic and the Pacific. If you carefully check to see if the vessels which have been reported sunk in the so-called Bermuda Triangle area have been lost in a mysterious way, you will find this not to be so. We can categorically say that it is usually due to extremely severe weather conditions.'

Or take Lt-Cdr James Howe, of the US Seventh Coast Guard District, which is based in Miami. He encounters vessels in trouble throughout his working life:

'We've seen no evidence whatsoever of these reasonings, the Martians, UFOs or the Atlantises coming up to suck down the boats, or giant turtles, or what have you. What we see are people who get into trouble because of the weather, or because their vessels aren't properly prepared.

'We see some pretty incredible things. Fortunately, there's a lot of good sailors out there, people who really take time to prepare and think about

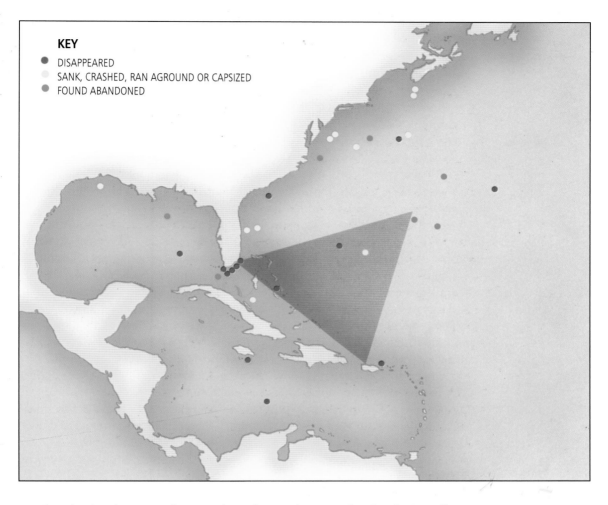

KEY
- DISAPPEARED
- SANK, CRASHED, RAN AGROUND OR CAPSIZED
- FOUND ABANDONED

what they're doing. Unfortunately we have other people who don't really give it a whole lot of thought. They're the ones that will try to navigate from Miami to the Bahamas using nothing more than a road atlas or a table mat that they got at a restaurant, or a place mat, which shows a picture of Miami and a picture of the Bahamas...there are people who have had no training whatsoever. They will go out fishing, not realising that the Gulf Stream is a current that's moving them at about four miles an hour. They get out to the Gulf Stream, they have a problem, and boom, the next thing you know they're off Fort Lauderdale and Cape Canaveral, and then the next stop's Europe.

'We have people tell us that their boat leaked suddenly, they sank and didn't have time to get off a May Day call. Those are things that people explained to us. We've never in my experience heard of anyone that comes back in and says, "Hey, I just ran into a UFO out there and they stole my wife, that's what our problem was." '

A map of the Bermuda Triangle based on one prepared by James Randi for his book 'Flim-Flam!'. It shows where some of the ships and planes that were said to have disappeared in the Triangle area actually met their end.

Thirty-odd years ago, the Triangle began to feature in numerous articles, such as 'The Deadly Bermuda Triangle' by Vincent Gaddis, which appeared in the February 1964 issue of *Argosy*. The following year he expanded the article – now entitled 'The Triangle of Death' – into a chapter of his book *Invisible Horizons*. This provided many of the basic – and most frequently repeated – stories about the Triangle. Gaddis's research was at best sloppy; for example, he reports the 'mysterious' disappearance in 1926 of the freighter *Suduffco*, without mentioning the dreadful weather conditions at the time. Others have lifted the story as fact, also without checking the weather.

In 1969 a writer called John Wallace Spencer wrote a book called *Limbo of the Lost* which also included the *Suduffco* story. But the holy text for Triangle fans is a book by Charles Berlitz entitled *The Bermuda Triangle*. This was published in 1974, and is an excitable account of scores of so-called mysteries. Almost every claim Berlitz makes is misleading, inadequately reported or contains so many important omissions that the story is warped beyond recognition. That didn't stop his book from selling around eighteen million copies worldwide in thirty different languages.

Fortunately for the cause of common sense, another author, Larry Kusche, set about researching Berlitz's claims. By analysing as many as he could, and by going back meticulously over the original sources, he was able to show how there was a perfectly sound explanation for almost every event. Kusche's book, *The Bermuda Triangle Mystery – Solved*, came out six months after the one by Berlitz. Of course, it did not sell anything like as well.

Little wonder. Kusche has no mystery to offer, only prosaic explanations. Take Flight 19, the first great and still the favourite Triangle 'mystery'. On 5 December 1945, five US Navy Avenger torpedo-bombers flew from Fort Lauderdale Naval Air Station in Florida, scheduled for a routine patrol. They were supposed to fly just 160 nautical miles due east, 40 in a northerly direction, then 120 miles back to base, and should have been out for just two hours. All the planes were in good working order and had full tanks of fuel. After an hour and a half, however, they began sending distress messages back to base. They said they couldn't see land. The patrol leader came on the air to say that everything was 'wrong', and that even the ocean looked strange. Two and a quarter hours later he radioed that they did not know where they were – followed by silence.

Immediately, a Martin Mariner flying boat, capable of landing on the roughest seas, took off with a crew of thirteen towards the last position of the five Avengers. As it flew towards the area, it sent back routine radio messages, followed by another ominous silence. The rescue plane had clearly met the same fate as those it was sent to save. Surely this could not be a coincidence.

A massive sea and air search began for the six aircraft and the twenty-seven men who had vanished. No trace was ever found. The planes had vanished into thin air without word or explanation, and no wreckage has been discovered since.

Or so Triangle adherents say. In fact, when Larry Kusche studied the official report by the Navy Board of Investigation which examined the affair, he found that there was a perfectly reasonable explanation, accepted by the Navy and fully documented in the report.

The compass on the leader's plane had failed and the flight was lost. The leader did hand over to another plane, but by then it was too late, since fuel had become too low to allow a return to the base, even if they'd known in which direction it lay from their present position. They were hopelessly lost and had to ditch the planes in seas described as 'rough and unfavourable'. Many of the strange radio transmissions quoted by Berlitz don't appear in the official report, even though the investigators had access to everything, and would hardly have ignored any clue which might help find the solution.

As for the rescue plane, the Martin Mariner was notorious for fuel leaks filling the crew area with fumes. Any spark, or a cigarette, could have caused an explosion, and indeed an explosion in the air was seen from a ship in the area at the right time. The reason why this story has such enduring popularity among Triangle supporters is that most of us find it hard to believe that a group of professional pilots could get lost so easily. Yet their leader was new to Fort Lauderdale and unfamiliar with the area. The other pilots were all in training. None of the planes had clocks, and the leader seems not even to have been wearing a watch; as Kusche points out: 'there is no better way of becoming disoriented than to fly for an unknown amount of time in an unknown direction'. The leader had also refused to use the emergency radio channel. In other words, we are looking at two dreadful and linked tragedies, but caused by separate problems and wholly explicable.

There are innumerable other non-mysteries turned over by Triangle fans. Another favourite is the Japanese ship *Raifuku Maru* which in 1925 disappeared in calm seas while inside the Bermuda Triangle. Except that in reality it had only recently left Boston. It was 700 miles north of Bermuda, and the seas were described as 'mountainous'. The ship's end was watched by crew of the liner *Homeric* who were unable to make a rescue attempt without putting their own ship in hazard.

Once the Triangle was discovered (and this is often true of other paranormal 'mysteries'), its influence can be detected, on a post-dated basis, back into the mists of history. Even the man who may have been the first western navigator to enter the dreaded region, Christopher Columbus, felt its terrifying powers. Berlitz has him reporting 'what appeared to be a fireball which circled his flagship,' to the utter terror of the three ships' crews. At another point, the crew were deeply worried when they saw the ships' compasses 'begin to turn in complete circles'.

That would indeed have been frightening, especially to a crew who had been out of sight of land for an exceptionally long time and had no real confidence that they were going anywhere at all. However, the merest glance at Columbus's log shows that he noticed that the compasses did begin pointing slightly further away from the Pole Star as the ships headed west. Nowhere does Columbus mention them spinning in circles. He simply worked out that compasses must point, not to the Pole Star, as had been assumed, but at something else – what is now known

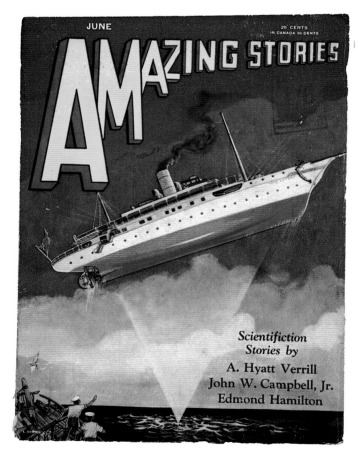

JUNE

AMAZING STORIES

25 CENTS
IN CANADA 30 CENTS

Scientifiction
Stories by
A. Hyatt Verrill
John W. Campbell, Jr.
Edmond Hamilton

This magazine from the 1930s included a fictional story called 'The Non-gravitational Vortex' featuring a sinister zone in the Atlantic Ocean. Maybe this was a forerunner of the Bermuda Triangle?

as magnetic north. As Kusche says, Columbus worked this out for himself 500 years ago, while Berlitz has not apparently grasped it yet.

As for the fireball, Columbus and his crew did spot a large meteorite which fell blazing into the sea, but which did no circling at all. Nor did it cause any recorded consternation.

But Berlitz, who has made a tidy living from the Triangle – it evidently brought no harm to him – has continued to discover newer, up-to-date horrors. In 1980 he produced no fewer than a dozen fresh mysteries, all of which were checked out by another researcher, Michael Dennett. Here's one which is typical: the case in 1978 of a 727 aircraft of National Airlines, which was flying from Miami to Newark, New Jersey. Suddenly, its engines lost power and the plane fell from 33,000 to 25,000 feet with 103 terrified passengers on board. Then, just as mysteriously, the engines started again, and the plane was able to land safely at Jacksonville. 'Despite a gruelling FAA mechanical inspection, officials [found] nothing wrong with the aircraft.'

True as far as it goes. What the account crucially omits, however, was the fact that a month later the flight engineer admitted that he had forgotten to turn on the fuel boost pumps. This caused a vapour lock and cut fuel to the engines. During the re-start procedures the boost pumps were selected, fuel returned to the engines, and the plane was able to land safely.

Here's another incident, which contains in itself most of the exaggerations and basic errors to which Triangularists are prone. In October 1978 a twin-engined fishing boat, *The Buddy Two*, vanished after leaving Miami on a five-hour fishing trip. Six people were on board. Already there's a crucial mistake in the story: they didn't leave from Miami. Instead they set out from Topsail Beach, North Carolina, 600 miles to the north. The boat was on an all-day fishing voyage rather than a five-hour trip, and the weather was poor enough for there to be a small-craft warning in effect when the boat left port. The weather deteriorated in the afternoon. Though it was due back by 5 pm, the coast guard was not alerted to *Buddy Two*'s absence until past 8 pm, long after dark. A search began, and among other debris, an aluminium locker belonging to the boat was found. Plainly it had gone down in rough weather – 300 miles from the Triangle.

Which was also the distance from the Triangle at which two Marine Phantom jets apparently disappeared into thin air while on a routine training flight from South Carolina in January 1980. Triangle aficionados are specially pleased with this one. What they don't trouble to mention is that the two planes were taking part in simulated *night-time* combat manoeuvres. At 7.45 pm that night no fewer than six people reported seeing a brilliant flash over Hilton Head Island, near the estimated position of the planes. This does not, of course, constitute proof of what happened, but it seems somewhat more likely than a paranormal force.

Not that that will discourage true believers. They hold that the force can extend hundreds of miles into the sky. It can even cause US meteorological satellites (Met-Sats), at 900 miles altitude, to malfunction while over the Triangle. Charles Berlitz quoted Wayne Meshejian, a teacher at a college in Virginia, as his authority. When the aeronautical scientist and author Philip Klass checked with the relevant government agencies, he discovered that – as a service to foreign countries and to individuals such as Meshejian – the Met-Sats do transmit simultaneous 'real time' cloud cover information about the areas they are passing over. However, their real job is a global survey, and so at intervals each transmits all its accumulated data to one of two ground stations, one in Alaska and the other on Wallops Island, Virginia.

If the satellite is not going to travel within range of the Alaska station, it has to transmit its data to the one in Virginia. This means it must briefly shut down its real time imagery service – while it is over the Bermuda Triangle. So, once again, no mystery at all.

Of course, there are unexplained accidents, tragedies and weird events at sea and in the air. There always have been, in the Bermuda Triangle as well as the rest of the world. It's in the nature of maritime disasters that the evidence tends to disappear. But none of them add up to anything like a powerful, malign, supernatural force.

But this won't stop people, even the otherwise sensible producers of 'Equinox' who, back in 1992, divided their programme into two: one, a series of experts pointing out that there was no evidence at all for the Bermuda Triangle 'mystery'; and two, the exposition of an 'explanation' involving underwater gas explosions. Which all goes to prove that perfectly intelligent people adore mysteries, and will probably continue to invent them where they don't exist.

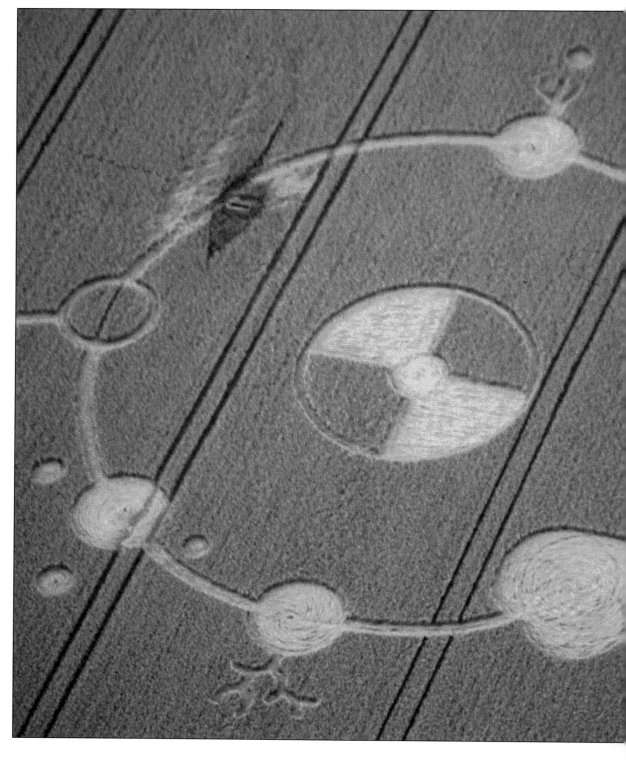

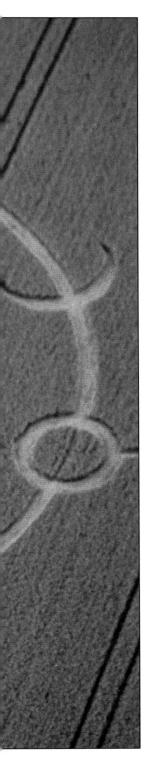

Crop Circles

CROP CIRCLES WERE THE BIGGEST paranormal thrill of the late 1980s and early 1990s. They were called the 'greatest mystery of the twentieth century'. The overwhelming majority seemed to be in England, particularly in the south, and TV crews from all over the world came to film them. Tourists paid farmers thousands of pounds to walk about in their fields and marvel at the patterns and the weird, inexplicable forces which must have created them.

Screeds of newsprint were filled with speculation about their origins. Were they the work of visitors from alien planets who had flown across the galaxies purely in order to trample down our crops (admittedly in attractive and perhaps symbolic designs)? Were they the result of bizarre, hitherto unknown, atmospheric phenomena? Those were just the mainstream suggestions. Some surmised they might be made by a race of semi-human creatures living inside the earth. Others wondered whether they could be caused by teams of hedgehogs, seized by some impulse which made them charge around in unison.

In fact the most obvious explanation is that they were all made by hoaxers. At least we know for certain that a very large number were made by hoaxers, who have not only admitted their deception, but have adequately demonstrated how they did it. As always, we willingly concede that it is possible – just conceivable – that some of the circles were created by little green persons, or 'plasma vortices', or even hedgehogs. We acknowledge that not every single circle has an *auteur* who has claimed the credit. So if anyone wishes to believe in the theory about beings under the earth's crust, they are welcome. The rest of us, however, can be assured that the circles and devices, even the most elaborate, were made by ordinary human beings, dwelling conventionally on the outside of the globe.

Jim Schnabel, one of the most celebrated of all the hoaxers, wrote a book about his experiences, called *Round in Circles*. It contains lyrical passages about the joys of hoaxing:

'I am unable to repress a few frank memories of circles swirled by myself or by my artistic colleagues: for instance, that set of big circles at Lockeridge, formed in lovely, soft, moonlit green barley with a garden roller and some string...the triplet near the town of Wroughton, so well wrought that George Wingfield [a famous student of crop circles, or "cereologist"] said of it, "If this is a hoax, I'll eat my shirt in public"...the 200 foot pictogram that appeared on the crest of a hill above Ogbourne St George, like a message from God, with a single pristine grapeshot for signature...I remember one night, which I swore would be my last, when I made several formations in separate locations, and how...an opaque downpour suddenly burst over my cereal canvas. I can still see myself afterwards, trudging a mile to my car, soaked to the skin, shivering in the pale blue light of dawn, hungry, thirsty, tired, triumphant.'

One of the favourite arguments of the true believers was that the circles could not be the work of hoaxers since there was no possible pleasure or satisfaction in it for them. Even if you ignore the fact that almost anybody, particularly someone with a mischievous cast of mind, would be delighted to see TV crews and hordes of 'experts' gazing in awe at their handiwork and declaring it an insoluble mystery, Mr Schnabel's evident pleasure in a job well done alone suggests that they were completely wrong.

The first crop circles appeared in Britain in the late 1970s. These have since become known as the work of two artists and UFO fans called Doug Bower and Dave Chorley, now pensioners, who were inspired by a 1966 formation in northeast Australia called the 'saucer nest'. They made their first circle at Cheesefoot Head near Winchester. It was 1981 before the press began to notice their work, and after that there was a steady rise in the number of circles appearing in the fields. In 1988 there were more than fifty, but in 1989 there were only thirty (Doug and Dave, as they are usually known, had had a falling out), followed by a remarkable 232 in 1990.

Two simple crop circles at Westbury, Wiltshire in 1988. These were fairly typical of the patterns which occurred before the era of the more complex pattern, or 'pictogram', which started in 1990.

The 'double pictogram' (right) which appeared at Alton Barnes, Wiltshire in July 1990 is perhaps the most celebrated of all crop-circle patterns. It also featured on the record cover of a Led Zeppelin album. The farmer, on whose land it appeared. charged visitors £1 for entry to the field. He is reported to have made £5000 from the sale of souvenirs.

In 1990 a surveillance operation called Operation Blackbird was set-up. This was funded by the BBC and a Japanese television company with electronic equipment said to be worth a million pounds. In a blaze of publicity this pictogram, which was filmed being made at night, was at first declared to be 'a major event' by circle specialist Colin Andrews. Upon close examination later, a zodiac board game and two wooden crosses were found in the pictogram. It is now known that it had been made by George Vernon, also known as 'Merlin'.

The year 1990 was particularly distinguished in cereological circles because it marked the arrival of 'pictograms', elaborate patterns comprising several circles, sometimes concentric, sometimes separate but linked by corridors in the crop, frequently reminiscent of ancient mystical signs and runes. A good example was the elaborate pictogram which appeared at Alton Barnes, Wiltshire; this soon became the most celebrated of all patterns, a sanctum sanctorum for croppies. (Sadly, two years later, the site was despoiled by the irreverent addition of a snail, complete with antennae and a 100-foot shell.)

In 1991 there were 181 patterns. (These figures are approximate; not all the sightings were logged.) That autumn, Doug and Dave admitted their hoaxing in a London newspaper. In spite of that setback another 179 appeared in 1992.

Not that the revelation of the hoaxes stopped true 'croppies' for long. (They hold an annual 'cornference' to debate their findings and, frequently, to row with each other.) As usual, supporters of the paranormal quickly found a way to rationalise everything. The confessions must be fraudulent, they said. Two elderly men could not possibly have created the circles; Doug and Dave then gave some credence to this view by making a mess when they were called upon to demonstrate their skills in a barley field in front of experts. What's more, when they were interviewed separately about everything they had done over the previous fifteen years, there were some contradictions in their stories. It became clear to at least some of the true believers that Doug and Dave were part of a conspiracy by the Establishment to discredit crop circles, and to fool the public into believing that there was no supernatural explanation.

Even when they grudgingly conceded that hoaxers were at work, croppies refused to give up the idea that at least some of the circles must be 'genuine' – that is to say, not made by human beings. Hoaxers were reviled for interfering with their own dispassionate quest for knowledge.

By 1991 cereologists had split, remaining united only by the belief that not all the circles were hoaxes. As the physicist Robin Allen, a member of Wessex Sceptics, keen student of the phenomenon, and adept hoaxer himself puts it:

'The discipline had evolved into two clearly defined camps, which we might label meteorological and mystical...Dr Terence Meaden, independent meteorologist and head of Circles Effect Research (CERES) attributes circles to the activities of a 'plasma vortex', a spinning mass of ionised air akin to ball lightning, envisaged as floating luminously through the summer air and punching its mark in the corn. Science did not recognise such an object, and some of its supposed properties – the ability to carve out circles with such repeated, flawless perfection whatever the weather or crop, for example – quite naturally engendered scepticism in its existence.'

However, Dr Meaden remained convinced. Writing in his own magazine *The Journal of Meteorology*, he said: 'The evidence is now overwhelming in favour of an atmospheric origin for the circles effect, and all open-minded people who have properly studied the evidence accept that this is so.'

Dr Meaden's views were eagerly seized upon by some ufologists, who saw the plasma vortex as an explanation for flying saucer sightings. Meaden himself said that the phenomenon he had discovered also accounted for Stonehenge; ancient man had built the monument on top of a crop circle.

As the number of circles and patterns continued to increase, so did the bodies devoted to their perusal. The Circles Phenomenon Research Group (CPRG) and the Centre for Crop Circle Studies (CCCS) both suggested mystical explanations. It was clear to these bodies that normal conventional science had failed to come up with the answer. Some thought they were dealing with the Earth's own energy, psychically manipulated. Others, quite literally, believed in fairies.

Innumerable tests were carried out by the researchers. Dowsers appeared at the circles and claimed to be able to detect which were genuine. Local people were asked to report on any strange sounds, lights or events which had occurred on the nights the shapes had appeared. That provided plenty of incidents to be tipped into the hopper: dogs acting strangely, cameras which refused to work, strange lights hovering over the fields. An unexplained crackling and hissing noise could be heard near the circles. Some researchers said they had found evidence of radioactivity in the flattened grain, and argued that it should not be fed to people or animals. Some claimed that the patterns represented messages to us written in ancient languages.

Meanwhile, the hoaxers kept up their work. Jim Schnabel, writing in *The Fortean Times*, identified at least seven groups who have been creating designs at one time or another. His article contained some wonderfully embarrassing quotes from cereal fans. One of the most open groups of hoaxers was the inventive Wessex Sceptics, to which Robin Allen belongs. In 1991 they co-operated with Channel 4 television to create a fairly crude set of circles at Clench Common, near Marlborough. Dr Meaden, on seeing the formation, declared it '100 per cent genuine...a textbook example...genuine in every way'. His subsequent exposure on national television infuriated the cereologists. To quote Allen again:

> 'Pat Delgado [of the CPRG] described the hoax as "vicious and unfunny". His colleague in the CPRG, Colin Andrews, minced no words in fulminating his sympathy in the pages of *The Cereologist*. "The cruel and unnecessary methods used by some of the sceptics groups leaves me almost speechless," he wrote. "There is always a place for scepticism...but it is the destructive type, that engenders such tremendously potent negativity and often hatred verging upon evil, that I have no time for." '

As so often when they are caught bang to rights, believers in pseudo-science shift the argument from facts to morals. They may have been proved entirely wrong, but it doesn't count, because the methods used were ungentlemanly.

Other groups identified by Schnabel include the Bill Bailey Gang – three youths from Northamptonshire who created the celebrated Woodford Rings in 1991 by spending six hours on their hands and knees pushing planks. A year later, using the knowledge they'd picked up from watching Doug and Dave's exposition on TV, they produced the 530-foot wide Cranford St Andrews complex, which boasted a five-pointed star, and was deemed by George Wingfield to be 'impressive' and 'wonderful'.

By the end of 1991, things were looking bleak for the true believers. Dr Terence Meaden had more or less retired from the fray, admitting that all the complicated designs were frauds. However, in 1992 more splendid circles began to appear, though by this time even the most ardent believers had begun to concede that many if not most of the patterns were hoaxes. Doug and Dave were busy once more, and created between twenty-five and thirty formations. The Dharmic Wheel at Silbury Hill was thought to be one of the finest patterns ever, a ring dec-

A pictogram which is either real, or it lays to rest the claim by believers that it is impossible for complex designs to be man-made at night. The bicycle was described (sceptically perhaps) by Barbara Davies, editor of 'The Circular' as 'V(ery) efficiently formed'.

orated with mystical symbols, like a gigantic charm bracelet. Unfortunately, this creation was eradicated by an angry farmer with a combine harvester the morning it appeared. It turned out later to have been made by Jim Schnabel.

In July 1992, a competition was held at West Wycombe, Bucks, for hoaxers to produce the best formation, including all the most difficult features spotted in earlier works. A dozen groups entered. Fundamentalist circle watchers said that their work was obviously artificial – an easy allegation to make when they already knew that they were – while sceptics said that the competition had adequately proved that human beings could make even the most elaborate patterns successfully.

Crop Circle maker extraordinaire, Doug Bower (above). The wire ring attached to his cap was used as a sighting device to make straight lines. He is demonstrating (right) how to flatten crops with a 'stalk-stomper'.

So how are crop circles made? Every team has its favourite techniques, and none of them are particularly difficult. Ordinary garden rollers are popular, since they are simple and neat. Doug and Dave, who were highly influential because of appearing on TV, favoured the 'stalk-stomper'. First, one member of the team stands stationary, holding a rope. The second stomper holds the other end of the rope, and walks round in a circle treading the corn down in front of him.

The stalk-stomper is then used to fill in the circle. It's a short plank with a loop of rope attached. A foot is placed on the plank while the rope is held in the hands. The plank is used to push down the corn in front of it, creating good-looking swirl effects. Small 'grapeshot' circles can be made with hands and feet. The United Bureau of Investigation, a large and fluid group of circle-makers centred in Somerset (many of whose members also posed as crop-watchers) favours a small instrument rather like a little surfboard. Pretty well anything which makes the job

fast and easy will do; at the height of circle-mania, devotees were prepared to take even failures, such as stalks still standing amid the flattened corn, as signs of magical properties, arguing that human beings wouldn't have been able to leave the crop looking exactly like that...

A large and elaborate formation can take a great number of hours to achieve, though with practice some groups attained considerable speed. Doug and Dave, for example, have been videoed creating a 60-foot diameter circle in just twelve minutes.

No doubt circles will continue to appear in what is left of the once unspoiled English countryside. No doubt a handful of obsessives will continue to say that at least *some* of these wonderful formations must have been made by unknown physical forces or by extraterrestrial powers. Meanwhile, the only real losers from the carnival which gripped Britain for so many summers are a few gullible believers who were made to look silly on television, and a number of farmers driven to distraction by the hordes of acolytes trampling all over the rest of their crop.

Cold Reading

ANYONE WHO'S EVER EXPRESSED DOUBTS about fortune-tellers, spiritualists, clair- voyants, palm-readers, crystal ball gazers, or wielders of the tarot pack, has heard it many times before: 'Well, I went to a fortune teller and she told me I was going to marry a blond man in the next year. One month later I met Jeremy. How do you account for that?' Or, 'it's all very well you saying there's nothing in it, but he knew that my mother was ill, and he even knew we had a blue car!'

This hardly matters if it's just end-of-the-pier fun, costing little more than a round of drinks. Some 'readers' however demand vast sums – hundreds or even thousands of pounds over time – while claiming to offer useful knowledge of the future, or comforting messages from the dead. An apparently miraculous piece of information, from the name of a loved one to something as banal as the colour of a car, obviously does wonders for the credibility of these people. Toss in human gullibility, grief at bereavement, ignorance of the techniques being used, plus everybody's longing to know what the future holds, and you have fertile ground for tricksters and charlatans. And also some people who, without doubt, gen- uinely believe that they have psychic powers – powers which occasionally need to be helped along by more mundane devices and ruses.

So you're sitting in your tent – or, more likely these days, your well-appointed office – and in walks a customer. You've never met him or her before. You know nothing whatever about him (of course, you might have prudently found as much as you could after he made the appointment, but that might not be necessary). Now you have to persuade this stranger that you know a great deal about him, including many things he doesn't even know himself.

So you use the art of 'cold reading'. Sherlock Holmes was probably the most famous cold reader of them all. He could tell a man's job from his hands, or whether he was married from the state of his clothes. A fine pair of boots, often repaired, told of someone who'd once been well off but had fallen on hard times. His visitors were mightily impressed, and only slightly less impressed when he explained how he'd done it. (Dr Watson expressed himself 'amazed' after Holmes had shown him how he'd followed his train of thought for several minutes.) But then Holmes, unlike his creator Sir Arthur Conan Doyle, was a rigorous believer in the power of rational thought.

All of us do some cold reading every day. A child comes home crying with mud on his shorts; it doesn't take supernatural powers to work out that he's fallen over playing football. A female colleague stops smoking and cuts down on drink, yet seems particularly cheerful; she's startled when you ask her when the baby's due.

Any of us could manage at least some professional cold reading without being trained. Simple common sense and sharp observation are a good start. A woman arrives in a state of some anxiety, nervously twisting her wedding ring. A tentative suggestion: 'your marriage is not always all that you hoped...' is hardly a big risk, and may well translate in her mind as 'he knew that my marriage was in trouble.' Cheap clothes, a plastic handbag and wet shoes which imply walking rather than driving – all these point to money worries. People consult soothsayers for a fairly limited range of reasons – usually love and sex, health, death and money – and it doesn't take much experience to work out which is the most likely.

In 1977 Ray Hyman, a professor of psychology at the University of Oregon, wrote a celebrated article explaining how cold reading works and offering thirteen points of advice. Most seers have used almost all of these devices to at least some extent at some time.

Hyman's first point was that the psychic must act with tremendous confidence. People will accept poor guesses and even outright mistakes if the person they are talking to seems to know what they are up to. The majority of us know next to nothing about clairvoyance, so a veneer of professionalism is easy to acquire.

Secondly, you should keep up to date with all the latest social trends through opinion polls, statistics, surveys and personal observation. A middle-aged woman in tweeds is unlikely to belong to a socialist fringe group, and a youth with tattoos and a nose-ring probably doesn't work as an accountant. There's a good chance an informed guess will be right; and the odd mistake will quickly be forgotten.

Third, be modest. Never claim to be infallible, and never turn a session into a battle of wits. Make it appear that you're happy to offer what you know; if the client doesn't respond to it, that's his problem, not yours. As a result, clients feel grateful for your time and effort, even though they've paid you well for them. The late Doris Stokes (see the chapter on Spiritualism p87) used to begin her performances by explaining how all the voices came in at once, jumbled in her head and difficult to separate. So at the same time she won sympathy for her difficult task, and had a perfect excuse for her many mistakes.

Fourth, a cunning clairvoyant quickly gains the client's co-operation: the reading is presented as a joint effort.

She tells the client that what she says might not be exactly right, or it may need interpretation in terms of his own life. This means that if she's wrong, the client may feel that it's his fault as much as hers. By sleight of mind, so to speak, the client has been saddled with the duty of explaining away the psychic's own errors and obfuscations.

Fifth, Hyman recommends using some kind of gimmick, such as a crystal ball, tarot pack, or palm reading. This adds to the air of professional competence, and also provides valuable thinking time. Another way of buying time to work out what to say next is Hyman's sixth technique: the use of repetition and stock statements which no one will challenge. 'He was a lovely child...' 'She adored having a bit of a laugh.' An extension of this is to repeat back what the client has just told you, as if giving them endorsement from whatever method you are using. 'He was always so generous to his friends', can be met with, 'Yes, I can see that. He hated to say "no" to anybody, didn't he?'

Ray Hyman, a psychologist who is also a highly skilled 'psychic' reader. In a test of his abilities on Canadian radio in 1990 callers into the programme were convinced he was genuine.

You should watch people's body language, which will give vital clues. For instance, you can recite a list of names, while waiting for the sudden excitement which marks one your client recognises. A tiny nod of the head, a widening of the pupils – few of us can avoid giving ourselves away.

Use 'fishing' skills. One method is to phrase every statement in the form of a question. If this gets a positive response, repeat it as an assertion, making it appear that you knew it all along. This has another advantage: you oblige the client to do much of the work for you. 'Was there unhappiness in your childhood?' might bring out anything from a violently abusive parent to a grazed knee. Either will work. As you pick up and digest the information the client feeds you, more and more of your questions are on the money.

Be a good listener. The ideal is to have the client do the work. It is astonishing how often people will talk for three-quarters of the session, while you nod sagely and make the occasional interjection. They will then declare that you did almost all the talking. Be dramatic, says Hyman, ham it up. Paint pictures: 'I can see your sister walking in. She looks deeply unhappy...' The client will usually fill in the gaps and supply an event – from a broken doll to 'he knew my sister's fiancé had died!'

Always make out you know more than you do – that you're holding something back. This creates an air of mystery, but also builds confidence. Use a single piece of information which you have managed to obtain, which the client believes you cannot possibly have found except through occult powers. That gives you authority, and encourages the client to open up. After all, he or she thinks, the more I tell this person, the more she'll tell me in return. Which is precisely how it works.

Hyman says that a good clairvoyant uses shameless flattery. We all love being flattered, no matter how much we deny it. It shouldn't be too specific. 'You are a wonderful pianist' would probably be wrong, unless you know already. But 'you are generous, even when you suspect others may be taking advantage of you' can be agreed to by almost anyone. Even if the flattery is blatantly wrong, it indicates a rapport between reader and client. A line like: 'you are deeply suspicious of flattery' is doubly flattering.

Always remember the Barnum effect, which we describe in the chapter on Astrology(see p100). People are more alike than dissimilar. An enormous number of statements could apply to almost anybody's self-image ('you are a spontaneous sort of person, though sometimes this makes you hot-tempered'). Uttered with professional aplomb, directed personally at the client, this kind of general nonsense can seem astonishingly perceptive.

Finally, a successful cold reader remembers always to tell the client what he wants to hear. No clairvoyant kept a business going with remarks like: 'your late husband is undergoing all the tortures of the damned', or 'the smallpox which carried off your child has left her face scarred for eternity.' People generally go to a psychic because they need reassurance, or confirmation that what they want to do is the right thing. A crucial part of the job is detecting what that is. Yes, you should leave your unfaithful partner. Or, alternatively, forgive him. Yes, your beloved mother is happy in her eternal rest. The more you get that right, the more the client will be inclined to take everything else on trust.

Because cold reading is so effective (see the chapter on Spiritualism p87 for examples of how Doris Stokes contrived to make people think she was bringing them messages from the dead), magicians who specialise in mind reading are learning how to do it. It looks terrific and it pays extremely well. They can buy books with titles such as *Cashing in on the Psychic*, *The Tarot Reader's Notebook*, *Psychometry from A to Z* and *Money-Making Cold Reading*. But the art can be learned without training. You can start with very general readings, then as you gain experience and confidence, become more specific. It seems to 'work'. Your clients are impressed by how much you seem to know, and how confident your predictions are. You are also impressed by yourself. Perhaps, you might think, you really are receiving messages from the beyond, or from some other paranormal force. Your increased confidence communicates itself. The reading becomes a brief *folie à deux* in which each side confirms the other in their delusion.

Ray Hyman earned money as a teenager doing magic and palmistry. When he started, he didn't believe in palmistry, but after a few years he did become a firm believer; he had convinced himself by his own insights. Then someone told him to tell people the opposite of what he read in their hands. To his surprise, even horror, the readings were as successful as ever.

The human mind loves to make connections. When someone is being given a reading they are positively striving to make them. After all, they usually have something invested in the reading: money, a yearning to know the future, or both. They need it to succeed, and without being prompted, work with the clairvoyant to make it succeed. So they forgive ambiguities, meaningless remarks and downright errors, while seizing on anything which looks like a 'hit'.

A typical statement used by cold readers is: 'I see a blue car outside your house.' Since blue is a favourite, perhaps the most popular of all colours for cars, most people know someone who has a blue car, even if they themselves don't. A friend or relation who often visits. A neighbour, who sometimes parks outside the house. The existence of any blue car looks fairly impressive, but if the client's car is blue, then it's a sizeable hit.

And it only requires one impressive hit to hook some clients for life – which is why a few people go from psychic to psychic searching for one who is 'good', i.e. the one who scored the lucky hit or, for all we know, cheated. Your local clairvoyant, specialising in one-on-one sessions, works in much the same way, using cold reading possibly laced with a little research. Any half-competent psychic, who knows how word of mouth can build a terrific reputation, will keep a close eye on the local paper for news of deaths, divorces and bankruptcies. Really useful information can be found there, and if you make it sound as if you're hearing it from the ether, or the tarot pack, or the crystal ball, no one's going to remember that it once appeared in a classified ad.

If a woman makes an appointment, her husband's name can be often found in the phone book. Or if it's an initial, guess 'John – no, James; I am hearing the letter J...' Initials are big in psychic reading, since they can refer to a christian name, surname or nickname. Easy to drive past the house and notice details there ('she actually knew that we have yellow curtains, and said that Ron liked them'). A good private detective can

The cover of a French manual on palm reading published about the turn of the century.

Visiting a fortune-teller. From Pierce Egan's 'Life in London' published in 1820.

obtain much of your life in twenty-four hours; a clairvoyant has it easier, needing only one or two 'hits' which will give a lustre to the whole session.

Good luck plays a part, too. Richard Mather, a magician and cold reader from Scotland who claims no special powers whatever, told us about a performance he gave to a group of around eighteen people at a Women's Institute. Mather used a system, by which he takes the letters in a subject's name, and associates it with some vague word which they can tailor to fit their own lives. For instance, 'A' means absence, 'B' means beautiful surroundings, and so on.

He gave a reading for an eighty-year-old woman whose name included an N – 'new beginnings' according to the system. He thought that since she was so old there was no point in mentioning marriage, but then decided to stick to his system anyway. It turned out that she *was* engaged, and the audience was duly astounded. Mather knows it was nothing but good luck.

Psychics often have a wide social acquaintanceship, and this can help. Suppose they meet someone who has an unusual name which they encountered before in a different part of the country. If they mention a connection with that area, and there isn't one, no harm is done. If there is, it's a valuable hit. If the subject doesn't learn about the connection until after the reading, the effect is magnified. 'He told me that I had a family link with Northumberland, which I didn't find out about until months later. How do you explain that?'

There's the small world factor. Mike Hutchinson recently met a woman who said she was going out with a man who lived in East London and had once been a monk. Hutchinson was able to describe the man's flat in detail, to his girl-friend's astonishment. But it just happened that he knew another woman who had sold her East London flat to a monk, and it turned out to be the same man. As we show in the chapter on Coincidence(see p210), the world is full of such links – there are coincidences everywhere – and they appear very impressive if they are said to have supernatural causes.

Take the advice of Ian Rowland, a self-styled 'psychic conman' who makes no pretence to having paranormal powers, but who makes money performing his act at parties and functions. He uses most of the techniques described above to give amazingly convincing readings to complete strangers. (He insists on telling them afterwards that his abilities have absolutely nothing to do with the paranormal. Often he finds that his subjects refuse to believe him, so convinced are they by his knowledge and insights.)

"Well, first of all, you're very naive."

In 1993 he demonstrated his skills to *New Woman* magazine. They had a young woman on their staff called Rebecca listen to his spiel, without telling her that he was a deliberate fraud. She was mightily impressed. He seemed to know about her boyfriend's car crash. He knew that she had had a talent which she had failed to pursue – it turned out to be dancing – and he knew that she had had a relationship 'where distance was a problem'. She nodded eagerly at all these, and said afterwards that it was the knowledge of the accident which had really convinced her. She said: 'There were too many significant things he picked up for it to be just guessing. He's definitely got some sort of power.'

Rowland explained to the magazine how he had done it.

'I do exactly the same reading for everyone's past and it always works well. That's how personalised it is. It gives me time to build up a rapport. [The accident was] what we call a stereotype statement and it's almost as useful as a Barnum statement...there are lots of events which are generally true for people at particular ages. Most people have something to do with an accident at school. That is the way readings work. You give people something general enough and they fit their own experience onto it.

'If I was doing a reading for a woman in her thirties I would make stereotype statements about babies and get at least one hit...If you do readings you get to know these things. The business about Rebecca having a talent she hasn't followed up is another stereotype, and so is having a relationship where it's difficult to keep in touch.'

Ian Rowland (who describes himself as a psillusionist - a term he coined). His ability to give accurate readings has been confirmed by subjects writing in magazines and interviewed on television.

He did make one glaring 'miss' with Rebecca, asking her about problems with her ankle around Christmas or New Year. She looked blank, even when he extended it to:

'something you were wearing or a problem with your shoe'.

'That's what I call a Push statement. You make a very definite statement which quite likely gets a negative response, but then you pursue it, changing the details. If it's not the ankle, it's below the knee, if it's not Christmas it's winter, if it's not at a party, it's on the way to one...sooner or later something fits and then the person is amazed.'

In the Channel 4 programme 'The Talking Show', Rowland gave the *same* reading to two women who were unaware of the other's participation. The first was asked if she was surprised by how much he knew about her. She replied:

'Yes, because there were quite a lot of specifics there. The creative side, which people wouldn't necessarily know, and being quite close to my brother. I was quite impressed. Having done it once, I think, gosh, maybe there are people out there that know things that you may – or may not – want them to.'

The second woman said:

'It was a bit amazing. There were a few things that he picked up on that kind of threw me. The fact that I had been sick and my parents were worried about me. He probably could have guessed that. Also about the sports, or the activities that they thought I could have done well at, which was gymnastics. I was quite good at gymnastics when I was younger and I did want to pursue it, but didn't. I felt unnerved.'

Rowland scored an even more startling success when he gave two identical astrological readings for different people on the BBC TV programme 'The Heart of the Matter'. They gave him 95 and 99 per cent scores for accuracy.

If people like Rowland and Mather can do so well without employing any mysterious powers, it seems extremely likely that psychics are using the same techniques – consciously or unconsciously. They are not necessarily crooks. As we've seen, many have come to believe in their own paranormal abilities. Perhaps they have had the occasional dream which has come true, the odd accurate foreboding that something is about to happen, even a disposition to daydream – all these can easily convince some people that they are receiving messages from another place. When this genuine conviction is blended with an instinctive feeling for people and their lives, and is strengthened by years of experience, it can create seers who positively radiate self-confidence and authority.

Psychics and fortune-tellers certainly bring comfort and reassurance to many people. One can argue that they provide a valuable public service. Yet it seems a shame that this requires such deception, even when it is largely self-deception. Telling clients that their problems are much the same as other people's is less exciting but more realistic than telling them that their fate is determined in advance, or can be predicted through the fall of the cards. In the same way, a £20 Rolex might make its buyer feel cheerful and contented, but it is nevertheless a sham.

Nostradamus and the Art of Prophecy

IT'S ONE OF THOSE JOKEY PRESS CLIPPINGS which are often read out on the radio: 'This month's meeting of the East Wittering Clairvoyants' Association has been cancelled due to unforseen circumstances.' It always gets a laugh.

But then what self-respecting clairvoyant, psychic or spiritualist bothered with something so mundane (or so precise) as a cancelled meeting? Did any seer or sayer of sooth ever gaze into their crystal ball and announce: 'I see the Church Hall has been double booked by us and the Scouts next Friday'? They are concerned with far grander events than that. Events so grand, sometimes so far into the future, that it may even be impossible to detect when they have actually happened. As for precision, that can be left to share tipsters and the like. Your average clairvoyant and prophet is more concerned with vagueness and innuendo, covering all his predictions in a miasma of ambiguity. This means that anyone can interpret the prophecies almost any way they like, including the psychic himself, who can, according to circumstances, pick and choose among all the interpretations he himself has placed on offer. Even Julius Caesar wasn't told of what he should beware on the Ides of March.

You and I might think that this was suspicious. We might imagine that, since all logic tells us it's impossible to know what the future holds, obscure and confusing prophecies are designed to cover up for the prophet's ignorance. We might even imagine that they are necessary since someone predicting public, rather than private, events in the future cannot make use of the cold reading techniques described in the previous chapter. But, as we know, things are rarely that simple in the world of the paranormal.

Take the most famous of all ancient prognosticators, the Oracle at Delphi. Any modern soothsayer would have been proud of that operation. The prophecies were credited to Apollo, which meant that if clients disagreed they were taking on a god, rather than a mere human. There was much exciting 'business', involving the submission of written questions to a priestess, who chewed bay leaves, drank a mysterious liquor, sat on a tripod and went into a trance. Best of all, the answers were almost impossible to interpret. But because there was so much authoritative mumbo-jumbo, suppliants who mistook or were baffled by the Oracle's message had only themselves to blame! It was a perfect arrangement, for the Oracle at least, if for no one else.

One victim was King Croesus of Lydia, who sent to the Oracle to ask whether he ought to cross the River Halys to fight against the Persians. The Oracle, working through the male priests who obligingly translated her words into hexameters, replied:

When Croesus shall o'er Halys River go
He will a mighty kingdom overthrow.

Confident of victory, Croesus joined battle and had his head chopped off. The Oracle had wisely declined to say which mighty kingdom would be overthrown. With hindsight, Croesus should have gone elsewhere – there are records of more than 250 oracles operating in Greece at the same time.

But small drawbacks, such as your clients getting entirely the wrong end of the stick, can usually be presented as yet further proof of your powers. Take Nostradamus, one of the greatest charlatans in the long history of charlatanry. One of his first modern admirers was the British writer Charles Ward, who 100 years ago wrote this magnificent example of tortured logic:

'It is obvious that many prophecies are of such a nature as that, if they were clearly understood previous to the event, they would prevent their own fulfilment, and so cease to have been prophecies. What they foretold would never have occurred.'

Suppose a racing tipster were to try this technique. He would eschew the names of horses and even the races they were in, but would speak in riddles instead. 'I see storm clouds, I sense many people shouting and crying, the long quest will reach its destiny...' After a horse called *Tempest-Tost* won the 3.40 at Chepstow, he could explain that the riddle clearly predicted the name, but that if he'd actually given it, the odds would have collapsed so that the nag wouldn't have been worth backing.

Such a tipster would be out of business in two days. Yet precisely this kind of nonsense is practised all the time by clairvoyants, who are paid vast sums of money, courted on television, and generally taken seriously.

Take Mystic Meg, who appears during the televising of Britain's National Lottery draw every week, making her possibly the best-known psychic in Europe, if not the world. She never, ever, says anything useful such as: 'The jackpot will be won tonight by Mrs Ivy Partridge of Lytham St Annes.' Instead she says, and these are real examples:

'An Aquarius with a Gemini who works in the world of flowers is going to win a big prize... A family who have just been reunited will celebrate a big win too... The house has a number 5, the town starts with the letter C or D and the name Green or the colour is very important to this person.'

'She's been right so often!' coo the presenters. For example:
'One of this week's winners is wearing blue and has dark hair, spiked with gray. The letters G and K are very important to him and he is holding a red pen.'

This was reported as a hit by a winning syndicate member the following week. He claimed that Mystic Meg had said: "A chap named John, watching the television, dressed in blue, with a red pen." I had a red pencil. That was the only difference.' His recollection was greatly mistaken. Also he had no grey hairs, though perhaps they had been grey before they fell out.

We wrote to the National Lottery Live programme asking for details of the predictions, the dates, the criteria for deciding which predictions were successes, and – since the lottery promoters are not allowed to divulge information about the winners – how did they know? A brisk letter from the producer said: 'We're in the middle of a series at the moment and that represents a lot of work for the programme staff. We can't do it at the moment.'

The fact is that dozens, if not hundreds, of people win a substantial prize in the lottery every week. Given that Mystic Meg's predictions are so scattered and so vague, it would be hard for her to avoid getting numerous 'hits'. Once she said that a winner would from among 'those who work in the dental world'. This was claimed as a hit because one of a winning syndicate *used* to work at a dentist's. No doubt the producers think it's all a bit of harmless fun, yet it seems a shame that the once rigidly honest BBC should connive at misleading their viewers even in this mild way. It suggests a contempt for their audience.

Debunking clairvoyants is a little like shooting fish in a barrel; it's too easy to be truly satisfying. Yet nothing seems to stop them swimming back. Take the British seer Kim Tracey, who crops up time and again in various newspapers and magazines. In January 1982, writing in *The Sunday People*, she scored a hit when she said that Prince Charles and Princess Diana's first child would be a boy. A fifty-fifty guess, to be sure, but incontrovertibly correct. Sadly, she was also quoted as saying that the royal couple would go on to have two girls. They would become King and Queen within five years when Elizabeth II would be forced to abdicate through ill-health. Kim went on to provide vivid descriptions of the personalities of the two young princesses who, it now seems sadly inevitable, will never be born.

The Sunday People did not go on to recall some of her other predictions, which appeared in *Women's Realm* back in February 1978. This was before Prince Charles married. She predicted that his bride would be 'of royal blood'. Oh, well. Can't win them all. However, Ms Tracey seems to find it hard to win any. Among her other misses were that the winner of the Grand National that year would be an Irish horse whose name included the word 'boy'. The winner was called Lucius, and the only 'boy', Churchtown Boy fell at the fifteenth fence. Germany would win the Eurovision Song Contest. Israel did; Germany came fifth. Her most spectacular mistake was saying that there would be an election in late 1978. James Callaghan would win, and Margaret Thatcher would resign as Conservative leader – an error on a world scale.

Even her non-mistakes (you could hardly call them hits) were noticeably vague. Paul Newman would act in his last film. One day no doubt he will. Carlo Ponti, aged 65, would be taken ill. A member of the Beatles would 'make the news'. John Lennon was murdered two years later, but Ms Tracey was not exactly specific about the event. It seems almost cruel to continue, and there are no newspaper psychics with any better records, only isolated 'hits' of which they tirelessly remind us.

James Randi, the Canadian magician and sceptic, has produced a convenient set of six rules for successful prophecy – or at least six rules for making a living and a reputation from prophecy, which is a rather different thing.

His first tip is to employ the scatter-gun effect. The more predictions you make, the more hits you'll have. For instance, over a four-year period the predictions of all the major psychics working for the American tabloid paper *The National Enquirer* were analysed. Of a total of 364 predictions, just four were right. You can bet that all four went down on the seers' CVs as proof of their amazing success.

Secondly, be vague. Notice how often clairvoyants and their ilk say 'I see...', 'I sense...' or 'I feel...' This has two advantages: it allows followers to interpret the world in any way which fits the message, and it makes it unlikely that the prophet can be deemed mis-

taken. An astrologer might say that the stars are telling of 'great upheavals in Europe', which could conveniently mean anything from Bosnia to the European Union. Or football fans on the rampage.

Thirdly, the successful prognosticator uses bags of metaphor and symbols. Animals are a good bet. 'I sense the eagle is falling from the sky' could mean almost anything: political problems in the US, strikes in Germany, or any other country which has an eagle as its symbol. Or a commercial undertaking which has the word 'eagle' in its name. Months later, when an avalanche kills three skiers on Eagle Mountain, you modestly say you suppose that's what must have been foretold by the prediction.

Fourth, you should cover yourself both ways. If at all possible, make quite contrary predictions at different times. Insist that Party A will win an election, then find another place to declare that you see Party B coming up on the rails. After the result is out, loudly repeat the correct guess. You will have the tape or the clipping to prove you were right.

James Randi, formerly an escapologist who has escaped from twenty-eight jails and is now the world's foremost sceptical investigator of paranormal claims.

One classic instance of this is Jeane Dixon, who is much the most famous 'prophet' in America. Mrs Dixon's greatest claim to fame is that she correctly forecast the assassination of President Kennedy. Since this was probably the most single shocking event in the United States since Pearl Harbor, the prediction has given Mrs Dixon a degree of charisma which none in her trade can match. That particular success is attached to her name as securely as a world record to a sporting hero.

And indeed here is her prediction, from the 13 May 1956 edition of *Parade* magazine: 'As to the 1960 election, Mrs Dixon thinks it will be dominated by labour and won by a Democrat. But he will be assassinated or die in office, though not necessarily in his first term.'

Pretty good. Okay, the election wasn't dominated by the labour unions, and she wasn't clear how the unfortunate winner would die, or when. At the time she was speaking, the odds against a twentieth-century president dying in office were seven to three against. And five of the last seven elections had been won by Democrats. Still, there it was. She had said that a Democratic president was likely to be elected and to die in office.

However in January 1960, ten months before the vote, Mrs Dixon changed her mind. She actually declared that John F Kennedy would *not* be elected, adding: 'the symbol of the presidency is directly over the head of Vice-President Nixon.'

Richard Nixon did almost pull it off in 1960, and went on to be elected president in 1968. So perhaps she was right. On the other hand the symbol of the presidency was directly over Nixon's head every time he stood in public with his boss, President Eisenhower. So even being wrong at the time, she was right in a more diffuse sense.

However, she has been spectacularly wrong on innumerable other occasions. Russia did not move into Iran in 1953. Eisenhower did not appoint the disgraced general Douglas MacArthur to 'an exceedingly important post'. China did not start a world war over Quemoy and Matsu, nor did it use germ warfare against the United States. She predicted that the Soviet Union would be the first country to put a man on the moon, and that the Vietnam War would be over in ninety days.

But imagine the excitement if any of those guesses had come true! As it is nothing seems to stand in the way of favoured prophets when the gullible get to work. In at least one book, *They Foresaw the Future*, by Justine Glass, it's said that Mrs Dixon predicted Kennedy's name, the date that he was shot – in the head – and even part of Lee Harvey Oswald's name. What an easy job a psychic has, where an admirer can take a vague guess, later rescinded, and turn it into an inexplicably accurate prediction.

Randi's fifth suggestion is, like Mrs Dixon, Nostradamus, the Delphic Oracle and many others, to credit God for all your skills (while keeping the money for yourself). This makes you appear becomingly modest, keeps the Inquisition at bay, and means that anyone who scoffs at you is taking issue with the Creator.

Sixth, ignore your mistakes. Keep going. Your admirers will only recall your successes, not least because you go on about them so much.

Seventh, when it comes to predicting public or world events, the rule we mentioned in the chapter on Cold Readings (see p63) – give people what they want to hear – is modified. In their personal lives, they want the good news. But in the wider world, they want earthquakes, assassinations, floods and general mayhem.

One celebrated astrologer who nearly came to a sticky end by muddling up these rules was Dr John Dee (1527-1608) who was a personal advisor to Queen Elizabeth I. In the early 1550s he predicted for the then Princess Elizabeth a very long life and a high position in the Kingdom (though the latter guess was perhaps not that astonishing, given that she was the daughter of Henry VIII). Dr Dee also predicted that Elizabeth's half-sister, better known as Bloody Mary, would have an unhappy and childless marriage. This was precisely what she did not want to hear, and had the prophet locked up in the Tower, whence he was rescued only after Mary's premature death.

Of course many disasters are entirely predictable. There are innumerable floods around the world every year, major earthquakes occur two or three times a week, and 'world leaders' are bumped off pretty frequently. Wars have an unpleasant habit of breaking out too. So predict a generous handful each year, and you are bound to get something right. How about 'a terrible earthquake will bring death and devastation to a prosperous region'? You can point to almost any tremor you like.

Dr John Dee, (1527-1608) astrologer and personal advisor to Queen Elizabeth I.

If you strike lucky, with a Los Angeles, San Francisco or Kobe earthquake then it won't be hard to claim that your vague prediction was in fact amazingly precise. *That* was the earthquake you meant, naturally. And there are many professional people who do make a genuine effort to predict the future by using the lessons of the past. Racing and share tipsters, and weather forecasters are among them. There's no reason why you shouldn't do the same. Foresee a spot of turmoil in Africa and you won't go far wrong. 'Scandal will end the career of a prominent politician' would work with almost 100 per cent success every year in virtually any country.

The seer who has stood the test of time better than any other is Michel de Notredame, a doctor and astrologer who lived in Provence during the sixteenth-century. It would be pleasing to report that Nostradamus, to give the Latin form of his name which is generally used, has lasted so well because his prophecies have proved uncannily accurate. Sadly, they have proved entirely useless.

When it comes to divining the future, the works of Nostradamus are no more and no less accurate than tea-leaves or freckle patterns. What they do have is the two great virtues of all similar twaddle: bulk and ambiguity. There is so much material that it would be almost impossible not to find something which fits some event, at some point in history. And the prophecies are written in such a weird, elliptical and disjointed fashion that almost any interpretation can be made.

Given that Nostradamus's admirers feel free to re-invent history to fit their case, to treat any individual word as it stands, or as an anagram, or as a metaphor, or as a foreign translation – whatever suits them best – it's no wonder that the Nostradamus industry has so much material to draw upon. This they have glee-fully done. Books claiming to be the 'true' interpretation of his works still pour from the presses, all of them 'proving' how he predicted events such as the rise and fall of Hitler, the death of kings and even the coming of AIDS.

Sadly, while it has been easy to interpret the seer's work in the light of events which have already happened, it has been more difficult to predict events in our future. For instance, in 1988 there was a panic in Los Angeles because, it was claimed, Nostradamus had predicted an earthquake there. This mass lunacy, which led to thousands of people fleeing the city, followed a TV re-run of a silly film about the prophet called *The Man Who Saw Tomorrow*. Various astrologers and interpreters of his work claimed that different quatrains proved that the quake would take place on one day or another in early May. The hysteria became so great that the Griffith Observatory had to set up a 'Nostradamus hotline' to assure anxious callers that there was no earth-quake due, and indeed none occurred, that week at any rate. Since it required the most agonising intellectual contortions to extract any such prophecy from the works, one could even twist the argument round and suggest that Nostradamus had scored by *not* predicting an earthquake on that occasion.

Nostradamus was born in St Rémy-de-Provence, in 1503, some twenty-two years after Provence had become part of the France. Thanks to an edict by Louis XI, his father was obliged to convert from Judaism to Christianity. This was the religion which his son Michel proclaimed vigorously all his life, no doubt to help avoid charges of heresy and witchcraft.

Nostradamus studied 'astronomy' at school (the topic included astrology, which was not then seen as a separate field). He read medicine at university and set up as a doctor.

By 1550, he had started to put his knowledge of astrology to use (his ancestors were descended from the Jewish tribe of Issacher, whose members were thought to have prophetic powers) and he published the first in an annual series of almanacs containing predictions for the future. Then in 1555 (the same year, oddly enough, that he published a recipe book for jams and sauces) he produced the first of his *Centuries*. These each consisted of 100 rhyming quatrains. Within the next thirteen years he produced a total of ten *Centuries*, though not all are complete, and different quatrains appear in different editions. However, between 940 and 948 of these mystical four-line verses are attributed to him.

The *Centuries* were an instant *succès d'estime*. Nostradamus was invited to Paris to meet the Queen of France, Catherine de Médicis. He was warmly received by the Court and returned south loaded with money and jobs. He set about expanding the *Centuries* and basking in the fame, influence and good fortune which his royal patronage had brought him.

Catherine de Médicis (1519-89) and the 'magic mirror of Nostradamus'. Nostradamus is in a circle using the tools of his trade (a skull, a cat, incense and a wand) to summon future kings of France for Catherine to see in the mirror.

What the quatrains have in common is almost total obscurity, which of course has made them a perfect hunting ground for his aficionados. If Nostradamus had ever said anything specific, such as 'In the New World a President named John will be assassinated in 1963', we could have hailed a remarkable prophet. But then he would have run the risk that 99 per cent of his other prophecies would have been wrong. However, the vagueness, as at Delphi, makes almost any interpretation possible. It's the fact that Nostradamus did not directly prophecy anything whatever which has kept his reputation intact.

Take for example what may be the most famous of all the quatrains, number 51 from Century 2. It is usually held by Nostradamians to refer to the Great Fire of London in 1666, more than a century later.

Le sang du iuste à Londres fera faulte,
Bruslés par fouldres de vint trois les six,
La dame antique cherra de place haute,
De mesme secte plusieurs seront occis.

Translation of such verse, with its archaic Provencal French and deliberate ambiguity is hard, but here's one attempt:

The blood of the just in London will be lacking,
Burnt by thunderbolts of twenty-three the six(es),
The ancient woman shall fall from high place,
Of the same sect many shall be slain.

Well, 'twenty-three the six(es)' could mean three twenties (sixty), with a six tacked on to either end, giving us the date 1666, or at least 666. If we are generous, that is. Nostradamians say that line one describes the events of that year when many good people died in London as a result of the fire. They suggest that 'La dame antique' means 'The Old Lady', and is a contemporary name for the old St Paul's Cathedral, which was burned down in the Fire. So were many other churches, a fact which explains line four.

All well and good, except that 'fouldres' means not fire, but thunderbolts. There is no evidence at all that St Paul's was ever called The Old Lady, and in any case, 'antique' at that time meant dotty rather than ancient, as in the English 'antic', which occurs later in Shakespeare. And, we may be sure, not only 'just' people died in the fire. In other words, as a prediction of the Great Fire the quatrain is a mess, offering only the name of London and a trio of numbers which can conceivably be twisted to mean 1666.

In fact, Randi discovered in the Bibliothèque Nationale in Paris a fascinating set of letters which reveal that Nostradamus – whose father was forced to convert from Judaism – had private leanings towards the Protestant cause, something which he kept carefully hidden from his royal clients. He even wrote to customers in Germany praising Lutheranism. After his death, his son César went to a lot of trouble to keep these letters secret, since such heresy was a capital offence for the living, and would certainly have severely damaged Michel's reputation.

Michel de Nostradame
(1503-66) - known as Nostradamus. Prophet or charlatan? From the frontispiece of one of his early publications.

As it had been in England, under the reign of Bloody Mary. At the start of 1555, the year Nostradamus was writing, she had begun the ethnic cleansing of Protestants. These were burned at the stake, in groups of six, with the 'merciful' addition of bags of gunpowder tied to them, in order to make their end sudden – and necessarily somewhat spectacular. Queen Mary, meanwhile, was known to be going insane, wandering half-naked round her palace. She died three years later.

As Randi points out, the quatrain, instead of being a barely credible prediction of events 111 years in the future, looks much more like a cunning commentary on current events. The blood of the 'just' or 'innocent' will be a 'fault' in London (the French 'faulte' could mean either). The thunderbolts refers to the explosion of the gunpowder, 'les six' to the groups of victims. As for 'vint trois', we don't know – possibly it refers to a report of the number of burnings. 'The mad lady will fall' fits the Queen more closely than the cathedral, and sounds like a hopeful prediction from a dissenter. 'Many more of the same sect will be slain', is a less optimistic, but highly realistic guess.

Many other quatrains have been tortured to make them 'reveal' events in the future. In several cases, however, they make more sense when applied to events in the past. Take number 49 in Century 5.

Gand & Bruceles macheront contre Anuers.
Senat de Londres mettront à mort leur roy
Le sel & vin luy seront à l'enuers,
Pour eux auoir le regne en desarroy.

This translates roughly as:
Ghent and Brussels will march against Antwerp.
The senate of London will put to death their king
The salt and wine will be against him,
To have them the realm in disarray.

And indeed, less than 100 years after those lines were written, King Charles I was executed by order of the English Parliament in London. Many fans regard that as an incredible success by their hero, though for him to hazard, once in around 3,800 lines, that an English king might be executed by order of some deliberative body, was hardly astonishing. All European kings and queens, including many English ones, were in permanent danger of their lives.

Even if we accept this as a good guess, though, it leaves us bewildered about the other lines. The Nostradamus author Everett Bleiler suggests that they might fit English history of the previous century. While Henry VI was dying in the Tower – without parliament objecting – the English were being driven out of Guienne, a region from which salt and wine were imported. The loss of this territory did create upheaval in Britain. As for line 1, the best anyone has come up with is that in the mid-1550s there was a great deal of diplomatic activity in those three cities, chiefly concerned with unpopular Spanish rule there. A loose fit? Most certainly, but it all matches the quatrain far better than the death of Charles I. One can only imagine the Nostradamians' excitement if he had got remotely as close to a prophecy of the future!

One could examine almost all the quatrains to analyse what prominent admirers of the sage have discovered. The outpouring of nonsense on this topic never seems to end. But we'll look at one more example, number 74 from Century 6:

La deschassee au regne tournera,
Ses ennemis trouués des coniurés:
Plus que iamais son temps triomphera,
Trois & septante à mor trop asseurés.

She who was chased out shall return to the kingdom,
Her enemies found to be conspirators:
More than ever her time will triumph,
Three and seventy to death much assured.

This may very well be a reference to Elizabeth I, the arch-enemy of Nostradamus's patron Henry II. Indeed some admirers, such as Charles Ward, deftly removed the word 'and' from the last line, so that what is clearly a poetic way of saying '73' becomes 'Three and seventy', permitting them to claim that the three refers to the year 1603, the year Elizabeth died, and seventy, her age at the time.

However, Nostradamus's celebrated obscurity has made it possible for his most devoted believers to find almost any meaning. Among other explanations offered, and no doubt devoutly believed by some, are that the quatrain predicts the return of Charles II to the English throne, the arrival of Communism in France, Nazis returning to Germany after the Second World War, an allegorical reference to the French Revolution, and a prediction that for seventy-three years communism will rule in Russia – an amazing hit, since one-party rule ended in the USSR in 1990, exactly seventy-three years after the October Revolution.

Which means that one half of one line, surrounded by apparently meaningless gibberish, might conceivably refer to some event in the future. As a prophecy, it's pretty feeble. But who cares? The Nostradamus industry marches onward.

Spiritualism

LIKE SO MANY PARANORMAL PHENOMENA, those which are associated with Spiritualism were late arrivals in the great march of human history. The year was 1848, and the place a town called Hydesville, New York State, where Katherine and Margaret Fox lived with their parents. Their ages at the time have been differently reported; they were somewhere between six and eight, and eleven and thirteen. They were the unwitting founders of a religion which has spread throughout the world, and now perhaps has its strongest base in Britain. (As a recognised religion, Spiritualism gets a capital 'S', though not if the spiritualist is just another psychic with no particular religious affiliation.)

Katherine and Margaret had no intention of founding a religion or anything of the sort. Things just got out of hand. In a confession forty years later Margaret, by then Mrs Kane, admitted that the whole thing had been a 'horrible deception'. They had been very mischievous children, she said, and had learned that they could terrify their 'easily frightened' mother by creating noises, which they did by cracking their knuckles and joints, especially their toes. Mrs Fox could not explain these weird sounds and concluded that they were the work of spirits. She invited the neighbours in to witness the manifestations and communicate with the spirits.

At first the spirits (or rather, the girls) merely rapped when asked to do so. Then they would spell out messages by rapping at the appropriate time when visitors recited the alphabet. Margaret said in her confession that 'when so many people came to see us children, we were ourselves frightened, and for self-preservation forced to keep it up.'

The agent of their greatest success was their big sister Leah, who was twenty-three years older than Margaret. She took the girls to live with her in nearby Rochester, where she arranged exhibitions which brought in as much as $150 per night, a vast sum in those days. Their fame spread rapidly, to New York City, then all over the United States, and to Europe, where Margaret conducted a seance for Queen Victoria and Kate performed in Russia for the Tsar.

Spiritualism grew with incredible speed. Two years after the first rappings there were one hundred mediums in New York City alone, and by 1858 there were said to be millions of believers. The spirits were becoming more ambitious. A Mrs Hayden arrived in England from the US in 1851 where she was greeted with excited acclaim. Tea and table-turning sessions were the latest fad. The amazing phe-

Preceding page
When this photograph was taken of Doris Stokes in 1985 and reproduced in 'The Sunday Mirror', she was Britain's leading psychic and is still probably considered the most famous medium the country has ever known.

nomena included the levitation of trumpets, through which spirits sometimes spoke if the audience was lucky, the playing of musical instruments and even full-size manifestations of the dead. All these were demonstrated in the dark, or near darkness.

Under such conditions, and with so much money to be made, fraud was rife. But the occasional exposure of a charlatan didn't put off the true believers. As so often with the paranormal, nothing deterred them, not even a full confession made by Margaret Fox in 1888. She was on stage at the New York Academy of Music, and her admission was confirmed by Kate who sat in a box overlooking the stage. Even now, faced with the choice of believing that the souls of the dead waited until 1848

to communicate with the living by means of cracking noises, or that two foolish girls got into something over their heads, the believers prefer to believe the former. The confessions were fake, they say; both women had been widowed, and were now destitute and drunk.

The confessions brought more fame, and the women set off on another US tour, this time demonstrating their tricks *as* tricks. A year later they recanted the confession, possibly because they thought there was more money in being real mediums, conceivably because their admission had been false in the first place. Again, Spiritualists prefer to believe the latter. They ignore the fact, though, that the Fox sisters had frequently been exposed long before their own admission. In 1850, a physician who investigated them said that the raps always came from the girls' feet or from tables and doors which were in contact with their dresses. In 1851 a relative of the girls, a Mrs Culver, admitted having helped the manifestations by touching Kate when the correct letter of the alphabet had been reached. There were other similar reports, though none have affected the true believers' faith. In the end, Kate and Margaret died in the 1890s, probably still in poverty. Leah, the first person in the world to see the money-making opportunities of spiritualism, had turned her back on her sisters and continued to prosper.

At that time, physical mediumship was what the public expected and was offered. The most celebrated of all nineteenth-century mediums was Daniel Dunglas Home, sometimes called The Medium Who Was Never Exposed. Home was born in Edinburgh in 1833, went to America when he was nine, and returned to Britain at the age of twenty-two, by which time he was already an experienced medium. The craze was just getting underway, there was a shortage of spiritual-

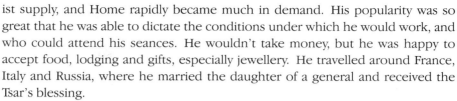

An artist's version (left) of the Fox sisters demonstrating table-levitation to a Revd Hammond. But were their demonstrations as unambiguous as the one depicted here?

Leah Underhill (née Fox) who was responsible for the promotion of her sisters Katherine and Margaret's spiritualist discoveries. She charged up to $150 a night for demonstrations.

ist supply, and Home rapidly became much in demand. His popularity was so great that he was able to dictate the conditions under which he would work, and who could attend his seances. He wouldn't take money, but he was happy to accept food, lodging and gifts, especially jewellery. He travelled around France, Italy and Russia, where he married the daughter of a general and received the Tsar's blessing.

Home's phenomena included elongating his own body, table tipping or 'levitation', fire-resistance, bodily levitation and the materialisation of spirit hands. He was never exposed, which could of course mean that he had genuine powers, but seems more likely to be the result of his skills as a magician, and the fact that he could pick and choose his audiences – admirers only invited. One of his greatest fans was Elizabeth Barrett Browning, and through her a rare sceptic, her husband Robert Browning, was able to attend a Home seance. He reported in 1855 on the difficulty of finding out what was really going on: 'It was a family party, met for family purposes, and one could no more presume to [grab] at the hands (for instance) of what they believed to be the spirit of their child, than one could have committed any other outrage on their feelings.' Browning was unable to tackle Home in his presence, but made his feelings known in a contemptuous poem, 'Mr Sludge the Medium'.

Another witness, a Mr F Merrifield, provided an account in August 1855, some weeks after he had attended a seance. Merrifield wrote that, with the lights 'removed', the spirit hand of a child could be seen near the medium, either at the same distance from him as his hand or his foot would be. 'When the object receded or approached I noticed that the medium's body either sank or rose in his chair accordingly.' And to settle the matter, when the spirit hand rose high in the air, Merrifield and a friend 'saw the whole connection between the medium's shoulder and arm, and the "spirit hand" dressed out on the end of his own'.

In spite of such reports, Home is still highly esteemed by spiritualists for his greatest *tour de force*, the occasion in December 1868 when he is supposed to have levitated in Victoria, London. The story is, that in the presence of three reputable witnesses, he floated out of the window of a third-floor room, and then floated back into another room on the same storey. The event clearly left a deep impression on the witnesses, and is still cited in Spiritualist literature today. But the impression wasn't deep enough to prevent the witnesses disagreeing about what they saw. None of them actually *saw* Home levitate, and they were all gathered in the room which he entered, rather than the one he allegedly left. There were no lights, and the moon had set hours before. As proof of anything, the event is absurdly unhelpful. What we

How an artist for 'The Strand' magazine saw Daniel Dunglas Home's levitation in 1921. Careful reading of the witnesses' reports suggest that the actual event might have been somewhat different.

can say for sure is that illustrations of Home floating outside the window in broad daylight are the product of wild imagination – such as Home himself possessed; that same night he went into a 'trance' and claimed that the sun was cold, 'covered with a beautiful vegetation, and full of organic life.' In a later, more cynical, age we might have concluded that both the medium and his admiring audience had been consuming restricted substances.

To list all the fraudulent spiritualists who have been unmasked at various times would be unnecessary (though a fascinating account does appear in Ruth Brandon's book, *The Spiritualists*. Few of the exposés trouble Spiritualists, who assume that the fact that cheating exists does not mean that genuine mediums don't exist too. One favourite argument is that some *genuine* mediums cheat as well, being under constant and intense pressure to perform. These occasional devices do not, they say, invalidate the claims.

One happy recipient of the benefit of the doubt was William Roy, who was caught in 1958 and confessed in a series of articles in *The Sunday Pictorial*. He had fooled doctors, clergymen, journalists, judges and politicians. He had an accomplice who rifled through the clients' coats and bags, and passed scraps of information to the medium through an earphone. Roy earned around £50,000 (again, a stupendous sum at the time) plus presents and favours from wealthy women. After his confession, many of his supporters said they were certain that he had produced genuine phenomena for *them* and that the press must have bribed him to confess.

With technological advance, there have been fewer physical mediums in recent times, possibly because it is so much easier to expose them. For instance, in 1993, Spiritualism in Britain was convulsed when a physical medium was videotaped with an infrared camera. Although he was supposed to be in a trance, the medium was observed standing up sixteen times during the seance, at which points a trumpet was seen to 'levitate'. The medium claimed that his 'spirits' must have lifted him, and a subsequent inquiry concluded that there was no evidence on the videotape to prove fraud. Spiritualists instead concentrated their fire on the man who had made the secret tape, who had, they said, used 'deceitful methods', and for having no respect for the safety of the medium. It has long been claimed that mediums may be harmed or even die if they are disturbed during a seance. We have yet to hear of a death actually happening, and suspect that this is just another ruse to keep clients sitting quiet and still, rather than checking out what is really going on around them.

Of late, physical mediumship has become very rare. These days psychics prefer to bring verbal message from the dead. William Roy claimed that he and other mediums exchanged information about clients 'like trading [postage] stamps'. He kept an elaborate card-index system of sitters and likely sitters, with information obtained at previous seances, voters' lists, and from Somerset House, where the national birth and death records were then held.

We don't know if mediums still swap information in the same way. It may still happen, but there is probably no real need. There are plenty of ways of obtaining advance information, to be served back to the clients with a flourish. People who

This nineteenth-century print shows how a medium might fake a levitation in the dark. Although the caption to this print suggests that sitters were allowed to feel the shoes, it is more likely that the medium touched people's heads as the illustration shows.

attend a lot of spiritualists' public meetings notice that the same people keep receiving much the same messages.

As Spiritualism had another bout of popularity in the 1970s and 1980s, mediums began giving public meetings in bigger halls and theatres – consequently earning larger sums of money. It was claimed by spiritualists that this ruled out cold reading, which generally needs to be performed one-on-one so that the reader can pick up subtle hints and body language, and would also prevent the use of plants in the audience, which would cost a lot of money and would add to the risk of exposure. In fact, the money generated would pay for many plants, and the fact is that a popular psychic can carry on a successful career even after being exposed. This was what happened when *The Mail on Sunday* wrote a devastating exposé of Doris Stokes, then Britain's leading psychic, and probably the most famous medium the country has ever seen.

Mrs Stokes was born Doris Sutton, just after the First World War, in Grantham, Lincolnshire, shortly before it became the birthplace of Margaret Thatcher. She came from a poor family, and her father died when she was thirteen. In 1943 she married and had a baby with a paratrooper called John Stokes, who was reported missing, believed dead, at Arnhem. According to her autobiography, she was then visited by her late father, who told her that her husband was alive and would return, but that her little son would die. Both these things happened. (The tragic death of small boys was a constant *leitmotif* in her performances.) She claimed to have had many similar paranormal experiences – for example, sensing which planes would return safely from bombing raids and which would not.

Over the years her fame grew; the marvels she could perform were constantly logged by the tabloid press, and she was the subject of adulatory TV programmes in Britain, the US and Australia. In 1984 the BBC made a film about her, and it provides us with a marvellous opportunity to watch a leading professional psychic in action.

She was on stage in London in front of a packed audience. She was warm, unpretentious and friendly to all the people who came up to speak. (The fact that they stood directly before her, just in front of the stage, made it easier to pick up cues.) Nevertheless, her white hair and gentle accent made her seem the quintessence of straightforward honesty. She joined in the audience's laughter, shared their pleasure at each apparent success, and generally behaved like a favourite aunt at a family reunion. Watching her, it is not remotely surprising that the people who paid to see her, many of them desperate with grief, yearned to believe in her powers. Most of them clearly did, in spite of a track record which at its best was mediocre and was often ludicrously bad.

Here, from the television tape, are three encounters she had with members of the audience, all women, all bereaved. We have left in all Mrs Stokes's hits as well as her frequent misses.

First she gazed around the hall.

DS: Somewhere in the back, near the middle, knows the surname of Rogers?

[A woman comes forward.] Do you know the name, spirit side? All the voices come in at once. I've got a man here who went over quickly with a heart attack, love.

Woman: [pause] Not exactly a heart attack.

DS: Pardon?

Woman: Cancer, with cancer.

DS: Oh, it's in his lungs, is it?

Woman: Yes, well, glands.

DS: I thought it was a heart attack. He did have a heart attack at the end. 'My chest hurt me,' he says. Where does your Rogers fit in, you're not Rogers are you? His name is Rogers? Who's Bill? [The woman looks puzzled.] Let's try and stick to the family. Who's Joan? It isn't, darling, it's John. Who's Tony? It doesn't mean a thing to you, does it?

For an old trouper like Mrs Stokes, that was a pretty rough beginning. She calls out a common surname, and asks if any of the hundreds of people 'in the back, near the middle' know it. She then gets the cause of his death wrong. Told it was cancer, she mistakes the specific type – though the woman appears quite willing to accept lungs.

Then Mrs Stokes recovers with aplomb by announcing that he did have a heart attack just before he died. The woman doesn't disagree, but how would she know? As far as the audience are concerned, far from being mistaken, Mrs Stokes knows more about how the man died than his own family does.

She seems to guess correctly that she was not dealing with the dead man's wife or daughter ('you're not Rogers are you?') but the statement was interrogative, so that if she'd been wrong it could have been a straightforward request for information. She then lists a series of common christian names – Bill, Joan, John and Tony – without, perhaps surprisingly, scoring a single hit. Finally she gives up with this particular woman – in spite of the fact that earlier she had been so confident about the identity of Mr Rogers that she could even offer the real story of his death, unknown to the family. One possible explanation is that she did know about some people involved with a Rogers who were in the hall; unfortunately the wrong ones came forward.

Luckily for her the name 'Tony' did strike a chord with another woman, who also came forward.

DS: Tony went quickly, he was a very young boy. He's talking about a pub called the Green Man. [Mentioned earlier in the performance.]

Woman 2: He probably was. He knew quite a few pubs, yeah. [Audience laughs.]

DS: It's all right, Tony. [As if talking to the dead man. Then softly, to the woman.] Luvvy, was his neck broken?

Woman 2: Well, he had head injuries with a motorbike accident, yes.

DS: [apparently quoting the deceased] 'My head and my neck' – I didn't like

Doris Stokes in November 1984, two years before 'The Mail on Sunday' accused her of trickery.

to ask him. As he comes in close, I feel the impact. He said, 'Yes, I never went home again.' He was on his way home, and he never got there. Is he the baby, darling?

Woman 2: That's right.

DS: The baby of the family?

Woman 2: Yes, my young brother.

DS: 'Cos he says, 'I'm the baby, I was very spoiled.'

Woman 2: [clearly surprised and delighted by this direct quote] Yes, he was.

DS: 'I was the baby, she's my big sister.' Is it the first time he's made it back? Yes, he says, 'I've waited a long time.' Who's Michael he's talking about?

Woman 2: His cousin.

DS: He's been to see Michael, our side? [woman nods] Yes, he was thrown. Says he was thrown?

Woman 2: Yes

DS: He says if you're worried about it, he said, will you tell her the last impression he got was 'Oh my God', and over, [makes rolling gesture with hand] and that was it?

Woman 2: Yes

DS: But he says, 'my face was all right.'

Woman 2: Yes, it was

DS: Everybody could look at me.

Woman 2: Yes

DS: And he says, 'don't you think I'm a handsome fella?' [loud sympathetic laughter from audience] He's got a great sense of humour!

Woman 2: Yes, he had!

Much better altogether, and the audience were clearly impressed. But an analysis of the conversation shows the narrow limits of Mrs Stokes's knowledge. Since the young man in question died in a motorbike accident, it's odd that she should first describe him as a 'very young boy'. For the same reason, she is caught unawares by 'he knew quite a few pubs', since she hasn't figured out that he was of drinking age.

But by this stage, we know he was a bit of a boozer, and the name Tony more often than not belongs to youngish men. So there's a good chance he died in an accident, and the 'neck broken' guess was well worth a try. It was close enough to impress the woman, even though, she says, it was head injuries that actually killed him. Mrs Stokes smoothly tacks on her guess – the neck – to the true cause, the head.

She's right, too, that he was on his way home rather than going in the other direction. Her stab about him being 'the baby' gets an excellent response, though since we are all babies for some time, that could easily be interpreted as a hit by anyone in Tony's family. The woman doesn't confirm that he was *the* baby, merely her little brother. Mrs Stokes adds that he says he was very spoiled, and this predictable suggestion seems to confirm to the woman that it is indeed her brother on the line from the beyond.

By now, the clairvoyant is coasting. She tosses out the name Michael, and scores a hit with a cousin. She then asserts that Tony has 'been to see' Michael, whatever that might mean. (There's no response, such as 'Oh yes, Michael said he'd felt Tony's presence.' And, we might ask, why did Mrs Stokes ask if it was 'the first time he's made it back' a few moments before?) Next she declares that he was 'thrown', and gets instant agreement, though it's hard to imagine a motorbike accident in which the rider wasn't thrown off.

With bravura style, she actually describes the thoughts that were going through his head at the moment of impact, and gets his sister to agree, as if she could have had the faintest idea – unless of course Tony lived for a time after the crash, a point which isn't touched on.

Finally Mrs Stokes scores a big hit by saying that Tony's face was undamaged. A bit risky that, even though her ability to skate over mistaken guesses is always superb. However, crash helmets are mandatory in Britain, and they can protect the face from mangling, so perhaps it wasn't such a gamble.

She finishes with a joke from the dead man: 'He says, "don't you think I'm a handsome fella?"' This warms the audience, and she caps it by saying that he has a great sense of humour – a view which the sister willingly endorses, as if she were likely to say, no, he was a miserable old curmudgeon.

The third example is a classic example of a cold reading which – by any rational assessment – goes horribly wrong, yet which was clearly a great success for the participants. Our running commentary is in brackets.

Mrs Stokes begins by gazing towards the back of the hall and asking, 'Little Daniel, who's little Daniel?'
A woman jumps up. 'Yes, I've got a Daniel.' [Note the use of the present tense. This is important.]
DS: Okay, has there been a birthday with little Daniel?
Woman 3: [louder, as she gets near the front of the hall] I've got a Daniel
DS: Little Daniel?
Woman 3: Very little? [An important clue on offer here.]
DS: You've a baby Daniel? [No response from the woman, implying that he might be small but he isn't a baby.] Did he have to go back into hospital,

love? [Pretty obvious, really – most sick children spend a lot of time moving between hospital and home.]

Woman 3: Yes, he had to go back into hospital.

DS: But he's all right now, love?

Woman 3: No...well, he might be all right on your side. But we lost him. [Thus we learn the stunning fact that the medium does not even know that the person she is 'listening' to is dead. However, the woman helpfully suggests that Mrs Stokes really meant he was 'all right' in the afterlife.]

DS: [Utterly unfazed. But how could she possibly have imagined that the voice in her head was of someone still living? Could it be the fact that the woman twice referred to him in the present tense: 'I've got a Daniel'?]

That's what he's saying, he's all right now, and they're [who?] saying they've brought little Daniel. And he went back home and he had to go back in the hospital. And he never went home again. [Tragically, at some point that must have happened. In any event, the woman doesn't respond.] But he said he's all right now [gratefully accepting the woman's kind offer of an explanation for her tremendous error]. And he's about three now, luvvy? [a fairly obvious guess, given that we already knew he was 'little' though not a baby.]

Woman 3: Yes, he would be.

DS: I can see him. He's got auburn hair, love.

Woman 3: [pause] Yes, he has. [This is a real hit.]

DS: He's here. He's looking at the flowers. Yes, Daniel, you can, love. He says, 'can I have some flowers for my Mum?' [Audience sighs with pleasure. Mrs Stokes is once again on the home stretch, or so she probably imagines.] So when you go home tonight, love, you take some flowers.

Woman 3: I wasn't his Mum. [Oh dear, it turns out that Mrs Stokes has assumed she's been dealing with the mother. However, an old pro like her doesn't let another first-class mistake put her off her stride.]

DS: But you knew his Mum! [Triumphantly, so that even this error is turned into a fake 'hit'.]

Woman 3: Yes.

DS: [recovering fast] I didn't say to you. He said, 'Can I have some flowers for my Mum?' And he's here, and he's a beautiful child. [As if listening.] Just a minute, Daniel, yes. [Back to the aunt.] He had a defect, darling.

Woman 3: Yes.

DS: With his heart. And they tried to repair it.

Woman 3: Yes [This is really subtle. Mrs Stokes has just surmised that this poor child had a 'defect'. Of course he did. The woman naturally agrees.]

DS: And it didn't work. [Naturally it didn't. That's why the boy died.] And he's going to give the flowers to where the children are, because I adore the spirit children, me. [She finishes with an unchallengeable statement which delights the audience and makes her appear even more kindly than before, if that is possible.]

We had an illustration of the power clairvoyants exercise when we mentioned this encounter briefly in *The Observer*, some years ago. Daniel's mother wrote a letter saying that, as a former non-believer, she had been deeply impressed by what Mrs Stokes had said, and regarded the fact that she had mentioned Daniel's 'auburn' hair as proof that she was really was in touch with the boy. (We had suggested that 'auburn' was a guess which, for a receptive listener, would have covered any shade of brown or reddish hair). The mother added that she had also been right to call the boy 'Baby' Daniel, since that was the family's pet name for him, right that he would have been three years old, and right that he suffered from a heart defect.

It seems to us that all these 'hits' are fairly safe guesses, especially as by now we're familiar with Mrs Stokes's numerous means of dealing with her own frequent mistakes. The aunt who appeared on the TV programme was a keen spiritualist, and as we know, the same information often crops up at several spiritualist performances. One possibility is that Mrs Stokes, having been misled into imagining that the boy was still alive, then recognised a familiar case from a previous spiritualist meeting and made use of information she already had. One might just conceive that she really was hearing Daniel's voice. But in that case, why on earth did she think he was still alive?

The Mail on Sunday exposure of her trickery appeared in April 1986. A good example was provided by a particularly astute woman, Janette O'Donnell of Glasgow. She had attended one of Mrs Stokes's shows and had received a 'message' there from her son Gary, who had died of a brain tumour just before his third birthday. In front of the amazed audience Mrs Stokes had given the names of Gary's parents, said that they were Scottish, correctly gave the cause of death, and identified the boy's aunt. In the theatre foyer afterwards, two women approached Mrs O'Donnell to say how lucky she had been and how wonderful Doris was. 'No, not at all,' she replied. 'Mrs Stokes rang me beforehand and got all the information she needed.'

Mrs O'Donnell told the newspaper that her sister-in-law, Gary's aunt, had written to a magazine, asking if they could arrange a sitting with Doris Stokes. Then, at her home in Glasgow, she received a call from the celebrated psychic:

'She told me my son was beside her and what he was like. I was crying and in the emotional shock I just gave out the information. My fear was that if I rejected her, then I might be rejecting my son. It was emotional blackmail.'

Fortunately, Mrs O'Donnell made careful notes of the conversation. *The Mail on Sunday* reporters, John Dale and Richard Holliday, wrote: 'By suggesting various names, Doris built up a picture of the family. She said Gary died of leukaemia – but Mrs O'Donnell corrected her. Doris was right in suggesting he was bald, but that is common among dying children.

'During her call, Doris had also confirmed that Mrs O'Donnell and her husband would be in London to attend one of her shows' – the show in which she demonstrated such apparently miraculous knowledge of the boy and his family.

Some time later, Doris Stokes appeared in Glasgow, and also brought a message from Gary. Mrs O'Donnell was not present on that occasion, but she surmised that the medium would have expected her to be there and so had expected to score another great success with the same material. 'She claims your child is with you all the time. If so, why didn't Gary know that I wouldn't be in the audience?' she asked, quite reasonably.

None of this cramped Mrs Stokes's style. The centrepiece of her act was often a display of breathtaking knowledge. For example, she gave a performance at the London Palladium in November 1986. It was highly successful, though what she did not reckon with was her audience included the writer Ian Wilson, and two TV researchers who made a point of getting further interviews with some of the people picked out during the show.

Mrs Stokes was formidable. At one point she seemed to 'hear' the surname 'Stennett' or something like it, and the first name 'Kelly' or 'Kerry'. This brought a gasp from a woman in the front row called Stenning, whose daughter Kerry had recently died from injuries in a road crash. After this Mrs Stokes produced a bewildering amount of accurate detail. She knew that Kerry had died of a blood clot, she knew where she had lived, the names of her grandfather and of her boyfriend. It was a stunning performance.

But there was more. Mrs Stokes said that she was getting messages from someone called Graham, and was hearing the name Dawn. A woman called Dawn, also in the front row, came forward to say that her husband Graham had died a few weeks before. Mrs Stokes then announced, quite correctly, that he had been a solicitor, and that he had died in a scaffolding accident. She appeared to be having a private conversation with Graham, who had assured Dawn she was quite right to agree to his 'ventilator' – presumably his life-support machine – being switched off. After scoring numerous direct hits with the names of Graham's mother, his in-laws, and the couple's baby daughter, she held another private chat with the deceased, which allowed her to tell Dawn that he'd said she should not feel guilty if she ever wanted to re-marry.

There were other equally dazzling successes, and the audience could hardly fail to have been thrilled and excited by this proof of life in the hereafter. Except that – as Ian Wilson reports in his book *The After Death Experience* – the TV researchers, Beth Miller and Siobhan Hockton, soon found out that there was much less there than met the eye.

Mrs Stenning told the two women that a friend of hers had written to Mrs Stokes telling her about Kerry's death. Mrs Stokes had phoned to offer a pair of free tickets for the Palladium show, a gesture which seemed no more than simple generosity. Mrs Stenning remained convinced that all she had given Mrs Stokes was her name and phone number. Yet we know that she also had all the information in a friend's letter, and that her address could easily be found in the phone book.

As for Dawn, she had asked to talk to Doris Stokes when the hospital told her they might need permission to switch off her husband's life-support machine. Mrs

Stokes had returned the call promptly and spoke at length to Dawn, then to her mother, and later to Dawn again, when she also offered tickets for the show. In other words, she had ample information about the cases of both women, information she happily relayed back to them. Mrs Stokes also had 'groupies', innocent fans who travelled round the country going to her performances. They were more than delighted when she picked them out to demonstrate her powers by knowing a wealth of detail about them. As admirers, they would not have dreamt of pointing out that she'd heard their stories many times before.

"Mr-Dodsworth-is-engaged-at-the-moment-please-state-your-query-at-the-end-of-this-recording."

The researchers attending the Palladium show were shocked, but the two women in the front row were plainly much impressed. Certainly neither challenged Mrs Stokes, who had demonstrated again the advantage psychics possess: people yearn desperately to believe in them. They yearn just as desperately to be told what they want to hear. For instance, it is inconceivable that the medium would have told Dawn that her husband deeply resented his life-support machine being switched off. She would have been appalled, and might well have gone on to look for indications that Mrs Stokes wasn't in any position to know. As it was, the suggestion that she had done the right thing was clearly very welcome, and was strongly reinforced by Mrs Stokes's evident expertise.

Other psychics use other methods. One is to have an assistant who hangs round the toilets and bars before the show and during the interval, eavesdropping. The smallest scrap of information – a child's name, the cause of a fatal accident – is enough to validate the conversation which follows. ('How could she possibly have known my husband's name and the way he died in a bus crash?')

The Palladium management confirmed to Ian Wilson that Doris Stokes always kept the front three rows of the theatre free for her own use. Clearly this was to 'paper' the audience with people she knew about (often they had rung her home, where her husband would say she was not available, but would offer to take down the details and pass them on. Oh, and would the caller like free tickets to her next performance in the area?) There's no record of anyone turning round and saying: 'You only know that because I told your husband.' Nobody who didn't have at least some faith in her abilities would get in touch in the first place. The desire to believe did the rest.

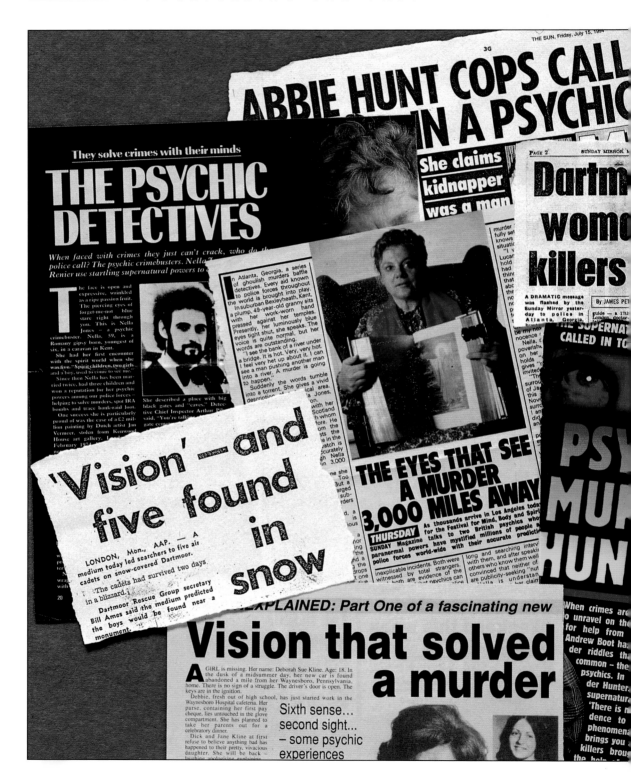

THE SUN, Friday, July 15, 1994

3G

ABBIE HUNT COPS CALL IN A PSYCHIC

She claims kidnapper was a man

PAGE 2   SUNDAY MIRROR,

Dartm woma killers

By JAMES PET

A DRAMATIC message was flashed by the Sunday Mirror yesterday to police in Atlanta, Georgia,

They solve crimes with their minds

THE PSYCHIC DETECTIVES

When faced with crimes they just can't crack, who do the police call? The psychic crimebusters. Nella ? Renier use startling supernatural powers to ?

The face is open and expressive, wrinkled as a ripe passion fruit. The piercing eyes of forget-me-not blue stare right through you. This is Nella Jones, a psychic crimebuster. Nella, 59, is a Romany gipsy born, youngest of six, in a caravan in Kent.

She had her first encounter with the spirit world when she was five. "Spirit children, two girls and a boy, used to come to see me.'

Since then Nella has been married twice, had three children and won a reputation for her psychic powers among our police forces – helping to solve murders, spot IRA bombs and trace bank-raid loot.

One success she is particularly proud of was the case of a £2 million painting by Dutch artist Jan Vermeer, stolen from Kenwood House art gallery, February 197?

She described a place with big black gates and "caves." Detective Chief Inspector Arthur Pil said, "You're talking gate ceme

In Atlanta, Georgia, a series of ghoulish murders baffle detectives. Every aid known to police forces throughout the world is brought into play.

In suburban Bexleyheath, Kent, a plump, 49-year-old granny sits with her work-worn hand pressed against her temples. Presently, her luminously blue eyes tight shut, she speaks. The voice is quite normal, but her words are outstanding.

"I see the bank of a river under a bridge. It is hot. Very, very hot. I feel very het up about it. I can see a man pushing another man into a river. A murder is going to happen."

Suddenly the words tumble into a torrent. She gives a vivid description of the local area.

with her Scotland h whom fore. He om the ts the e in the atch is ccurately gh Nella in 3,000

ne she Too but a arged sub- rders

THE EYES THAT SEE A MURDER 3,000 MILES AWAY

THURSDAY SUNDAY Magazine talks to two British psychics who

As thousands arrive in Los Angeles today for the Festival for Mind, Body and Spirit paranormal powers have mystified millions of people police forces world-wide with their accurate prediction

inexplicable incidents. Both were witnessed by total strangers, both are evidence of the that psychics can

long and searching interv with them, and after speakir others who know them well convinced that neither of are publicity-seeking "nut Nella is understan

'Vision' – and five found in snow

LONDON, Mon., AAP. — A medium today led searchers to five air cadets on snow-covered Dartmoor.

The cadets had survived two days in a blizzard.

Dartmoor Rescue Group secretary Bill Ames said the medium predicted the boys would be found near a monument.

EXPLAINED: Part One of a fascinating new

Vision that solved a murder

A GIRL is missing. Her name: Deborah Sue Kline. Age: 18. In the dusk of a midsummer day, her new car is found abandoned a mile from her Waynesboro, Pennsylvania, home. There is no sign of a struggle. The driver's door is open. The keys are in the ignition.

Debbie, fresh out of high school, has just started work in the Waynesboro Hospital cafeteria. Her purse, containing her first pay cheque, lies untouched in the glove compartment. She has planned to take her parents out for a celebratory dinner.

Dick and Jane Kline at first refuse to believe anything bad has happened to their pretty, vivacious daughter. She will be back laughing, apologising, explaining.

Sixth sense... second sight... – some psychic experiences

When crimes are to unravel on the for help from Andrew Boot ha der riddles tha common – the psychics. In der Hunter supernatura 'There is n dence to phenomena brings you killers brou the

Psychic Detectives

PSYCHIC DETECTIVES ARE THE LATEST menace the police have to cope with. Over and over again they crop up in the newspaper headlines, claiming to have 'solved' baffling cases, to have trapped murderers and to have found missing people. The headlines are so persistent, the claims so immense, that undoubtedly some policemen have turned to them for help with difficult cases, so giving them even more credibility.

In fact, it is almost certainly true that no psychic has ever given the police information which has led to a missing person – or their body – being found, or to a crime being prevented, or a criminal arrested. Instead they clog up the system, wasting time, opening up non-existent 'leads' and diverting officers from useful work.

Afterwards they claim immense success, but this has always been achieved by the usual means: wild exaggeration of 'hits', omission of all misses, claims that vague hints were actually specific instructions, and in some cases outright lies.

None of this stops the headlines from appearing. Here's a typical fistful:
'THEY SOLVE CRIMES WITH THEIR MINDS', *News of the World Magazine*, September 1991.
'VISION THAT SOLVED A MURDER', *Weekend*, April 1989.
' "VISION" – AND FIVE FOUND IN SNOW', *Melbourne Herald*, Australia, April 1981.
'ABBIE HUNT COPS CALL IN A PSYCHIC', *The Sun*, July 1994.

Psychic detection is not entirely new. One of the earliest claims of a psychic success came in 1692 when a French dowser, Jacques Aymar, is said to have located the murderer of a wine-grower and his wife. The alleged perpetrator was executed, which must have been rough luck if there was no corroborating evidence.

Psychics crop up only occasionally in the 250 years since that forensic triumph. One psychic claimed to have solved the Jack the Ripper murders in 1888, but this was discredited many years ago by the research officer of the Society for Psychical Research himself – a fact which doesn't stop other spiritualist writers from repeating the claim as fact.

However, we've seen an upsurge in psychic sleuthing over the past few decades, matching the growth in fascination with the paranormal. Even some policemen have been impressed by the results. One detective, quoted in *Psychic*

Preceding page

A selection of headlines about psychic detectives which have appeared over the past fourteen years.

News in 1977, said of the British psychic Nella Jones that he would dig up the pitch at Lord's, England's leading cricket ground, if she said a body was buried there. It would be hard to get more confident than that.

The headline ' " Vision" – and five found in snow' referred to a story which happened in England. On Saturday 25 April, 1981, five teenage air cadets had been caught in an unexpected blizzard while on a training exercise on Dartmoor in Devon, a bleak and inhospitable place. When search teams were unable to find them, a medium called Frances Dymond from Cornwall contacted the police to say that the boys were three miles from the spot where they had last been seen. Her vision included a derelict farmhouse with a roof almost down to the ground, where an old man had died, and an 'ancient monument sticking in the air like a needle'. She is also reported to have said that 'one' of the boys was still alive.

In fact, all of them were still alive. This did not stop Ms Dymond's claim from going round the world. *The Melbourne Herald*'s report quoted one of the rescuers, Bill Ames, as saying: 'The only monument I knew was Widgery Cross, near Brat Tor. So we went there and saw the boys walking through the snow.' (It's not clear if this quote is entirely accurate or was taken out of context.)

Writing in *The Sunday Times*, Elizabeth Grice poured cold water on the medium's claims. The boys were not 'rescued' but had survived on their own wits. When 'found' they were only ten minutes' walk from a main road, and were on the opposite side of the moor from the location nearest to the medium's description.

This had been identified by Fred Barlow, an experienced member of the rescue team. It was White Moor Stone, not far from a ruined farmhouse. But Royal Marines had already searched the area without success. It was the following day when Bill Ames and the others came upon the boys, who were on the far side of the moor from the site apparently identified by the clairvoyant. They were half a mile from Widgery Cross – yet that was only one of thirteen monumental crosses on the moor. It had been erected to mark Queen Victoria's diamond jubilee, so couldn't by any stretch of the imagination be considered an 'ancient' monument. According to Grice, however, Ames had thought it worth investigating Widgery Cross because of the medium's description, but he stressed that his men planned to comb the west of the moor in any case.

However, Frances Dymond made full use of the publicity. She sold her story to another Sunday newspaper for a reported £400, and gave interviews to journalists at £35 a time. On the strength of her 'success' at Dartmoor, *The Sunday Mirror* sent details of her other predictions to police in Atlanta, Georgia, who were investigating the serial killing of twenty-six young blacks. She said the murders were the work of a team of three or four young racists, led by an older man who worked with coloured children in some kind of park. The paper reported an Atlanta detective as saying 'We will take careful note'. In fact, the only person ever charged with any of the murders was Wayne Williams, a young black man.

Dymond has one incontrovertible success on her record. She predicted that the then pregnant Princess Anne would have a baby girl. A fifty-fifty chance, but then you can't lose 'em all. She was less helpful in the matter of Genette Tate, a thirteen-year-old girl whose disappearance while on her newspaper round in Aylesbeare, Devon, in August 1979 caught the imagination of psychics all over the country. Dymond told the press that she knew exactly where the girl's body was hidden. When police called to find out where, she was unable to help, telling them that her spirit guide, an eighteenth-century London doctor, had told her to concentrate on faith healing and leave prediction alone. Another wasted journey for the men in blue.

Others tried to be more helpful in this dreadful case. Devon and Cornwall police told us that by 1981 they had amassed 2,000 items of information sent by psychics and mystics, though tragically none of them have helped to find the girl or her body. One man drove hundreds of miles from Leicester to tell an officer:

'I've solved it. Genette's in the boot of a car.'

'Can you tell me what make of car?'

'I'm sorry, I can't.'

'Registration number?'

'Afraid not...'

The man was given a cup of tea and sent home.

Undoubtedly much of the information was given in good faith. However, most of it was much too vague to be of any use. 'She's in a country cottage with honeysuckle round the door' – no shortage of those in the West Country. 'She's been devoured by a wild animal which escaped from the zoo. You won't know the animal's escaped because it ate its keeper first.'

Even ufologists offered help. One group told police that Genette had been kidnapped by a Venusian space craft. The evidence for this was a crescent-shaped scorch mark from its exhaust found in a field near where Genette had disappeared. It turned out the mark had been made by a farmer spilling lime.

But we might look at the figures given to us by the police. Even if a fraction of the 2,000 scraps of information were followed up, they amounted to a serious waste of time. There is no way of showing exactly how much the cost was, but in one case a financial estimate has been made. Det Sgt Michael Riley and Det Chief Insp David Thompson were students on an advanced CID course in West Yorkshire. Members of the seventeen different forces attending the course were asked to find out from their home forces about the use of psychics and mediums in their investigations. Writing in the 16 January 1987 edition of *Police Review*, they reported that over 600 unsolicited letters were received from psychics who wanted to help find a particular missing girl.

It was estimated that it would have taken an average of six hours for an officer to visit or contact the medium, and to assess the information. Two more hours would have been taken up by administration and evaluation by the control room team. Thus a total of around 4,800 hours would have been used. Taking an average cost of £7 per hour, this exercise would have cost about £34,000 at 1987 rates of pay.

No one has calculated how much police time was wasted by psychics in the search for the Yorkshire Ripper, the most notorious British mass murderer of the

'Psychic Detective'
Nella Jones whose work has been praised by the press and Scotland Yard detectives. Did she help to solve the Yorkshire Ripper murders?

past two decades. The manhunt, which lasted six years certainly cost around £4,000,000 for the investigation between 1975 and 1981. Innumerable bits of information were sent in, and we know that many of them were followed up. One can only speculate how much quicker the investigation would have been if the police had been able to follow up only genuine information, how many lives would have been saved, and how many other crimes solved or averted.

One psychic who has created a reputation for herself, enhanced by her claims in the Ripper case is Nella Jones, probably the best known psychic detective in Britain. She claims to have solved several crimes, especially those which have foxed police, and these claims are eagerly lapped up by the tabloid press. In 1991, *The News of the World* asked: 'When faced with crimes they just can't crack, who do police call?' Mrs Jones of course.

If so, they are probably wasting their time. There are difficulties in proving this, since contemporary newspaper accounts of psychic successes usually take the claims without the usual checking – which might, indeed probably would, spoil the story. This means that psychics are constantly being judged at their own valuation.

For instance, Mrs Jones describes her first great success in her first autobiography, *Ghost of a Chance* . In 1974 a Vermeer painting was stolen from Kenwood House in north London. When Mrs Jones saw the theft reported on TV, she 'slipped into a semi-trance' and a 'picture' appeared in her mind. She made a sketch of what she'd seen and placed two crosses on it. She then phoned the police and told them where they could find the missing frame from the painting. A short while later they called her back to say that they had found the frame in the spot she'd described.

Two days later, she says, she helped police find part of the alarm system from the house, buried in mud at the edge of a lake. Since she had such incredibly accurate information at her fingertips, some policemen thought she must have taken part in the crime. Others became convinced of her amazing powers. This came to a head when she told them (so she claims) that the missing painting would be found in a cemetery – as it was.

Our problem is that it is impossible to judge these marvellous claims. Both detectives involved in the case have retired and have proved impossible to track down. If she was right about the cemetery, that would indeed be a great success – unless the criminal, wanting to get rid of his annoyingly hot property decided to leave it in a graveyard so that it might be found earlier. Either way, the case brought Mrs Jones to public attention, and started her on her long career of phantom crime-busting.

By the time her book came out in 1982, she was a familiar figure to readers of the tabloid newspapers. Naturally her high profile demanded her engagement in the Yorkshire Ripper investigation. It's worth looking at the claims she made for herself (and were parroted by the media) and the reality.

Claim: *The Daily Mirror*, 21 November 1980, reported Mrs Jones as saying 'It's tragic, but I feel he will strike again almost immediately. I see him coming back to claim another victim within the week'. We are told that six weeks previously (i.e. in October 1980) she had predicted that the Ripper would strike twice within a few days.

Eight days after *The Daily Mirror* article, *Psychic News* quoted another national newspaper: 'In *The Daily Star*, the clairvoyant said the Ripper might already have struck again, and left his victim undiscovered.' Jones said, 'The next victim will be older and may work in a hospital.'

There wasn't another victim, either within one week or ever. The Ripper, Peter Sutcliffe, had struck for the last time, and was arrested on 2 January 1981. In her book, Mrs Jones admits that she had predicted two more murders: 'I saw...the scene of the Ripper's next attack...my eyes were drawn to two legs sticking out of some small trees or bushes.' She added, 'He will try to do another, but it will go wrong, and he won't finish the job. He will be caught before he gets the chance.'

Sutcliffe was arrested in the company of another prostitute, though he had not at that stage offered her any violence. In her book, Mrs Jones went on to say that on 19 November, she 'still had an uneasy feeling that there could be a second murder in Leeds in a few days time, this time in the grounds of a medical building.' She was wrong about Leeds, and wrong about the murder. (It's intriguing, that unlike many clairvoyants, Mrs Jones is prepared to admit some mistaken claims. One possible explanation is that her autobiography was written 'with' a *Yorkshire Post* journalist called Shirley Davenport, who told us that she had used notebooks filled with Mrs Jones's predictions. Being an honest reporter, she had included those which failed as well as the handful which worked.)

Claim: we are told in her autobiography that after the murder of the final victim, Jacqueline Hill on 17 November, 1980, Mrs Jones 'inexplicably...felt that the killer had...dressed up either as a clergyman or a woman...it was almost a year after this that I learned from a magazine that several clairvoyants had had the same uncanny feelings about the Yorkshire Ripper's mode of dress.'

That makes it sound as if Mrs Jones didn't realise until a year later that any clairvoyant had predicted this disguise. In fact, it was only weeks; later that she was told this. *Psychic News* of 6 December 1980, reported: 'Another medium "saw" the Ripper disgusted as a woman. When told this, Nella Jones said, "That's right. I told the police about that months ago. He could also appear as a priest." '

Peter Sutcliffe had a beard, an improbable feature for a female impersonator. During the recording of the TV programme 'Esther' in November 1994, Dr Chris French, a psychology lecturer at Goldsmiths' College, London, mentioned Mrs Jones's claim that Sutcliffe dressed as a woman. She denied having said this, and credited it instead Doris Stokes. Dr French sent a copy of the *Psychic News* story to the BBC who had already edited out both the accusation and the denial.

> *Claim*: a detective told a newspaper: 'In the Ripper case she predicted the date, place, time, initials and even the weather conditions of Jacqueline Hill's death'.

This refers to a prediction she made in October 1980, a forecast which was a great deal less specific than the detective's encomium might suggest. She predicted two different dates, 17 or 27 November (the first was right). She said the murder would be in Leeds – which is where four of the previous eleven had taken place. She predicted that it would be 'on a small patch of wasteland', without saying where. (She had made this same prediction over a year before about the death of the twelfth victim, who would be found in the grounds of a house. Not surprisingly, none were killed in a busy high street.) As for the time, she predicted 'night'; at least eleven, and probably all the murders took place at night. (In *The Mail on Sunday* for 7 July, 1991, Mrs Jones was quoted as saying she had predicted the correct time for the murder, at 9.30 pm. It's odd that she didn't mention this claim before.)

She predicted that the murder would take place on a 'damp, misty night, when it is raining'. This is not exactly unusual in November, in Leeds. So far as the initials J H are concerned, she first mentioned them around October 1979, before two other murders, including Miss Hill's, and two other attacks.

> *Claim*: 'Eighteen months before police arrested the man they said was the Yorkshire Ripper I had drawn the killer's face, described where he lived and worked, and predicted two more murders before he was caught.'

The drawing in her book bears no resemblance to Sutcliffe and could not have helped in any way. Her description of where the Ripper lived was this:
> 'Stop him at the city centre. Go to Chapel Street...the number 6 flashed across my mind, the name Joyce..a grey house with a wrought iron gate in front...a small garage nearby but I didn't know if it belonged to the house or was a separate business.'

Sutcliffe's house was at 6 Garden Lane, so she was right about the number. But she was wrong about the city centre, and wrong about the name Joyce. She claims a hit with the 'low garage at the side' but in fact she had mentioned only a 'small garage' which could have been a 'business'. Telling the police that the killer's home was near a small garage would be utterly useless information.

Shortly before September 1979, Mrs Jones says that she 'had the strongest feeling that the police had already spoken to him'.

This was hardly surprising. The police interviewed tens of thousands of people, many of whom like Sutcliffe spent time in red light areas and whose jobs involved their travelling around West Yorkshire. In January 1978, police said: 'It is more than likely that we have interviewed the person who received the fiver.' (The £5 note was found in the sixth victim's handbag and traced to a bank in Shipley, Yorkshire. Some 5,000 people who might have received it in their pay were interviewed.)

Claim: she predicted the initial 'C' for the name of the company the Ripper worked for. In her book she said 'All I could see was the first letter, a "C" '.

This was a hit. Sutcliffe was a driver for a company called T & W H Clark. (Though if all she could see was one letter, how did she know it was the first of anything?) On page 117 of her book she admits also seeing the initial 'A'. Later she mentions 'C' and 'J H'. But were there other letters she saw which she had decided not to mention? And what on earth could the police do with nothing more than the letter 'C'?

She also mentioned many names and places in the period up to October 1979, including Dudley, King's Cross, Darlington, Dinsdale, Jean, Peter, Charles, Len, Leonard, Hull, Joyce and Harry. The last was said to be Sutcliffe's father's name. In fact he is called John. Only 'Peter' was a hit; none of the others matches the name of any of Sutcliffe's family, friends or victims.

Does Mrs Jones mean what she says? Do people like her really imagine that they are making a useful contribution to the fight against crime? Quite possibly so. As we try to show in the chapters on Cold Reading(see p63) and Spiritualism(see p87), many people who clearly aren't getting supernatural assistance have managed to convince themselves that they are. If Mrs Jones knew herself to be a

Doris Stokes in June 1979 describing the Yorkshire Ripper to an artist for 'The Sunday People'.
Inset: The real Yorkshire Ripper (Peter Sutcliffe).

fraud, it's unlikely that she would have agreed to be tested on television in 1991, by the world's most high-profile sceptic, James Randi.

In the programme she was presented with six objects, any or all of which might have been involved in a serious crime leading to loss of life. Her job was to say which. She settled on three of the objects, a corkscrew-cum-bottle opener, which she said might have been used to open a lock, a hammer which she connected to broken glass, and a fireman's axe, which she connected to 'a heavy vehicle tyre'.

The corkscrew and the hammer were new, and had been bought specially for the show. The fireman's axe had been used in a particularly brutal murder, an event whose psychic auras evidently eluded Mrs Jones. Later, in *Psychic News*, she complained that she had been given just one minute to look at all the items. 'I picked up the bag containing the axe. But I didn't get time to go into details about the murder.' In his book of the TV series, Randi wrote that she had actually taken four minutes and thirty-one seconds to judge the objects, and – offered more time – had refused to say anything else.

If the media and the psychics themselves are to be believed, the police will sometimes call on psychics to help them with particularly baffling cases. This may be the case with some individual officers, but there's no evidence that this is common policy for any police force in the world. In 1991 Scotland Yard told Randi: 'We never go out of our way to seek psychic help, and no psychic has ever cleared up a single case for us.' The Los Angeles Police Department went so far as to conduct two trials to see if psychics could be of any use to them.

The first, reported by psychologist Martin Reiser in 1979, used twelve psychics, eight of whom were professional or semi-professional. They were all selected from the most 'reputable' psychics in Los Angeles. Physical evidence from four crimes, two of which had already been solved, were presented to the psychics who gave their impressions of the crimes and the criminals who committed them.

This table shows some descriptions of the Yorkshire Ripper as seen by psychic detectives and which appeared in print before Peter Sutcliffe was caught. Although Nella Jones claims many successful predictions about Sutcliffe there is only a record of one which appeared in print before he was caught. Many others appeared in her books and in the press afterwards.

	NAME	AGE	HEIGHT	WEIGHT	HAIR	EYES	MARRIED
Nella Jones							
Doris Stokes July 1979	Johnnie or Ronnie Morris or Morrison	31 – 32			Mousy/dark, covers ears. Right parting covers bald patch		Married – wife left him
Thelma Welham Aug 1979							
Gerard Croiset Nov 1979		32	5ft 8in		Long		
Kay Rhea 1980			Nearly 6ft	Thin face	Straight Dark	Prominent	
David Walton Nov 1980	Cecil or Cyril						
Daily Star Nov/Dec 1980	12 names. None significant	40 – 45	5ft 3in	Stocky	Fair Recently dyed	Blue	Single
Daily Star Nov/Dec 1980							
Perpetrator	Peter Sutcliffe	34	5ft 9in – 5ft 11in		Dark	Dark	Yes 10.8.74

The researchers reported that in this test 'little, if any, information was elicited from the twelve psychic participants that would provide material helpful in the investigation of the major crimes in question.' The use of psychics, they said, had not been validated.

A further test was reported by Reiser in 1982. In this, two additional groups were brought in for comparison with the psychics, one of college students, the other of homicide detectives. The psychics produced a torrent of information – roughly ten times as much as the comparison groups. Reiser said:

'The data provided no support for the belief that the identified "sensitives" could produce investigatively useful information. Additionally, the data also failed to show that the psychics could produce *any* information relating to the cases beyond a chance level of expectancy.'

In his first report Reiser summed up the whole problem facing police who imagine that they can crack an impossible case by paranormal means: 'A psychic may generate relatively accurate information on one case, but be totally incorrect on another; correct information may be generated only in parts of each case; all information from some psychics may be incorrect; a psychic may have picked up correct information about one case, but may have reported it for another case (displacement); a psychic may be more accurate on one day as opposed to another, and personal motivation may be required on the part of some psychics to provide accurate responses.'

How any detective might pick and choose from that collection of maybes, possibles, lies and stolen factual bric-a-brac, we cannot say. Our advice to the police would be, even in a desperate case, to ignore everything that comes from a sceptic and to stick to techniques which get results, such as DNA, fingerprints, and good old-fashioned leg-work.

HOME	BORN	OCCUPATION	FATHER	MOTHER	MISCELLANEOUS
					Would strike again after Jacqui Hill
Tyneside or Wearside Address includes Berwick or Bewick				Dead, of cancer Called Molly or Polly	Distinctive scar on left cheek, mark on right cheek. Full bottom lip
Lives with sister and family					'Beware of a violent end to it. He will fight not to be taken alive.'
Sunderland					
Terraced house in Leeds		Machinery or engines – works in a factory	Dead		Disguises or dresses as a woman
House called 'Roselea'	London	Plumber Ex-miner		Alive	Moles on face. Blue van. Figures 297 could link with a car
Lancashire/Bolton area					Has already been questioned by police
4-bedroom detached house in Heaton, Bradford	Bradford	Lorry driver for engineering firm	John Alive	Kathleen Died of heart attack 8.11.78	Was questioned by police 3 years before finally arrested

Astrology

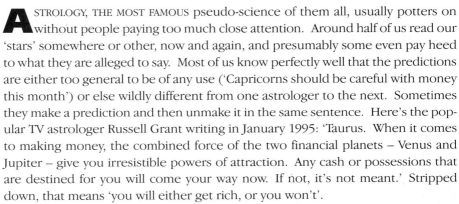

ASTROLOGY, THE MOST FAMOUS pseudo-science of them all, usually potters on without people paying too much close attention. Around half of us read our 'stars' somewhere or other, now and again, and presumably some even pay heed to what they are alleged to say. Most of us know perfectly well that the predictions are either too general to be of any use ('Capricorns should be careful with money this month') or else wildly different from one astrologer to the next. Sometimes they make a prediction and then unmake it in the same sentence. Here's the popular TV astrologer Russell Grant writing in January 1995: 'Taurus. When it comes to making money, the combined force of the two financial planets – Venus and Jupiter – give you irresistible powers of attraction. Any cash or possessions that are destined for you will come your way now. If not, it's not meant.' Stripped down, that means 'you will either get rich, or you won't'.

When astrologers attempt to be precise about world events, as opposed to being vague about personal lives, they court disaster. In his book *Return of Heroic Failures*, Stephen Pile records 'the world's least correct astrologer', R H Naylor, who wrote prognostications for *The Sunday Express* during the 1930s and 1940s. In the space of a few weeks, he predicted that General Franco would never rule Spain, the Conservatives would win the next election (Labour won by a landslide) and firmly declared that there would be no war in 1939. 'Hitler's horoscope shows he is not a warmaker,' he told his readers.

As even Jonathan Cainer – described by his newspaper as 'Britain's most authoritative astrologer' – said on BBC radio in 1995, 'the whole thing is a load of cods...how can you say that a twelfth of the population are going to have the same day, for crying out loud?' Journalists tell a (perhaps apocryphal) story about the reporter who had the job of making up the regular horoscope in *The Daily Mirror*'s Manchester office. Once, bored with the usual nonsense about romantic opportunities beckoning and the need for diligence at work, he wrote: 'All the sorrows of yesteryear are as nothing to what will befall you today.' The paper was flooded with complaints, and the stargazer was fired.

(So-called 'serious' astrologers scorn many newspaper columns, which they regard as little better than guesswork, compared to their own more scholarly approach.)

But except when a famous person turns out to use astrology to take important decisions – such as the revelation in 1988 that Nancy Reagan had consulted a San

Francisco astrologer to determine the most propitious days for her husband, President Reagan, to undertake engagements – there's precious little news about astrology in the papers.

However, in January 1995, there was a positive sunburst of publicity. Dr Jacqueline Mitton, spokeswoman for the British Royal Astronomical Society, pointed out that – thanks to the precession of the equinoxes – all the traditional star signs were one place out in the sky. People who thought they were born under Aries were in fact under the influence of Pisces. Virgos had become Leos, Cancers turned into Geminis, and so on, right around the heavens. What's more, said Ms Mitton, there should be a thirteenth zodiac sign, the constellation Ophiucus (a man wrestling a snake, sometimes called Serpentarius), tucked in between Scorpio and Sagittarius.

Now, the precession of the equinoxes has been known about for thousands of years. Even Ptolemy, the man who invented the zodiac used today, knew that the dates of the year at which the sun is in each constellation shift slowly but constantly. In another 2,166 years they will have moved round one more place. In about 26,000 years they will have made a complete revolution back to where the ancient Greeks first logged them.

This phenomenon is not easy to grasp, but it is the result of the fact that the earth's axis wobbles slightly, thanks to the gravitational pull of the Sun and the Moon. This wobble makes the axis describe, over time, a cone shape. The effect is that through the 26,000-year cycle the heavens, or the celestial sphere, appear to have moved relative to the vernal equinox. Since Ptolemy drew up the signs of the zodiac in AD 140, they've moved – from our point of view – about 26° out of the total 360°.

Ptolemy was a superlative scientist, working at a time when there was no distinction between astronomy and astrology. Among other achievements, he was able to predict the motions of

the planets and named many stars. He also believed firmly that all these bodies had a direct, and very specific influence on human beings, even down to our physical appearance.

It was Ms Mitton's statement, plastered over the front page of several newspapers in 1995, which brought the subject to the attention of millions of people who might have thought there could be 'something' in astrology. They were perhaps forced to ask how it was that one's personality and future might be determined by random patterns of stars billions of miles away – when the stars themselves appear in a quite different place from where they were supposed to be.

Arabic astrologers with instruments for taking measurements of planets and stars from a print c.1498.

As usually happens with pseudo-scientists, astrologers decided to ignore the evidence. *The Daily Telegraph*, an otherwise reputable newspaper whose weekly magazine nevertheless employs an astrologer, asked for his view. Robert Hyde said that whatever scientists find in today's sky, astrologers continued to base their predictions on the stars as they were 3,000 years ago. 'A thousand years from now people will laugh at many of today's scientific beliefs,' he said, 'but astrology will still be going strong.'

He may well be right. After all, real scientists have to measure their beliefs against the acid test of demonstrable truth. Many of their theories do collapse. Astrologers have no such problem. They can go on churning out reams of meaningless, unprovable twaddle for as long as they like. Why should the facts ever trouble them at all?

As it happens, all astrologers with any claim to half-competence knew about the precession of the equinoxes. Naturally they responded with a *post hoc* rationalisation. What mattered were not those particular stars, they said, but the part of the sky in which they had once appeared to be. Signs such as Virgo and Cancer were simply a shorthand way of identifying sectors of the heavens, and the fact that those constellations had since moved on to a different sector of the sky was irrelevant. Many modern astrologers argue that it is only the position of the sun and the planets which matter. If someone is born when the sun is said to be 'in Sagittarius' (i.e. set against the background of those stars when viewed from earth) it actually means that it is in Scorpio. They could have done us all a favour by calling these segments something less confusing, or just allocating each one a number.

A horoscope written in both Arabic and Latin figures from a text of 1641 describing the making of an Astrolabe.

Certainly many of their customers seemed willing to take their work on trust, however misguided it turned out to be. The BBC interviewed several followers of astrology about the shift in the stars' positions. 'I wouldn't believe it,' said one, 'because I'm a Scorpio and that's the way I am, and nothing is going to change it.' 'I do think I'm very much a Leo, so I'd be a bit dubious that

The horoscope for the formation of the United States of America, from 'A Complete Illustration of the Astrological and Occult Sciences' by E Sibley 1790.

it was wrong, actually,' said another. People seem to want to be pigeon-holed, and resent attempts to tell them that they might have been given the wrong stereotype.

This is not surprising, since polls in the United States suggest that 52 per cent of the population 'believes' in astrology, and as many as one person in three (G A Dean, 1983) believes in it strongly enough to shift their self-image in the direction their star sign suggests. In other words, these people tend to think of themselves as caring, extrovert, shy, creative, or whatever they are supposed to be.

However, the suggestion that the constellations themselves have nothing to do with the case now leaves us with the somewhat limp conclusion that the real influence upon us comes from the time of year we are born. If you're induced a day early, then you escape being moody and morose, and instead are lively and generous. A gynaecologist decides on a caesarean section because he's booked a golfing holiday and, as if by magic, instead of being a cheerful extrovert, you are doomed to be shy and retiring. A cartoon in *Punch* summed up the whole ridiculous claim. It showed a puzzled man listening to the radio news: 'And the science of astrology took a major leap forward today when all persons born under the sign of Scorpio were run over by egg lorries.' A Monty Python sketch satirised the same nonsense. For those born under a new sign of 'Nesbit', they predicted: 'in the

Feng Shui is a 2000-year-old Chinese system of divination which has been used by telephone company Hutchison Telecom and by Richard Branson head of Virgin Atlantic. This is an illustration of a compass used by Feng Shui practitioners whose main occupation is to recommend alignment of proposed buildings.

morning an old school friend of Duane Eddy's will come round and whistle some of Duane's great instrumental hits. In the afternoon, you will die.' (This may not be quite as ludicrous as it sounds. The sixteenth-century Italian astrologer, Girolamo Cardano, who cast horoscopes for Edward VI of England, predicted the day and the hour of his own death. When it came, and he found himself regrettably fit and healthy, he committed suicide rather than ruin his reputation.)

The belief that the heavens can influence life on Earth goes back to almost every society in history. It is not surprising. Early man had little or no scientific knowledge to explain all that went on around him, but he did know that certain things happened at regular intervals. Hot weather, cold weather, rainy seasons and harvests all came at much the same time of year. The Moon and women's bodies worked to a monthly cycle. The Sun and the Moon indubitably had a direct effect on Earth; why not other heavenly bodies too? Since certain events occurred at a time when other heavenly bodies were at a particular place in the sky, it was natural to associate the two and imagine that the heavens caused the events to happen.

The planets were of particular interest, since they appeared to have their own independent motion against the backcloth of the stars. It is no wonder that ancient man pondered what effect they might have. As scholars began to keep records, it was possible to recall what had happened the last time when one planet was in a particular constellation; perhaps the same kind of thing would happen again.

The human mind likes to make connections and to categorise. Over the centuries, in different societies and in the light of different religions, the hidden meanings of the night sky were codified by 'experts'. In China, astrologers who made mistaken predictions were sometimes executed; an excellent reason for being exceedingly vague, or simply changing what you'd written after the event. No mediaeval king or potentate would be without an astrologer to suggest the most propitious times for important events such as marriages or wars. (Louis XI of France had a court astrologer whose unpleasant predictions displeased him. He decided to have him killed, but thought better of it when the man cunningly told him: 'I shall die three days before your Majesty.') Over the centuries, astrologers learned the most important trick of their trade: to combine meticulous and impressive record keeping with ambiguous predictions.

As Carl Sagan records, many familiar words derive from these beliefs. 'Disaster' is from the Greek for 'bad star'; 'the Hebrew 'mazeltov' means 'good constellation'. Romeo and Juliet were said to be 'star-crossed' and blues singers bemoan being 'born under a bad sign'. (There is a considerable human vanity to all this. As one nineteenth-century writer said: 'How we should pity the arrogance of the

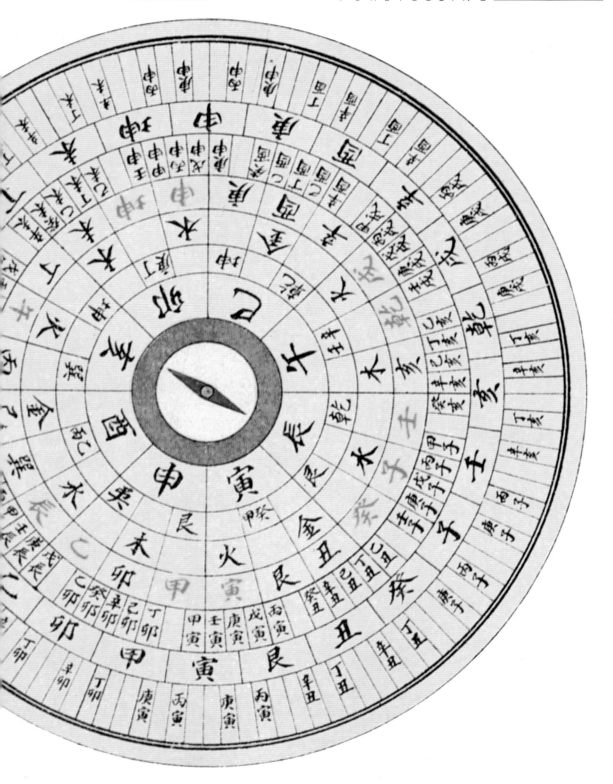

Aries

Alia terrea Taurus

Alia aerea Gemini

Alia aquea Cancer

Leo

Virgo

worm that crawls at our feet, if...it...imagined that meteors shot athwart the sky to warn it that a tom-tit was hovering near to gobble it up.')

Even now, when Man has landed on the Moon and space probes visit the stars, we retain a hunger for something which will explain the mysteries of life and anticipate our future. Most newspapers, even 'serious' ones, now print horoscopes. A tabloid which offers an annual horoscope can see its circulation rise by a quarter million or so, helped by expensive TV advertising. In the Library of Congress there are no fewer than 12,000 works on astrology. Add together fees for 'consultations', producing media horoscopes, books, lectures and seminars, and it's estimated that astrology may bring in as much as $100 million a year in the United States alone.

There are two main types of astrology used in the modern West. The most common is tropical astrology, the kind familiar from newspapers and magazines. This is the one which, to all intents and purposes, says that your personality and your future life are determined in part by the time of year you are born. Because the constellations are now in the 'wrong' places, tropical astrologers ignore them. Sidereal (or 'planetary') astrology is less common. It plots the actual constellation which the sun is in at the time of birth. It also considers where the moon and planets are in relation to the twelve signs of the zodiac, plus potentially another twenty-nine constellations. The two systems are not compatible and produce quite different results, often dramatically so, because adjacent signs are often deemed to have opposite qualities.

All that astrologers can agree on is that in some ways heavenly bodies do influence life on earth – quite apart from the heat and light provided by the Sun, or the tides caused by the Moon. They do not generally claim to know how this happens, suggesting that it might have something to do with gravity, or electromagnetism, or so-called 'planetary vibrations'. Many astrologers admit that they don't know how the influence is transmitted, merely that it must be transmitted somehow because the system 'works'. (In fact, the gravitational pull of the Moon is minuscule compared to that of a midwife attending a birth. A planet in outer space has an undetectable pull on a human being on earth. Some astrologers claim, however, that the influence may be similar to the effect of the Moon on the oceans.)

The stars in the sky are billions of miles away. However, when we look up on a clear night, we can imagine them as being dotted onto the inside of a vast black ball, with us on Earth at the centre. This is the 'celestial sphere' (it's possible to buy globes of this, depicting the stars as they appear from Earth, only printed on the outside of the ball).

An astrologer generally draws up a horoscope by examining the relative position of objects in the sky in the celestial sphere and on the Earth's horizon at the time of a subject's birth. But there are other factors to be considered too. Astrologers divide the sky into twelve notional 'houses' which rotate with the Earth. The effect a planet has upon someone is supposed to vary with the house it's in when the person was born. Saturn would have a different influence at its highest point in the sky than if it were on the horizon. However, there are three quite different 'house systems' which all lead to different results.

Some astrologers include other objects in the sky, such as comets and asteroids, and some even reckon on 'esoteric' planets, which don't actually exist. Some of these are held to give excellent results. (On the other hand, they are loth to include the recently discovered planets, and ignore quasars, black holes and so on. Apparently only those heavenly bodies which we can actually see have any influence.)

Then there are 'aspects', which are the angular relationships between any two planets. 'Major aspects' indicate that the planets are separated by 0, 60, 90, 120 or 180°, 'minor aspects' refer to 30, 45, 135 and 150° of separation. Unfortunately few astrologers can agree on what these signify, or even how an aspect is defined. For example, what does a 52° angle indicate? However, all is not lost. These aspects are recorded by mediaeval-looking symbols, so instead of boring statements such as 'Jupiter and Uranus are 150° apart' you have a chart filled with the most wonderfully mysterious squiggles. No wonder clients came away impressed by the astrologer's ancient, arcane wisdom.

Given that astrologers agree on very little, apart from the most general statements – we might call them 'untruisms' – such as 'Mars is associated with aggressive, warlike behaviour', or 'Geminis are outgoing and lively', one would assume that their science would have long been abandoned as useless. Yet for a lot of people it does seem to work, and to work well. There seems no doubt that many astrologers sincerely believe in what they are doing. Their enthusiastic customers may range from those who found a 'hit' in a newspaper column ('It said "expect a financial reward" the very day my Premium Bond won!') to people who have spent good money on a personal consultation ('It was amazing, she knew all about me. Apparently it's because Jupiter was in the ascendant when I was born').

Astrologers are also always keen to point out that numerous 'scientific tests' have proved that astrology works. And it is certainly true that a very few experiments have produced some statistics which might suggest a better-than-chance correlation between events on Earth and the movement of heavenly bodies. The trouble is that these tests have always proved impossible to duplicate, they frequently suffered from flawed methodology, and what they suggest is usually based on quite different premises from the beliefs of individual astrologers. And there are far, far more scientific tests which indicate the contrary, that there is nothing in astrology at all.

One thing the pseudo-sciences tend to have in common is that they generate vast quantities of data. Astrologers create innumerable 'facts' by considering anything in the heavens, and any relationship between an object there and any other object. It would be amazing if many coincidences didn't occur, some of them quite startling.

For astrologers one of the most exciting studies was the biggest ever carried out in their field. In the early 1980s, Professor Alan Smithers of Manchester University examined the jobs and the birth dates of 2.3 million people listed in Britain's 1971 national census. What he found was reported over four days in *The*

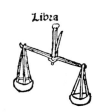

Libra

Scorpio

Sagittarius

Capricornus.

Aquarius.

Pisces

Guardian in March 1984. Before beginning his analysis, he asked sixteen recognised expert astrologers to make predictions of the correlations that would be found between sun signs and occupations. One of these experts was Charles Harvey, president of the Astrological Association, who predicted that people in the caring professions, such as nurses, would crop up more frequently in alternate zodiac signs, starting with Taurus. Another was that the average number of trade union officials would be born in alternate signs, starting with Aries. These predictions turned out to be correct for nurses, and almost correct for union officials.

Professor Smithers, who said however that he 'remained unconvinced' about astrology after his search, suggested that some of the results could be explained by seasonal trends, often caused by patterns of birth among different social classes. Nevertheless, the survey produced such a flood of tables and statistics, supporters of astrology have found enough correlations to claim that it 'proves' their beliefs beyond doubt.

For instance, Professor Smithers identified ten occupations where his astrologers generally agreed that certain star signs would predominate. They were:

Coal miner	Scorpio, Capricorn
Car mechanic	Aries
Tailor/dressmaker	Libra
Baker	Taurus
Clerk/cashier	Virgo
Typist	Virgo
Hairdresser	Libra
Optician	Virgo
Civil engineer	Capricorn
Author/journalist	Gemini

Of these ten, seven were 'hits' in that there was a higher than average number born under the correct sign. On the other hand, astrologers don't presume that signs will be merely somewhat above average, but will be clearly dominant. We can see what position each of these specially chosen signs were for each trade:

Coal miner	Scorpio (4th); Capricorn (3rd)
Car mechanic	Aries (4th)
Tailor/dressmaker	Libra (2nd)
Baker	Taurus (4th)
Clerk/cashier	Virgo (joint 3rd)
Typist	Virgo (12th)
Hairdresser	Libra (joint 6th)
Optician	Virgo (2nd)
Civil engineer	Capricorn (11th)
Author/journalist	Gemini (1st)

A clairvoyant and astrologer checking a horoscope using a table of planetary positions.

At first sight, this table is not bad news for astrologers. On the other hand, they managed only one direct hit – authors and journalists – which is precisely what would have been expected by chance. And this table only considers those occupations where the astrologers broadly agreed with each other.

However, even if the results get nowhere near to matching astrologers' claims, sceptics need to ask why the results are marginally better than chance would predict. There are several reasons.

Social class is an important factor. A 10 per cent sample from the same census showed the remarkable fact that the professional and managerial classes in Britain are significantly more likely to have their babies in spring and summer, whereas the opposite applies to manual workers and the unskilled. For instance, babies born into social classes 1 and 2 are 2 per cent more likely to be born under Aries and Taurus (21 March to 20 May) than the national average. They are more than 2 per cent less likely to be born under Capricorn (23 December to 20 January). The exact opposite applies to social classes 3 through 5. They are two per cent less likely than average to have children in Taurus (21 April to 20 May) and 1½ per cent more likely to have them in Sagittarius and Capricorn (23 November to 20 January).

An illustration from a sixteenth-century Turkish Treatise on Astrology showing Virgo.

Whether this is to do with central heating (most of the sample were born before that became widespread), or comes about because the middle classes are more likely to plan their births, with spring being a favourite time, no one is sure. But the sample (of 2.3 million people) is too large to be skewed, and the survey agrees with several others, suggesting that it is accurate.

In a long critique of *The Guardian* survey, four psychologists (Dean, Kelly, Rotton, Saklofske) also suggested that the results might have been affected by self-attribution – people plumping for a particular line of work because it matches their star sign. This may seem far-fetched, though the psychologists argue that it would only require one person in sixty to think this way to account for *The Guardian* results. Since polls show that one person in three believes in astrology enough to shift their sense of self-image, it would only need one in twenty of those to choose a job accordingly.

However, *The Guardian* survey did seem to offer a little prima facie support for astrology, and it keeps cropping up when astrologers defend their work. Sometimes it is not only used to bolster belief in the subject, but as source material in itself. For example, the astrologer Nicholas Campion, writing in *The Daily Mail* in 1991, pointed out that Aries was the sign for politicians as well as show-business people. According to *The Guardian*'s sample of 3,317 people engaged in show business, Aries occurred 12 per cent above the norm, with Taurus next at 5 per cent. However, before the survey, fifteen astrologers picked Leo and Pisces for actors and musicians. These came in at ninth (-5.5 per cent) and fifth (+3 per cent) respectively. But this is typical of pseudo-science. Make a prediction. When it turns out to be untrue, blithely incorporate the actual outcome into your 'science'.

Campion also said that Virgo was dominant among the caring professions. Of course it's not always easy to define which the caring professions are, but if we take a wide selection it's easy to see that the spread is as wide as chance would predict:

Virgo's position

Clergy	7th, fractionally below average
Dentists	12th, at -12 per cent
Doctors	10th, at -6 per cent
Nurses	5th, at +0.5 per cent
Opticians	2nd, at +27 per cent
Radiographers	joint 9th, at -9 per cent
Social workers	7th, at -1 per cent
Teachers (school)	3rd, at +1.5 per cent
Teachers (FE)	7th, at average
Teachers (univ)	11th, at -8 per cent

This table makes some interesting points: Virgo fails to come top in any of the caring professions, and for only one (opticians) is it substantially higher than average. The three jobs which might be thought closest to each other, teachers at various stages of the education process, are instead widely apart, with Virgo ranked from third to eleventh. Most intriguingly, Virgo is top for accountants (+7 per cent), and for bakers and pastry cooks (+10 per cent). The same sign is above average among fishermen (+8 per cent), bus conductors (+4 per cent), farmers (+1 per cent), and – of all people – politicians and civil servants (+5 per cent). In all of these trades there were more Virgos than among either doctors or nurses.

If Virgo is the sign for caring people, then it embraces a pretty broad definition of 'caring'.

The other survey which has been seized on by delighted astrologers was the one carried out in 1950s and 1960s by the French scientists, Michel and Francoise Gauquelin. This couple had long been critical of traditional astrology. However, their own work suggested a clear connection between three planets and three occupations: Saturn with scientists, Jupiter with military men, and Mars with successful sportsmen and women. There appeared to be a particularly close link between sports champions and Mars. Michel Gauquelin divided the sky into twelve sections in which Mars appears as it orbits the sun. He claimed that his sample of 2,088 French sporting champions were likely to be born above chance expectation when Mars was in the first section (rising) and the fourth (at its culmination).

"D'you think there's anything in this astrology business?"

This seemed quite sensational news, and many scientists around the world began testing to see if Gauquelin's results could be duplicated. Almost immediately doubts set in. In Belgium the Para Committee tested 535 champions, and found that Gauquelin's outcome *did* occur, though they pointed out that the distribution for the other ten sectors were not what either chance or Gauquelin had predicted. They also suggested possible bias in the data selection – exactly what is a sporting 'champion'? How is he or she chosen to be thrown into the statistical pot? Marvin Zelen, now a professor of statistics at Harvard, also suspected the selection. He and two colleagues conducted a test of 408 American champions, and got negative results.

Michel Gauqelin disputed these American tests. In 1979 he tried another replication, with 438 Europeans, saying that he had deleted 423 'lesser' champions from his study. His results were positive again. Clearly there was an impasse. In 1982 a committee of French sceptics agreed to co-operate with Gauquelin to run a definitive test. Both sides worked out the protocol together. When the results began to emerge, it became clear that of the 1,066 champions under examination, only 200 (18.76 per cent) were born in the first and fourth sectors, compared to 18.2 per cent which chance would predict. This is statistically insignificant. (The reason why 18.2 per cent is slightly higher than the 16.66 per cent which might be expected is to do with Mars's orbit around the sun, compared to Earth's. A control group of non-athletes produced the figure of 18.2.)

Through 1990 and 1991, Gauquelin fought against these results, repeatedly demanding changes in the sample. He kept putting forward the names of sportsmen and women who, he said, ought to be considered; these included a substantial number born in the key sectors. He demanded the deletion of other people, none of whom were born in the key sectors. Finally the Committee concluded that the so-called Mars effect was probably attributable to Gauquelin's bias in choosing his sample.

This issue may never be cleared up altogether, since Gauquelin committed suicide in May 1991, allegedly leaving orders that all his data should be destroyed. None of this will, however, prevent astrologers from claiming his work as proof of their beliefs.

The Gauquelin and *The Guardian* surveys got a lot of attention largely because they appeared, at first sight, to offer some backing for astrology. But there have been far more surveys which do the opposite. For example, John McGervey of Case Western University looked up the birth dates of 16,634 American scientists and 6,475 politicians: he found the distribution of their signs as random as for the public at large. Bernard Silverman, a psychologist at Michigan State University, used the records of 2,978 couples who married and 478 couples who divorced in Michigan during 1967. This offered no hope to astrologers who claim that people should choose partners born under 'compatible' star signs. There was no link at all, either among those marrying or divorcing.

In 1985 *Nature* reported a test of thirty American and European astrologers carried out by Shawn Carlson, a physicist at UCLA. The astrologers were asked to interpret natal charts for 116 unseen 'clients'. For each chart, they were supplied with three anonymous personality profiles, one from the client and two others chosen at random. These personality profiles were obtained using an accepted personality test, which measures traits such as aggressiveness, dominance and femininity from a series of multiple choice questions. The astrologers had predicted that they would match half of the charts provided. Instead they scored one in three – exactly as predicted by chance.

Several tests have simply succeeded in making astrologers look foolish. One classic occurred when the psychologist Geoffrey Dean sent a large group of astrologers a natal chart which, he told them, belonged to the singer Petula Clark. They speedily came up with descriptions which matched her bubbly, amiable, outgoing personality. Unfortunately, the chart was actually for the mass murderer Charles Manson.

And yet, people continue to believe. Something which tends to convince more than reading any newspaper star-gazer is a personal visit to an astrologer. Without doubt, many customers come away convinced that the astrologer has been able to understand their true nature and has even been able to describe events from their past without having any way of knowing them. Many astrologers believe in what they are doing, and the warm and admiring feedback they get from clients helps encourage them. This is why they don't feel the need to explain how it works; they simply know that it does.

So how does it work? Overwhelmingly the main reason is the same as the one which seems to validate fortune-telling, palm reading, tarot cards and – in the last century – phrenology, the reading of bumps in the skull. We are all more alike than different. Indeed, our self-images are so much alike that it is quite easy to create character analyses which the overwhelming majority of people think apply to them. These are known as 'Barnum statements', after the American showman P T Barnum, who recognised that we are much more similar to each other than we imagine. Here's a typical Barnum statement:

'You have a need for other people to like and admire you and yet you tend to be critical of yourself. While you have some personality weaknesses, you are generally able to compensate for them.

'You have considerable unused capacity that you have not turned to your advantage. Disciplined and self-controlled on the outside, you tend to be worrisome and insecure on the inside. At times you have serious doubts as to whether you have made the right decision or done the right thing.

'You prefer a certain amount of change and variety and become dissatisfied when hemmed-in by restrictions and limitations.

'You also pride yourself as an independent thinker and do not accept others' statements without satisfactory proof. But you have found it unwise to be too frank in revealing yourself to others.'

There are few of us who could not find ourselves in that description. Think, for a moment, of what the opposite might be: 'You have a need for people to dislike you, though you never criticise yourself. You have no personality weaknesses...you like being hemmed in by restrictions... you regard yourself as a slave to other people's opinions...' It's obviously nonsense. Yet people reading the full statement above might well be astonished at how closely it matches them.

Another intriguing fact is that people are much more likely to agree with a Barnum statement when they are told that it is specifically about them. Offer someone the description above and ask if it fits, and most people will say that it does. Tell them that it has been drawn up after careful consideration of the position of the stars and planets at the time of their birth, and even more will find it an amazingly close match.

For example, C R Snyder, a psychologist at the University of Kansas, drew up, with his colleagues, a personality description similar to the one above. Three groups were asked to rate the description on a scale of 1–5, with 1 meaning 'completely unlike me' to 5 indicating 'a perfect fit'. The first group was given the description and told that it was a universal personality sketch. Asked if it matched them, they gave it an average rating of 3.2. The second group had been asked the month in which they were born and told that they were receiving a horoscope for their own sign. They esteemed it more highly, and gave it an average of 3.72. The third group had been asked for the date on which they were born, and were told that the self-same description was actually based on their own birth chart. They gave it an average rating of 4.38. Almost every test in this field shows that people rate a reading more highly if it appears authoritative and personal to them.

Astrologers also use the same techniques of cold reading (discussed in the chapter on Cold Readings see p 63). Since people seek counselling for a limited number of reasons, usually connected with severe emotional stress, an experienced astrologer can usually figure out quite quickly what the main cause of anxiety is. A few 'fishing' questions ('Money's not always been easy, has it?' 'People don't seem to realise your talents and abilities, do they?') plus a few safe universal guesses ('I see deep grief, connected with a relative' – who hasn't lost a relative at some time?) and the client is likely to be struck by the astrologer's obvious sympathy and – occasionally – amazing knowledge. This is helped by the fact that the client yearns to believe; he or she is paying a lot of money to be reassured, comforted and understood.

Show people the mysterious natal charts, tell them the splendid gobbledygook about Jupiter being in the ascendant, and the most vague prognostications take on an impressive air of authority. Furthermore, numerous studies show that people will continue to admire a fortune-teller of any kind if they've been told what they want to hear – even when it's wrong. A client who is, say, worried about not having a partner will continue to patronise an astrologer who sees marriage in the stars even if their love-life remains as bleak as ever. The astrologer is offering hope, which is the next best thing.

And of course it always does work. Here's the astrologer D Hamblin who became chairman of the UK Astological Association, describing how he forces it to work:

'If I find a very meek and unaggressive person with five planets in Aries, this does not cause me to doubt that Aries means aggression. I may be able to point to his Pisces Ascendant, or to his Sun conjunct Saturn, or to his ruler in the twelfth house; and if none of these alibis are available, I can simply say that he has not fulfilled his Aries potential.

'Or I can argue (as I have heard argued) that if a person has an excess of planets in a particular sign, he will tend to suppress the characteristics of that sign because he is scared that, if he reveals them, he will carry them to excess. But if on the next day I meet a very aggressive person who also has five planets in Aries, I will change my tune; I will say that he had to be like that because of his planets in Aries.'

Some psychologists argue that there is little wrong with this kind of nonsense, since combined with a sympathetic hearing and what might well be good, practical advice, an astrologer offers a service which could cost far more if provided by a psychiatrist. But the rest of us don't have to believe it.

Graphology

LIKE MANY PSEUDO-SCIENCES, graphology looks, at first sight, as if it's based on ordinary common sense. But nonsense has a habit of getting its start in life from reason. Look at astrology. Observations of the night sky led to the creation of a great body of 'science', the codified gibberish which modern astrology grinds out all the time.

In the same way, graphology seems almost logical. We *can* guess something about someone from their handwriting. Tests show that on average everyone can distinguish a man's writing from a woman's roughly 70 per cent of the time. If you were shown three examples of handwriting and were told that one was by a German, one by a Briton and the other by an American, there's a fairly good chance that you could work out which was which: the styles of writing taught in schools in those countries are quite different. In any event, 100 people asked to make a judgement would almost certainly do better than chance.

Journalists get a lot of handwritten letters from strangers. Even without reading the content or seeing the signature, one can generally make a good guess about the writer's sex and even their age. Some personality characteristics are very obvious in handwriting, just as they are in any other human activity, whether playing football or making love. Someone who writes a letter in a fast and unhesitant hand may very well be efficient and unhesitant. An elegant hand implies to most people someone who is artistic, and who may well have a meticulous side to their character as well.

Social class is an important clue. One of the few tests which gives any credibility to graphology, conducted by H Hönel in 1977, suggested that by a small margin, graphologists could tell the difference between the handwriting of criminals and that of non-criminals. But class seems a likely cause of that rare success. People who had poor schooling, or came from a labouring background in which good handwriting was not thought important, are slightly more likely to become criminals than those who went to good schools, lived in homes where good handwriting was highly regarded, and were diligent enough to learn how to do it. This would show up often enough to skew the results away from chance. (It does leave unanswered the universal puzzle of doctors' writing.)

Paradoxically this same test might indicate to us that graphology was positively misleading. Suppose a firm used a graphologist to help pick their senior executives. He might believe from H Hönel's experiment that he can identify criminal traits, whereas what he is really doing is detecting people from the lower social classes. But a candidate in that position has clearly struggled to recover from a difficult start in life, and might therefore make a better executive than the person with a more obviously 'educated' hand.

Some graphologists are really fortune tellers using a different gimmick from the tarot cards, palm reading, crystal balls and astrology. He or she may well believe that they are practising a reputable science, and positive feedback from the client confirms them in this view. What they are generally doing is providing a blend of cold reading (see p63), Barnum statements – using the knowledge that we are all more alike than different (see the chapter on Astrology p100) – and guesswork based on the client's appearance and handwriting which, as we know, can contain important clues. This kind of 'reading' may do little harm. Some people find it comforting. Observations such as 'your writing tells me that you are sometimes quick to anger, but almost always regret losing your temper' apply to nearly all of us but may be helpful for someone who has trouble with relationships. It's very comforting to think that there is someone non-judgemental who seems able to understand you better than even your friends and family do even when what they tell you is of little or no value.

However, most graphology is used in business, for personnel selection. It is clearly very appealing to some managers. It's hard to judge who is going to fit into a job from an interview alone, when people are, consciously or unconsciously, likely to dissemble, or from a glowing testimonial, which might be a sly means of getting rid of an unwanted employee. There's no easy way to measure the qualities of hard work, loyalty, honesty and competence which an employer wants. Graphology poses as a scientific, quantifiable system which can't be fiddled. If there were anything in it, it would be a personnel manager's dream.

One estimate is that around 3,000 American firms use the technique. For example, Van Deventer, writing in the journal United States Banker, of which he was the managing editor, said in 1983: 'Graphoanalysis reveals capabilities and aptitudes in an individual, many of which the applicant may not even be aware of.' (Notice how the last clause can be translated as 'which nobody but the graphologist can see'. As so often with pseudo-science, the supporters claim that even when they seem wrong, they are actually right, because they perceive things which are invisible to others.)

British firms are less inclined to admit using graphology, presumably because it sounds a little too much like superstition, but a few are quite open about it. The giant Heron Corporation told the BBC in a 1989 edition of the science programme 'QED' that very few of their top executives are appointed without their handwriting being analysed. Warburg's, the merchant bank, has used graphology for thirty years. Trevor James, managing director of the IPS group, which provides executive recruitment services, also told the BBC that many British companies use graphology to screen their top executives, though not necessarily for junior appointments. His company has been using graphology for more than twelve years and, he says, it enables them to choose the people they want much more accurately. The company won't take on anybody who has been rejected by the graphologist.

Another keen believer is Mr J Reid, a British personnel expert. Writing in the British magazine *Personnel Management* in 1983, he said how impressed he and his wife had been by a graphological analysis of his own character. (All surveys show that Barnum-type assessments are much more convincing to people when they're described as having been based on the individual's own particulars, such as birth-chart, palm-reading, or in this case, handwriting.) Mr Reid went on to give instances where, he said, graphology had worked. One man was up for a job shortly after his release from prison for embezzlement. The graphological analysis showed that 'his declaration that he was reformed needed to be taken with some caution'. The man was put in a job where 'there was no possibility of his being exposed to temptation' and, hey presto, he did not re-offend. Mr Reid saw this as a sign that graphology works. In fact, all it shows is that someone put in a position where they can't steal money, won't steal money.

A French manual on graphology from around the beginning of the century. Graphology is now probably more popular in France than any other European country.

But it is in Europe that graphology is of huge importance. Some 85 per cent of European firms are believed to use the technique, at least to some extent. In France, Peugeot and Air France have their own full-time graphologists. (These have not saved Air France from making horrendous operating losses. Clearly graphology is not especially good at finding people of an economical bent.) The TV programme 'QED' showed Odile Ellison, a member of a leading group of 200 French graphologists who are actually recognised by the State, going through applications for the post of laboratory technician. In some cases she rejected applications after the swiftest possible glance at the handwriting.

It is appropriate that interest is so high in France, since it was a group of French clerics in the 1830s who launched modern graphology. The term was coined by one of their number, Abbé Michon. He published three books in which he set out to give the new 'science' a systematic basis, and to show how each individual element in a person's handwriting, such as the dots on the 'i's and the crossing of the 't's, is linked with one character trait or another.

According to Joe Nickell's 'A Brief History of Graphology', included in the book *The Write Stuff*, the French dominated the field until the end of the century, when German researchers started to make the running. Georg Meyer, a psychiatrist, argued that handwriting was 'brain writing'. All psychomotor functions, not only writing, expressed the emotions present in the brain. Ludwig Klages took this forward, with the theory that we are all dominated by two forces: our 'mind' which binds and inhibits, and our 'soul' which frees and develops us creatively. All 'expressive movements', such as walking, gesture, speech and handwriting, express the tensions between these two forces, in a way which is consistent within each human being. Handwriting was merely the easiest expressive movement to analyse, being conveniently available on paper.

Over the years there have been innumerable attempts to codify the study. Some argue that the force and the angle of strokes are important, others look for loops and slopes. Thin, angular writing is contrasted with round writing. Some give importance to margins. (People who leave wide margins are told they are 'generous'; who would disagree with such a kind assessment? If a client leaves narrow margins, he can be told that he is 'careful, thrifty', qualities which most of us can find in ourselves if we look hard enough.) Then there is the amount of the page that is used and the precise area of the page where the writing appears.

The trouble is that there are many different ways of analysing handwriting. There are at least thirty-two graphological societies in the US alone, many of them having a quite different set of rules and guidelines for their practioners to follow. Some of these are incompatible, so that one might provide a completely different interpretation of a piece of handwriting from another. (Imagine if the lab technician so carefully selected by Mme Ellison were to arrive at work saying that he believed in different laws of physics from everyone else.)

Nor has anyone managed to find out how our personalities are expressed through such details. *Why* is someone who leaves a wide margin likely to be generous? How is loyalty communicated through the down stroke on a letter 'T' ? Another similarity between graphology and astrology is that its practitioners do not bother to answer these questions; they are satisfied that it 'works' and leave it at that.

The TV programme 'QED' tested four of the most prominent graphologists. They were Jane Paterson, Erik Rees, described as 'Britain's top earner', a 'radio show pundit' called Maureen Ward, all from Britain, and the Israeli Anna Koren, who then (in 1989) charged as much as £700 for a single reading. Graphology is very big in Israel.

The four experts were asked to use their skills in three tests. They had to look for qualities such as loyalty and efficiency from writing samples provided by fifty secretaries, half of them the Brooke Street Bureau's very best, the other half ex-secretaries with a long record of poor performance. They had to distinguish between thirty self-made businessmen and thirty 'low-fliers', bank clerks and librarians. Finally they had to separate sixty samples of actors and monks. Here were the results:

Secretaries: Good/Bad

	Right	Wrong	Pass	Per cent
Rees	30	20	0	60
Ward	36	14	0	72
Paterson	34	16	0	68
Koren	26	10	14	66

(Overall average: 66.5 per cent correct)

High fliers/Clerks:

Rees	39	20	1	66
Ward	36	24	0	60
Paterson	36	24	0	60
Koren	27	14	19	61

(Overall average: 61.75 per cent correct)

Actors/Monks

Rees	38	22	0	63
Ward	35	24	1	59
Paterson	44	16	0	73
Koren	35	11	14	70

(Overall average: 66.25 per cent correct)

At first sight, these figures look pretty good. Peter Armitage, Professor of Statistics at Oxford University, who administered the tests using the 'double blind' method, described the results as:

'very clear cut indeed and very consistent. If the graphologists had been guessing at random with absolutely no skill they would have got about half of their assessment right. In fact they got a little less than two-thirds right. Now that means that there is virtually no chance of this occurring by random happenings.'

That is certainly true. Yet it certainly doesn't mean that graphology as practised by these people 'works'. For one thing, we can assume that the writing would certainly have given helpful and legitimate clues. It would be surprising if, on the whole, one could not detect some bad secretaries on the basis of their handwriting. Monks lead life at a slower pace than most of us, and one might think that they were likely to have a neater, more painstaking hand than most actors do. The evident difference between high-fliers and people in more lowly, ill-paid jobs, might be attributable to social class, as we discussed earlier in this chapter. However, these were self-made businessmen, so class may have been less of a factor – hence the fact that overall the graphologists did worst on this test.

The percentages we've quoted are particularly kind to Anna Koren, who did not to make any judgement at all in forty-seven out of the 170 samples, 28 per cent. Indeed, on the toughest test of all – high-fliers versus clerks – she made correct guesses only twenty-seven times out of sixty, fewer than half. It may be significant that Ms Koren was the only non-Briton taking the test, and so was able to read fewer of the signals which we might be able to glean from the handwriting of people who've been raised in the same country and culture as ourselves.

To put the figures another way, the proportion of correct judgements made by all the graphologists for all the samples was just 65 per cent. This is even more remarkable when you consider that as a control, the producers asked several ordinary people with no graphological skills or training to take the same test. Their score was 59 per cent. This is close to the professionals – astonishingly close when you consider that, whether or not graphology works as a science, its practitioners study samplings of handwriting all the time, many from people about whom they know a great deal already. They ought to know an awful lot about handwriting. If, however, they can perform only fractionally better than untaught members of the public, then their skills must be very dubious indeed.

The worst performance was undoubtedly that of Anna Koren, who charges such lavish sums for executive assessment. Faced with 170 samples, she managed to make a correct choice only 51.7 per cent of the time. This, remember, was on a test to distinguish between two groups of people with very widely different characters, skills or lifestyles. Quite how she expects to find much more subtle qualities, such as loyalty or leadership, it is hard to see. Or indeed how the others can pose as serious scientists at all. On the most generous estimation, they could spot these marked differences less than two-thirds of the time. It's hard to imagine a conventional recruitment agency doing as badly as they did and staying in business for long. To be of any real use to an employer looking for the very best staff, they would need to be at 80 per cent or higher.

There are many other test results which are even poorer than the BBC results. Adrian Furnham, a psychology lecturer at London University went through these and found a series of results ranging from the equivocal to the damning. After a test at Wright State University, Ohio, in 1976 in which six handwriting experts rated forty-eight specimens of handwriting on fifteen personality variables, 'it was concluded that the analyst could not accurately predict personality from handwriting'.

Lester, McLaughlin and Nosal reported in 1977 in *Perceptual and Motor Skills* on a test in which sixteen graphological experts had tried to predict from handwriting samples the degree of extroversion of 109 people whose personality test scores were known. 'No evidence was found for the validity of the graphological signs,' they said.

Another survey, by Rosenthal and Lines in 1978, found much the same. They tried to correlate three graphological indices with the extroversion scores for fifty-eight students, and ended up saying: 'the results did not support the claim that the three handwriting measures were valid indices of extroversion.'

In 1986 at the Hebrew University in Jerusalem, a team headed by G Ben-Shakhar asked graphologists to judge which out of eight professions were followed by forty successful people. 'The graphologists did not perform significantly better than a chance model,' they concluded.

The handful of tests which do indicate that graphology 'works' tend to be flawed. For instance, A Drory in 1986 did find significant correlations between job ratings and graphological analysis. However, his samples were based on hand-written autobiographical sketches, which are inevitably filled with clues. In other studies based on the handwriting of people writing about themselves, graphologists and amateurs have had remarkably similar scores.

The jury is still out on how stress affects handwriting. In 1986, G Keinan found that graphologists did no better than chance when they were asked to distinguish between samples from soldiers in a highly stressful situation (half an hour before their first night parachute jump) and those who were in a non-stressful, relaxed situation. However, C J Frederick found in a 1968 test that graphologists could distinguish between suicide notes written by people who had actually killed themselves, and the same notes copied out by normal people from typescript. This result caused much excitement among graphologists, who frequently quote it. But Frederick's methods were not altogether reliable; for example, the graphologists tested had the age, sex and suicide method available to them. They (and the suicides) were European whereas the lay persons' control groups were American.

The fact is that there is little or no serious evidence that we can learn anything from handwriting beyond the obvious. As Ben-Shaktar put it:

'Although it would not be surprising if it were found that sloppy handwriting characterised sloppy writers, stylised calligraphy indicated some artistic flair, and bold, energetic people had bold, energetic handwriting, there is no reason to believe that traits such as honesty, insight, leadership, responsibility, warmth and promiscuity find any kind of expression in graphological features....indeed, if a correspondence were found between graphological features and such traits, it would be a major theoretical challenge to account for it.'

He added that one problem was that there were not enough constraints in graphological analysis.

'The very richness of handwriting can be its downfall. Unless the graphologist makes firm commitments to the nature of correspondence between handwriting and personality, one can find *ad hoc* corroboration for any claim.'

Graphology once again resembles astrology, another pseudo-science in which the practitioner can find pretty well anything to prove what he wants to prove.

Fire
Walking

THERE ARE FEW SIGHTS MORE RIVETING, even awe-inspiring, than a demonstration of fire walking. A great trench, ten or twenty feet long, is filled with paper, tinder and wood. This is set alight, creating a massive blaze. At dusk, the fire glows a lurid orange colour, settling to a luminescent scarlet as darkness falls. Anyone standing too near the pit is forced back by the intense heat, which can be as high as 700 °C (1,300 °F) at the surface. Fresh wood tossed on to the fire is burned up in seconds.

Then, barefooted, the walkers stride confidently on to the burning embers, marching smoothly to the far end of the trench, showing no sign of either pain or fear. Some happily to go back again and again, and appear to suffer no ill effects.

It is a baffling and astounding sight. From childhood we learn that fire causes excruciating injury and pain. People who've been burned are often disfigured for life. Every instinct warns us to avoid letting fire anywhere near our bare flesh.

It is hardly surprising that for centuries people have been fascinated by the apparent miracle of fire walking. It's one of the few phenomena described in this book which crops up in the Bible. The Book of Deuteronomy lumps fire walking in with various other foreign 'abominations unto the Lord', such as divination, witchcraft and necromancy. The Book of Proverbs asks 'Can one go upon hot coals and his feet not be burned?' – which is clearly meant as a rhetorical question, inviting the answer 'impossible'. Isaiah has God promising: 'When thou walkest through the fire, thou shalt not be burned,' suggesting that it's a feat which could be managed only by someone under the protection of the Lord.

Since fire walking appears to be miraculous, it has acquired powerful religious overtones. It has also acquired plenty of hucksters and charlatans who've found it a convenient way of raising money, often very large sums. In California especially, entrepreneurs have made hundreds of thousands of dollars persuading people that they could make their minds take control of their bodies – and to prove it, they would be able to accomplish a fire walk. This, they were promised, would both increase their self-esteem and open up limitless opportunities in their lives. (Of course, it is possible that some of the people who teach others how to fire walk might sincerely believe that it does need unique mental powers.)

For centuries travellers have reported many instances of fire walking as part of religious ceremonies. In 1901 an American professor, S P Langley of the Smithsonian Institute in Washington, witnessed a priest in Tahiti walk through a

Preceding page
A demonstration of fire walking by Ahmed Hussein at Carshalton, Surrey in April 1937.

fire, claiming to be under the protection of various spells and a goddess who had lived on the island. The ceremony was accompanied by terrific noise and excitement together with what actors call 'business', such as the priest thrashing the hot stones with palm leaves before he began his walk. After the walk was over, Langley levered out a stone from the hottest part of the fire and threw it in a bucket of water, much of which immediately boiled away.

In 1931, *The National Geographic* reported a Hindu fire walk in Singapore. 'The devotees, including quite a number of women, approximated 400.

Fire walking has mainly been used in religious ceremonies all over the world. Here, Brahmans of the Soivrasta sect perform a fire walk near Madras, India in 1908. Today fire walking is used in seminars by people hoping to increase their self-esteem.

Some were kneeling and touching the earth with their foreheads, while others, more devout, were literally grovelling in the dirt. A few were endeavouring to crawl or roll completely around the temple...

'Many of those who had made a vow to undergo torture had prepared their bodies the preceding month by some form of penance, and had refrained from eating for a day before the event.'

This particular pit was fully 24 feet deep. At the end was a pool of milk, surrounded by images of gods. As seems to be usual on these occasions there was a great deal of loud noise, this time from drums, and the crowd was steadily worked up into a state of frenzy. Priests used whips to lash the walkers over the coals. Some of the women even carried babies in their arms.

Similar events were reported from many other countries, including India, Sri Lanka, and even Greece, where the ceremony is adapted to Christianity; walkers believe they are under the protection of St Constantine.

Kuda Bux having his feet washed and examined before his 1935 fire walk at Carshalton, Surrey.

In the days when people did not fly off on cheap package tours of the Orient, such events seemed unutterably exotic and remote, existing in the half-world between myth and exaggerated travellers' tales. Then in 1935 a young Indian called Kuda Bux arrived in Britain claiming to know the secret of fire walking. He was taken up by Harry Price, a celebrated ghost finder whose work on the haunted Borley Rectory was thoroughly discredited years later. Price arranged a fire walk for Bux in a suburban garden in Surrey. He assembled a team of onlookers and had the walk filmed. There was a howling gale on the day, and it needed 7 tons of logs, 1 ton of firewood, 10 gallons of paraffin, fifty copies of *The Times* and a load of charcoal to fill the 11-foot pit and get a satisfactory blaze going. When it was tested the centre of the fire had reached 1,440 °C (2,550 °F), and the surface ash 430 °C (800 °F). Some of the onlookers were afraid that the gales would blow away the surface ash and make the walk especially hazardous.

However, Bux appeared to have no particular anxiety. His feet were carefully examined for traces of any chemicals or ointments, and were washed and dried. A small plaster was attached to one of his soles as a test. Then he walked 'steadily and deliberately' the length of the pit, and promptly back again. Arthur C Clarke, in his *World of Strange Powers*, reports the assessment of the doctor who examined his feet afterwards:

'By careful scrutiny could be seen here and there the whitened appearance of the skin which occurs when the very surface of the epithelium is scorched without blistering. There were no signs of hyperæmia or blistering. The patch of plaster was quite unharmed, except that the fluff of the cotton at the cut edge looked very slightly scorched. If this were so, these cotton fibres must have reached a temperature approaching 120°C (250°F).'

Two Britons at the fire walk tried themselves, but were burned, one of them badly. The onlookers decided that Bux's secret was his manner of walking across the fire. Speed and nimbleness meant that his feet were not in contact with the coals for more than half a second at a time.

Fire walking continues to exert a powerful hold over people's imaginations. Often this is heightened by means of obvious but impressive trickery. For example, Buddhists at a temple in Nagoya in Japan hold fire walks which include children. The actual bed is composed of burning straw as kindling, covered in sticks which, by the time the walk takes place, have cooled down considerably. But the pit is flanked on either side by 3-foot high piles of wood. These continue to blaze away and subsequently make the whole spectacle far more spectacular and, apparently, dangerous.

Something so impressive is bound to attract New Age cultists, all of whom are to be found in abundance in California. In 1984, for instance, Bill McCarthy, a research psychologist at UCLA (his speciality is investigating why people choose to do things which damage them, such as smoking and injecting heroin,) in the course of his research attended a fire walking seminar in southern California. The brochures promised that participants would find their self-esteem increased, their anxieties reduced, and their deepest hopes and greatest ambitions at last within their grasp. It certainly brought a great deal of money within the grasp of the organisers. The charge was $125 to attend the event, and since eighty people turned up on the occasion McCarthy attended, the take must have been $10,000 for a single evening's work.

The session began with pep talks about dragging up deep personal fears, developing positive thinking, enlarging one's expectations and aiming for important personal goals – all of which is fairly normal California-speak. The organiser, one Tony Robbins, claimed amazing powers for what he called 'neurolinguistic programming'. This would not only enable perfectly ordinary people to perform fire walks but could cure tumours, end impotence, prevent drug addiction and even allow women to have orgasms without being touched.

Like the ceremonies in the mysterious East, this one was also accompanied by loud music and dancing. Participants were encouraged to give each other supportive back rubs. By midnight, when the actual fire walk was due to take place, a mood of relaxed and happy optimism had infected almost everyone there.

Just before the fire walk itself the participants were given brief instructions on how to survive it. They should believe strongly in the likelihood of success, breathe deeply and noisily, focus their eyes at a point in the sky rather than down at the coals, walk confidently at a normal pace, chant a mantra of 'cool moss' over and over to themselves, and wipe their feet on wet grass at the end. As McCarthy noted at the time, apart from the last, these are similar instructions given for the

Lamaze method, which prepares women for the pain of childbirth.

Participants were taken down to see the pit while repeatedly shouting 'Yes, yes, yes!' as they worked themselves into a lather of excitement. In this heightened state, roughly 90 per cent of the audience then walked across the pit, and few reported any injuries at all – though of course it's possible that some were hurt but did not want to admit failure.

Anyone who knows the mundane secret of fire walking might think that all the elaborate preparation was at best a waste of time, at worst a misleading of the people who had paid. But in 1995 the same Tony Robbins was invited to the presidential country house, Camp David in Maryland, to pass his message to Bill Clinton. This is perhaps not surprising; reality in the form of the mid-term elections of 1994 had proved unpleasant for the President, so perhaps he thought a touch of New Age fantasy might prove preferable.

The same kind of hucksterism, in a more downbeat (and less expensive fashion) has also come to Britain. In 1985, Jeremy Cherfas reported in *New Scientist* on a seminar run in Chiswick, London, for which participants paid £50 each. Cherfas said that participants were obliged to listen to a stream of 'West Coast psychobabble, especially est'. The organiser, Hugh Bromiley, then

Mike Hutchinson at a test conducted by the Wessex Skeptics in Southampton doing the first of five fire walks. It was on this occasion that Simon Hoggart also did his fire walk. At a charity event held some weeks later, over 100 people succeeded in fire walking without special training.

> 'explained that fear was simply False Expectations about Reality, and took us out to show us the blazing fire and consign our fear to the flames.
>
> 'Back inside, for more preparation, mostly a mild form of self-hypnosis [sic]. We were encouraged to visualise a variety of good things that had happened to us, and given a gesture to hook into those good feelings. Repeating this gesture as we crossed the coals would give us the power we had dredged up from within.'

No injuries were reported from this session, which is not at all surprising. The fact is that fire walking is, under the right conditions, perfectly easy, perfectly safe and no more uncomfortable than walking along a hot sandy beach. In fact, it's somewhat less uncomfortable, since few beaches are a mere 10 feet long.

Both the authors of this book have done it, without the aid of any 'neurolinguistic programming', special mantras, loud noise, fasting, religious fervour or even special gestures, tempted though we might have been. Our fire walk was at the University of Southampton, and had been organised by Wessex Sceptics. They were planning what turned out to be a successful charity fire walk a few weeks later, and hoped to show as many people as possible that all the expensive New Age seminars were so much unnecessary claptrap.

The fire, made out of branches which had been knocked down by a hurricane, was ferocious at the start and even more impressive at the end, since darkness had fallen and it glowed threateningly red and orange. The first step for a newcomer is extremely difficult. Even after you have watched other people walk without any apparent difficulty your instincts scream at you to stay away from the fire. In Simon Hoggart's case, the attraction was the beer-drinking camaraderie of those who had dared to walk across the pit and were now celebrating their success. Four steps, walking quickly, light yet flat-footed, and the effect was no worse than a slight prickling sensation. A small blister appeared, but had gone the next morning. None of us was in anything remotely like a trance, religious or otherwise, nor had we spent any time at all in self-esteem or assertiveness training. Apart from a degree of forgivable anxiety we had the mental preparation of someone setting out for a stroll to the pub.

For centuries people have tried to work out the reason for the phenomenon of the fire walk. The explanations suggested have included trances, religious or chemically induced, which make the walker resistant to pain. Some onlookers have imagined that the walkers use special ointments or secret preparations made to local recipes from little-known plants. As might be expected in Victorian times, there were racist explanations too: 'natives' had feet which were specially thick and could resist burning in a way no white man's soles could. New Age gobbledygook suggests that particular strong beliefs held in the mind can cause body tissue not to burn.

A Sri Lankan fire walker. Although flames are commonly seen in artist's depictions of fire walks it is unusual to see them in reality. Judicious avoidance of scattered flames should not be much of a problem though.

In fact, the secret of the spectacle is simple physics. The heat conductivity of wood is very low. (The same is true of pumice stone, which has frequently been used for fire walking in Fiji.) Even if the surface temperature is as high as 700 °C (1,300 °F), the half-second the foot is in contact is not long enough to transfer a significant amount of heat.

It's like an oven in which you're baking a cake. The temperature of the air inside is at, say, 200 °C (400 °F). So is the cake, and so is the metal shelving. You can put your hand into the oven for quite a few seconds without any discomfort. You can comfortably prod the cake with a finger to see if it's ready. But if your finger brushed against the metal shelf, you would be badly hurt. If it was in close contact for one second, there might be a permanent scar.

This is not to say that a fire walk is like a cake walk. There are examples of people who have been severely burned because they spent too long on the coals, or tripped, or had bits of burning material stick to their feet. But the fact is that performed properly, under normal conditions, there isn't time for the fire to burn your feet. It would be a very different story if you tried to walk on a bed of metal. The heat energy of the metal would transfer itself instantly to your skin, which would be hideously injured by the first step – even if the surface temperature was very much lower than that of a wood fire.

Some physicists have wondered whether the so-called Leidenfrost effect might have some influence. This suggests that water vapour on the feet may serve as a form of insulation. Cooks know that if you let a drop of water fall on a warming frying pan, it will evaporate quickly. But if the pan is hot enough, the drops will dance on the surface, often for quite a long time. This is because the water quickly turns to vapour, and vapour, being a gas, is a poor conductor of heat. The drop of water is protected from the heat. (It's the same if you lick your finger before touching a hot iron.) Some people believe that the minuscule layer of vapour is just enough to give a crucial few extra milliseconds of protection.

However, Bill McCarthy and his co-author Bernard Leikind, who have studied fire walking at length, don't attach much importance to this. They point out that in other experiments, people have walked in rope-soled sandals, or with bandages on, and none of these have been harmed. In the Kuda Bux demonstration of 1935, the onlookers were careful to make sure that his feet were quite dry before he started out.

There is something of value in these modern, lucrative, fire walking seminars, even if it isn't what the organisers claim. Anyone who accomplishes a fire walk is sure to feel better about themselves, if only for having conquered an innate, atavistic fear. A successful walk creates a remarkable sense of exhilaration, and the fact that the laws of physics show that it's little more dangerous than baking a cake does not dampen the feeling down. But whether you can build on this achievement to win that big promotion, or find that perfect partner, or generally take a grip on the problems of your life, is another matter altogether.

As Jeremy Cherfas wrote after his fire walk in London, what distressed him was that some people honestly and sincerely believed that, if they hadn't attended the £50 training seminar, the fire would have burned their feet.

'That, I believe, is a false belief, based on a mistaken claim. At no point did anyone involved in the seminar say that walking on coals was indeed impossible. But there was a definite emphasis on things that were seemingly impossible, on tapping unknown reserves, and repeated affirmations that "my body will do whatever is necessary to protect itself"...if no protection is actually needed, and if people think that the training did protect them, they have been misled, and may end up investing the technique taught in the seminar with unwarranted power. In short, I believe it's a bit of a con.'

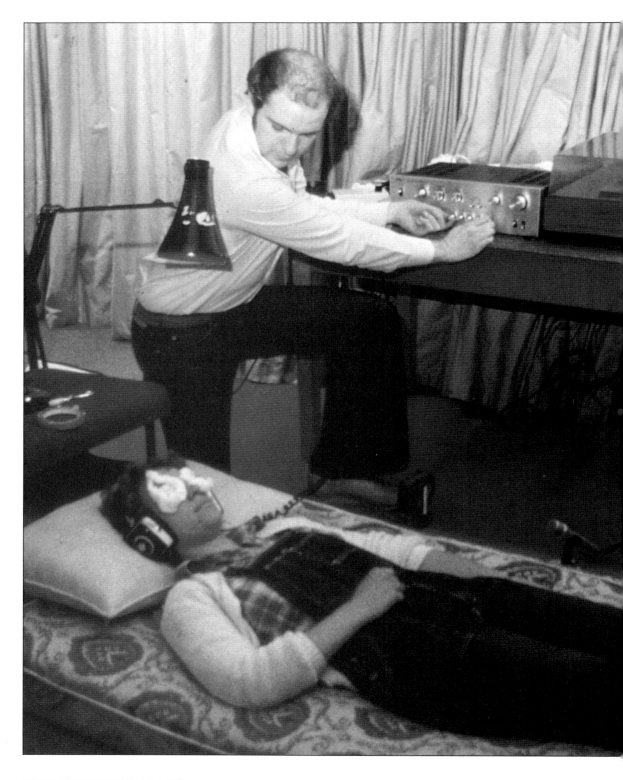

Psi

PSI IS THE WORD SCIENTISTS USE for what most people think of as telepathy. It includes extra-sensory perception, or ESP, plus PK, or psychokinesis, the ability to move or control objects by the power of the mind alone.

It has one great advantage over other bizarre beliefs, such as astrology, prophesy and re-incarnation: it can be measured scientifically in the laboratory. Not easily, to be sure, but in theory at least it should be possible to set up a series of experiments which would settle the question of the existence of psi, one way or the other, for good and for all.

In theory at least. The trouble is that the history of research into psi is littered with failed experiments, ambiguous experiments, and experiments which are claimed as great successes but are quickly rejected by conventional scientists. There has also been some spectacular cheating.

Even the very best results have been disappointingly ambiguous. We can forget any resemblance to the stage magician, or 'mentalist', using his tricks to guess right virtually every time. For more than a century now gullible people – often distinguished scientists themselves – have been convinced by various charlatans who claim to have telepathic powers. Routine magic stunts which people might ignore at a children's party acquire a mysterious fascination when it's claimed they are the result of paranormal powers.

A fascinating article appeared in *The London Daily News* in 1911. Douglas Blackburn, one of the most celebrated and investigated mind-readers of his day, confessed to decades of telepathic trickery. Blackburn and his partner, G A Smith, always refused to take money from anyone but found themselves pursued by 'spiritualistic cranks' wanting to see demonstrations of their astonishing powers. In fact Smith and Blackburn had invented a complicated set of signals, some of them undetectable by onlookers, such as apparent nervous tics, adjusting spectacles, or taking long and short breaths. They became so ingenious that they could communicate the subject of drawings to a partner who was blindfolded, deafened and wrapped in blankets. Their failures – usually with a hard to describe shape such as an inkblot – were always forgiven by their admirers.

'Smith and I, by constant practice, became so sympathetic that we frequently brought off startling hits, which were nothing but flukes...the delight of the investigators caused them to throw off their caution and accept practically anything they were offered.'

Preceding page
Dr Carl Sargent at
Cambridge University in
1981 adjusting the
sound and lighting
during a Ganzfeld
telepathy test.

They had wanted, Blackburn said, to disabuse their 'personally charming and scientifically distinguished' victims after the experiments, but found 'it was too late to recant. We did the next best thing. We stood aside and watched with amazement the astounding spread of the fire we had in a spirit of mischief lighted.' How little changes.

Psi has nothing to do with our common experience of 'knowing' what someone else is thinking. This usually means that we have a pretty good idea of how the mind of a partner, a family member or a close friend is likely to work. Or it is what we'd have thought ourselves in the same circumstances. It does seem startling if your spouse says: 'I bet the Hendersons will cancel their visit tonight,' at the very moment you're thinking it. But it isn't evidence for psi.

The scene is much more likely to be a laboratory where the same dreary test is being repeated literally millions of times. The reason is that the sheer volume of material is needed to prove anything, or even suggest it. If someone tossed a coin ten times and you guessed seven tosses correctly, that would be statistically meaningless. But if you had to call a million times and got 500,700 right, that would be very significant. For this reason, psi research has to be repetitive, grinding, and numbingly dull.

Even the most successful experiments imply that if psi does exist, then it is remarkably weak. For example, one researcher who has produced consistent results is Helmut Schmidt, a quantum physicist, who has been doing work on psychokinesis and random number generators since 1969. An RNG usually produces a long sequence of two different numbers, often zero and one. If it really is working without bias, then each number will crop up, over the distance, almost exactly 50 per cent of the time. Schmidt has an operator try to affect the RNG, bending all his or her mental efforts to making it produce the number one.

Over the years, Schmidt had a hit rate of 50.5 per cent, which certainly looks significant. Given the number of trials, this could not be the result of pure chance. It might well indicate that there is a PK effect, though a very feeble one. Other results, even those which point in the same direction, have been even less clearcut. The Princeton School of Engineering and Applied Science ran a series of no fewer than seventy-eight million trials. Their results were just 50.02 per cent.

That may look minuscule, but it would still be significant. After all, through all those millions of trials, the subjects got it right around 15,600 times more often than might be expected by chance alone.

However, figures like that expose the central problem in psi research. Even if they do imply a very faint effect, the fact that psi existed *at all* would force us to rewrite the known laws of the universe. Therefore all the results must stand up to the most stringent examination. And when the effects are as faint and as marginal as this, then the chances that some bias has crept in – probably quite unconscious and unwitting – is all the more likely. The tiniest, most unnoticeable factor could have skewed the overall result.

For instance, in the Princeton tests, one particular subject was responsible for 23 per cent of the total data base. This subject's hit rate was 50.05 per cent. Cut

all those trials out of the reckoning, and the average for the rest is only 50.01 per cent, a much less interesting figure. Does this mean that that subject had stronger PK powers than most other people? Or, given the tiny variations involved, does it only mean that some bias crept into his part of the tests?

The result is that, on the whole, regular scientists put these results down to imperfections in the methodology – the rules and procedures by which the trials are carried out. Is the RNG really as random as its makers believe? Left to its own devices would it invariably produce each number 500,000 times (give or take a handful) in every million trials? Does it sometimes create patterns which a subject might be aware of, even subconsciously? Is there some giveaway which the operators haven't noticed, such as a barely audible sound associated with one number coming up? Are the testers totally and entirely unbiased, or – when there's a technical problem or an interruption – are they ever so slightly tempted to junk more failed guesses than successful ones? Are they absolutely certain that no one is cheating?

Even in the most rigorous and well-run labs glitches like this can creep in. If the results were more clear-cut, they wouldn't matter. To take a simple example: water always boils at a lower temperature under reduced air pressure. This is why scientists are so certain of the fact, and why it's hard to make a good cup of tea on Mount Everest. But if this phenomenon was noticed only 200 times in a million tests, then we'd have to ask whether there was anything in it, and whether these marginal results might be the result of some error in the experiment.

The five ESP or Zener cards used since 1930 in telepathy experiments. Modern technology has mainly taken over, with subjects being asked to transmit impressions of a photograph, or more recently, excerpts from a videotape.

Scientists also wonder about the experiments which haven't worked and which aren't reported. No doubt the people who've conducted them genuinely think they are not worth mentioning, but they ought to be part of the whole data base.

Psi researchers have, over the years, tended to become impatient with more sceptical scientists. They argue that on several occasions they have come up with results which demand examination and explanation. All they meet, however, is a stone wall of rejection. In their view there are so many experiments which suggest psi exists that it should be admitted by the sheer weight of numbers. This is sometimes called the 'faggot' theory, and has nothing to do with American slang. The individual sticks in the faggot might be thin and fragile, they concede, but the bundle taken as a whole has an unassailable strength. Quite often one has the sense that because science hasn't been able to prove psi does *not* exist, believers in it have felt justified in claiming victory. Occasionally you see it alleged, in serious newspapers, that almost no one worth mentioning denies the existence of telepathy any more.

Mainstream scientists don't accept this kind of thinking. They demand replicability. If something is true, then it is true every single time. An experiment which seems to work proves something only if it works again and again and again. If it doesn't work sometimes, then there may be rules which explain why. You can try to find out what they are. What you can't do is pick and choose between experiments, accepting only those which seem to prove your case. You especially can't do that when your results, if confirmed, would overturn all our knowledge of the universe.

Some of the more extreme believers in psi (not, to be fair, most of the serious researchers) tend to believe that the phenomenon doesn't lend itself to scientific research at all, and that it's pointless even trying. Psi, they say, is too elusive and too fragile to be measured as crudely as a chemical in a test tube. It may be more like human emotions: evanescent, fleeting, liable to be changed by any passing circumstance. Nobody denies the existence of love, but no one demands that it is proved to exist in laboratory tests.

Believers often accuse sceptics of having a negative influence on tests. The sceptics usually reply scornfully that this only means that the psi subject can't perform when proper strict controls are applied. Parapsychologists frequently respond that the presence of someone who doesn't believe does have an inhibiting effect. In the same way, if a man isn't aroused by a particular woman, that doesn't mean he is impotent; unscientific emotions necessarily must play a part.

Another approach is the 'white raven' theory. The fact that all the ravens we see are black does not prove that white ravens don't exist. Indeed, some psi researchers say, we *have* found a very few white ravens, but you ignore them. The scientists say, look, we haven't got time. We're working on things that are really happening and which lead to real, useful results. And whenever we have examined your white ravens, they turn out to be misshapen seagulls, or covered in white paint.

Real science is also *cumulative*. It builds on itself. The discovery of radio waves led to more research which led to broadcasting, X-rays, radar and space travel. Parapsychologists are still stuck with people trying to force a machine to come up with a one or a zero, or sitting blindfold figuring out whether someone in the next room has drawn a picture of a ship or a house. Parapsychologists believe that if they finally do enough experiments, they'll show how people can communicate with anyone without sensory contact. Meanwhile real scientists have invented the mobile phone. The psi researchers' record is pitiful by comparison.

The way that even allegedly dispassionate scientists can make an emotional commitment to one side or the other is intriguingly demonstrated by the Soal case. S G Soal was a mathematics lecturer at London University and a sceptic about psi. He had been scornful of J B Rhine's celebrated experiments in the States, but decided, in the mid-1930s, to do his own card-guessing experiments. After 120,000 guesses he found no results better than chance.

However, a colleague suggested that he should look again at all his discarded data, searching for examples where subjects had guessed the card just before or just after the one they were aiming at. Soal was astonished to find that, by these criteria, two of his subjects produced remarkable results. One was called Basil Shackleton. Soal had him back for more trials; he did extraordinarily well at predicting the *next* card to come up in a sequence. When the speed of calling was doubled, he was able to spot the card two ahead. This was when the cards were selected in advance (they were pictures of five different animals, picked according to a random but predetermined list of the numbers one to five). In some exper-

A psychokinesis experiment in progress at Duke University in the 1930s. A machine was used to throw the dice to ensure that no manipulation by the experimenter could take place.

iments the cards were chosen only at the moment of guessing, by taking counters out of a bag. This seemed to argue for precognition. Since the cards he was aiming for had not yet been selected, Shackleton, it seemed, was not only detecting by telepathy what had already happened, he was perceiving future events. The odds against him performing like this by chance were calculated at 10^{35} to 1 (or one hundred thousand million billion billion to one), so the evidence for psi seemed pretty conclusive.

Mathematics lecturer S G Soal whose mid-1930s card-guessing experiments withstood all critical attack for many years before Betty Markwick finally showed how he had cheated.

And so it seemed to many. The Soal experiments proved to a lot of quite rational people that telepathy and precognition did exist, and had now to be assimilated into our general knowledge, like the theory of relativity. However, many other scientists remained doubtful. For one thing, it was all very well claiming that something *did* happen, but an explanation of how it happened was also needed. The parapsychologists were noticeably short of one. (Recently, they have been playing with the idea that it might have something to do with quantum physics. This has been angrily rejected by physicists working in the field.)

Numerous scientists came up with suggestions about why Soal's results might have been so spectacular. Some thought that one or more of his 'agents', the people whose thoughts were supposedly being read by Shackleton, might have been colluding with him. But no one could prove this and Soal angrily rejected the idea. Then in 1956 he was obliged to reveal that he no longer possessed his original records – he said they had been lost on a troop train. Then in 1960 came the most damaging admission of all: one of his participants, a Mrs G Albert, said she had seen Soal covertly changing the results, most often turning the figure one into a four or a five. Much later, Mrs Albert's recollection proved to be rather hazy, which allowed a few true believers to claim that her evidence was worthless. But the Soal data was beginning to crumble.

But it was a woman called Betty Markwick, a specialist in data correlation and member of the Council of the Society for Psychical Research, who finally destroyed Soal's claims. To quote Chris Scott, writing in *The British & Irish Skeptic* (now just *The Skeptic*):

'after an astonishingly tenacious pursuit...she showed that the target digits contained many runs of consecutive digits that were repetitions of runs used in earlier sessions, and that this could not have arisen by chance.

'This in itself was not particularly serious. However, she also showed that in many such cases the repetition was not exact, but there were intrusions – digits inserted in the sequence – and that these intruded digits were nearly always hits. The implication of improper manipulation seems almost inescapable.'

The true believers were, once again, faced with the disagreeable choice: either all the laws of physics have to be rewritten, or we were looking at the sad case of yet another scientist who, desperate to preserve his theory and his reputation, had resorted to cheating. This has not stopped believers in psi from continuing to quote Soal's results.

Modern researchers include Russell Targ and Harold Puthoff, called by some sceptics the 'Laurel and Hardy of Psi'. Working at the Stanford Research Institute in California, Targ and Puthoff have produced a stream of positive results, all of which have melted away like spring snow when examined rigorously and independently. These embarrassing facts did not stop a paper of theirs called 'Information Transmission Under Conditions of Sensory Shielding' from being published in the British journal *Nature*. This is an extremely prestigious publication, and its decision to print Targ and Puthoff's paper (unlike any serious American journal) brought the pair considerable prestige. But *Nature*'s editors were clearly very doubtful about the value of Targ and Puthoff's work; in the same issue they called it 'weak', 'disconcertingly vague', 'limited', 'flawed' and 'naïve'. They explained they were printing it only to show the kind of work which was being done in the parapsychological field. Oh well.

Targ and Puthoff's work is, for the most part, a sorry study in the range of human credulity. Like the investigators who clustered around Douglas Blackburn a century ago, they wanted to believe and, after a single success by one of their subjects, they were willing to believe almost anything about him.

One of these subjects was a Mr Ingo Swann, who they took to Stanford and placed next to a huge magnetometer, a device which registers the decay of a magnetic field. They told Swann that if he were to affect the magnetic field paranormally, this would register on the chart recording. According to them, 'Swann placed his attention on the interior of the magnetometer, at which time the frequency of the output doubled for about...thirty seconds.' Next, they reported, Mr Swann was asked if he could stop the field change as indicated on the chart. 'He then apparently proceeded to do just that,' they wrote. As Swann described his efforts to them, the recorder shifted again. When he stopped thinking about the magnetometer, the trace went back to normal, then switched when he mentioned it – and so on.

Most impressive, except that Randi contacted the designer of the machine, Dr Arthur Hebard, who was present throughout the experiment. His report of events was rather different. Changes in the machine's output could be caused by many different things and often were. Mr Swann was not asked to 'stop the field change' before he started. Instead he had stood in front of the machine for ten or fifteen minutes, staring at it. When the curve on the chart 'burped', Hebard says that Swann asked Targ and Puthoff 'is that what I'm suppose to do?' They agreed that it must be, without troubling to ask Dr Hebard whether there might be some perfectly natural explanation. You might as well stare at a bus stop for a quarter of an hour, then claim credit for materialising a number twenty-seven.

At this point Mr Swann went to a different part of the room while his companions continued to look at the chart recorder. When the same irregularity happened again, they asked, 'Did you do that, too?' and Swann said that he had, accidentally. Or to put it another way, he claimed credit for the next bus, as well. One is reminded of Uri Geller claiming he had 'stopped' Big Ben in London – but only after it had happened.

Some parapsychologists have claimed success with what are called 'ganzfeld' experiments, and which became popular in the mid-1970s. The word is German for 'whole field' and the theory is that by blanking out someone's ability to hear and see, you create excellent conditions for psi. In a typical ganzfeld experiment, the subject relaxes in a chair, wearing headphones through which 'white noise' – meaningless sound – is transmitted. Each eye is covered with half a table-tennis ball, and a bright light shone towards them. After about fifteen minutes of this most people report being in a 'pleasantly altered state' and it's time to start the experiment.

In another room the 'agent' is given one of four photographs, frequently of travel scenes. He concentrates hard on describing the picture to the subject, telepathically. The subject likewise concentrates on receiving the picture. Afterwards he or she returns to the real world and looks at the four pictures, choosing the one which came closest to his or her mental image. If it's the right one, this is deemed a hit.

Quite a few ganzfeld experiments did achieve better than chance results, and for a while it looked as if this might be a promising area of research. But then Ray Hyman, a research psychologist at the University of Oregon, a man held in high esteem on both sides of the argument, examined the studies with immense care and found serious flaws.

Again these might not have mattered if the results had been truly impressive – if even one person had been found who could get, say, half the pictures right rather than just marginally over 25 per cent. But the variations from chance were so small that they might well have been accounted for by errors.

Many of Hyman's conclusions were based on advanced statistical analysis, bewildering to the layman, which showed that the results were not quite as good as had been claimed. But he also pointed to more obvious faults. In some cases, the subject had been handed the photographs by an experimenter who knew which one was the target, leaving the way open for lots of sensory clues. In some cases the investigators gave inadequate accounts of their controls. For example, if the agent and the subject were friends, they might make cheating conceivable, or at least imply the possibility of some advance knowledge. In other cases there were 'failed' tests which simply weren't reported, or were abandoned half-way, making the published data base look more impressive than it was.

Few experimenters agreed on procedures, making it impossible to compare like with like. There was picking and choosing of statistics. For example, some experimenters used six or eight pictures. If a subject got the right one, this was scored as a direct hit. If they arranged all the pictures in descending order, and the chosen picture was in the top half, this was called a 'binary hit'. So at the end of the test, there were two separate groups of statistics, and all too often it was only the more successful one which saw the light of day.

Other breaches of procedure were more complicated and highly technical, but the net effect is that the ganzfeld results were at best ambiguous and at worst meaningless. You would need to be a true believer already to feel that they had confirmed the existence of psi.

And here is the problem. Psi either exists or it doesn't. This ought to be a matter of fact, and no more likely to arouse strong emotions than the question of what killed the dinosaurs. Yet life and people aren't like that; ironically, it's the very marginality of the claims, the fragmentary nature of the 'proofs', which mean that perfectly honest investigators find themselves taking up committed positions on one side or another. Psi becomes a matter of faith rather than of science.

To be fair, this is not always the case. Professor Robert Morris, the Koestler Professor of Parapsychology at Edinburgh University, for example, says that he remains a doubter – he is 90 per cent sure that psi exists, but feels he lacks the remaining 10 per cent. Many sceptics and parapsychologists get on perfectly well, since both are looking for the elusive proof of what they already tend to.believe.

Others are less broad-minded. This was certainly the experience of Susan Blackmore, a British psychologist who came to believe in psi during her time as an undergraduate at Oxford. She then set about ten years of experiments, none of which produced any positive results. Parapsychologists told her that this was because she was not a believer; only believers got results (this is true, but the believers don't draw the obvious lesson, which is that their belief is probably skewing the figures in their direction).

Ms Blackmore pointed out that she had been a believer; they replied with magnificent circularity that she could not have been *really*, or else she'd have avoided getting her negative results. She concludes:

'The structure and definition of parapsychology are to blame. The negative definition of psi, the hundred years of bolstering failing theories, and the powerful will to find something are at fault. They not only force us to ask, 'Does psi exist?' but force us to answer in terms of belief. Where there is no rational or convincing answer, belief takes over, and that is why there are two sides, and such misunderstanding.'

Biorhythms

BIORHYTHMS ARE A CLASSIC EXAMPLE of a pseudo-science and have all the right hallmarks. They appear to offer a way of planning your life to the last detail while demanding minimal mental effort. One simple rule explains everything you need to know, and a single set of figures can be used to generate a flood of magical statistics. Naturally, the sheer weight of numbers means there are some pretty impressive coincidences – even more, when you spot that, in common with nearly all pseudo-sciences, followers feel at liberty to massage the numbers any way they please. And because it's so hard to prove a negative, it is difficult for a real scientist to say that biorhythms are, beyond the faintest shadow of a doubt, total claptrap.

Which they almost certainly are. But it's not altogether surprising that recently this theory did gain a wide degree of acceptance. We rightly sense that rhythms control many aspects of our lives. The seasons; festivals such as Easter and Christmas; our own heartbeats and breathing. Indeed, conventional scientists use the term 'biological rhythm' to mean any more or less regular change in a living organism. Women put up with the menstrual cycle, and know all about feeling bad, physically and mentally, on a timed, predictable basis. Everyone has the daily circadian rhythms, which govern when our minds and bodies are most active and when they're ready to rest. These help make jet lag such a problem when we cross several time zones in the course of a day.

Sportsmen and women know there are spells when they're on top form, followed by weeks when they can't seem to do anything right, even though they are just as fit, rested and alert as before. Many authors know that a sustained period of speedy creative work can be followed by the agonies of writer's block. And few of us – not only manic depressives – don't have the experience of feeling particularly cheerful for no apparent reason on some days, then a while later being quite dejected, again with no obvious cause.

So there are undoubtedly biological rhythms and they do have a considerable influence on our lives. But what the New Age Biorhythm Theory teaches is much more precise than that. It offers a pattern for living the whole of the rest of our days. We learn that we are subject to three cycles, each of which is identical for everybody in the world. It starts on the day we are born (or, according to some proponents, on the day *after* we are born – a disagreement which brings about some confusion) and which never varies throughout the course of our lives.

Preceding page
Much of life is dictated by biological rhythms. Are there three 'biorhythms' by which we can predict our mood, and our physical and intellectual performance?

These rhythms are unchanged by anything – including illness, injury or stress – anything at all except death.

Because the rhythms are so predictable and so exact, we can plot the best times for anything we might want to do – getting married, coping with a difficult task, or just setting off in the car. If the 'science' of biorhythms is true, it would be enormously helpful. You could calculate every day of your future, marking the times when you could expect to be at your best, and those when you would be enervated, fractious and obtuse. You could literally decide, thirty years in advance, to spend the day in bed.

Another characteristic of pseudo-sciences is that, though they all appear to offer an astonishing breakthrough in our understanding of human life, they are as relentlessly subject to fashion as rock groups or kipper ties. In 1978 biorhythms were extremely popular and many books were published describing how you could use them to take control of your life. Nor was this material confined to the 'Occult' or 'New Wave' shelves in bookshops. Women's magazines published long articles describing how to put biorhythm theory to use. In America, biorhythm machines in airports and hotel lounges offered personal printouts for a few coins. Many American newspapers printed daily biorhythm charts, usually somewhere near the horoscope, along with other nonsense which editors weren't quite sure about but sensed that the public wanted.

Companies offered to prepare individual biorhythm charts, a pretty easy task since these simply require plotting three different coloured interlacing sine waves on a roll of paper. One company, Time Pattern Research, claimed sales of 100,000 charts at between $10 and $20 each over three years, presumably making some lucky person a millionaire. Since to produce a chart you only need to know the customer's date of birth, this is not a service which involves expensive research.

In 1978, even Britain's well-respected – if, these days, somewhat money oriented – Automobile Association was sufficiently concerned about biorhythm effects on traffic accidents to offer readers of their magazine *Drive* a cut-price 'biorhythmic computer', which could be used to predict days when members might be specially dangerous on the roads.

Since then biorhythms have fallen off somewhat in popularity, though as late as 1994 the computer magazine *PC Answers* gave readers a free disk containing a biorhythms project for spreadsheets, together with a long article explaining how to use it, and providing reasons why the theory was sound. There are still plenty of biorhythm books in print. A typical subtitle is 'How to Understand and Predict the Cycles in Your Mind and Body that Hold the Key to Success and Happiness'. What offer could be more tempting? Many of these books are produced by reputable publishers and sold in the good mainstream bookshops.

These articles tended to attract pseudo-information like burrs on a dog's back. Swiss surgeons were alleged to use biorhythms to decide which days to operate. American telephone companies had used them to increase productivity. One of the most popular 'facts', repeated endlessly in the literature, was that many Japanese firms now use the theory, to their great advantage. This suggestion was simply copied from one article to another; when the *Toronto Star* contacted the Japanese Embassy in Washington, the Japanese Trade Centre, and the Japanese Chamber of Commerce in New York, they all reported back that they were unaware of *any* Japanese company using biorhythms.

William Bainbridge, a sociology teacher at the University of Washington in Seattle, decided to investigate biorhythms back in the 1970s, and enrolled on a course taught by Benjamin Steele, who was then head of the Northwest Biorhythm Association. He quoted Mr Steele's introduction:

'The essence of the biorhythm theory is that from the moment of birth all human beings are programmed by nature to have cyclical ups and downs. The theory suggests that man's behaviour is characterised by three innate cycles. The cycles include a 23-day physical cycle, a 28-day emotional or sensitivity cycle, and a 33-day intellectual cycle. The physical cycle influences tasks of a physical nature: physical strength, endurance, energy, resistance, and confidence. The emotional curve takes on increased importance in situations of high emotional content: sensibility, nerves, feelings, intuition, cheerfulness, moodiness, and creative ability. And the intellectual cycle is of particular importance in pursuits requiring cognitive activity: intelligence, memory, mental alertness, logic, reasoning power, reaction and ambition.

'Each cycle begins at the moment of birth, then oscillates up and down with absolute precision for the entire life. When our cycles are 'high' we are most likely to be at our best. When our cycles are 'low' the opposite is true. But beware of 'critical days' – they occur whenever our cycles are changing. These are unstable days on which we're easily distracted and most prone to accidents.'

This is a fine example of the creative number crunching which pseudo-scientists are so good at. It would be difficult to measure in any useful or accurate way whether people feel vaguely up or down at a particular time, or whether they're somewhat fitter than usual, or more alert and mentally astute – though of course you could chart a sportsman's performance on different days. However, you can measure accidents – occasions when something specific goes wrong, such as a car crash. It should be easy to match the biorhythms of drivers who've been involved in a car crash with the day the crash took place. Indeed it's perfectly straightforward. More of that later.

However, biorhythm theory teaches that the danger times don't necessarily come in the low part of the cycle, but on the crossover or 'critical' days, of which there are two per cycle. This adds up to roughly eighty every year (naturally some critical days overlap). Add the two days on either side of each critical day, as some 'researchers' do, and *voilà*! we are dangerously prone to accidents on fully two-thirds of all the days we pass in this vale of tears. Throw into the pot, as writers on the subject frequently do, the low periods of all three cycles as well, and you turn pretty much the whole of everybody's lives into one long danger zone. It would certainly be a pretty feeble statistician who could not spot at least some intriguing correlations amidst those multitudinous figures.

And there are plenty to be found. One particular favourite among biorhythm buffs is the death of Marilyn Monroe, at a time when she was, according to their lore, low in both her emotional and intellectual cycles. Another is about the swimmer Mark Spitz, who won a record seven Olympic gold medals while he was near both physical and emotional high points. Impressive, until you remember that the supporters of biorhythms are, to put it mildly, somewhat selective about which celebrities they choose. For example, when Roger Bannister ran the world's first ever four-minute mile in 1954 – one of the great athletic achievements of all time – he was supposedly in a physical and emotional trough.

Biorhythmicists are not usually keen to make predictions in advance, since these have an annoying way of going wrong. But one did make the mistake of pointing out that the famous baseball star Reggie Jackson would go into the 1977 World Series at a time when all three of his cycles would be in the negative phase. Jackson went on to have one of the most successful World Series ever enjoyed by any player.

The modern interest in biorhythms started with the 1973 publication in New York of a book called *Is This Your Day?* by George Thommen. He claimed that the theory was based on the work of three European researchers working near the start of the twentieth century: Wilhelm Fleiss, Hermann Swoboda, and Alfred Teltscher. Fliess was a friend, or at least a correspondent, of Freud, and the psychologist's letters to him survive. Fliess's replies do not.

All three men were surprisingly unwilling to commit their exciting research to paper – or when they did, it unfortunately disappeared. For example, Teltscher, who allegedly came up with the idea of the thirty-three day emotional cycle, remains a considerable mystery since not one word of his research has turned up since. Mr Thommen had to base his own *oeuvre* on secondhand articles and reviews which discussed Teltscher's findings.

He did have a correspondence with Hermann Swoboda, but again this produced no concrete evidence for anything. Thommen reported in his book:

'In one of his letters, Dr Swoboda indicated that eight trunks of research documentation that he had stored in the vaults of the University of Vienna fell into the hands of Russian troops during the occupation of Vienna in 1945. This loss was a bitter blow to Swoboda.'

As William Bainbridge points out, while it might have been a bitter blow to Swoboda, it was a terrific advantage for the progress of biorhythms. Freed from the shackles of proper scientific method, the supporters of the theory have been able to make it up as they go along, occasionally citing research and findings which have long vanished from the face of the earth. This is another characteristic of pseudo-science fans; they often love all the trappings of real science, solemnly citing sources and authorities (the better if these have Germanic names and were active a conveniently long time ago.) On the other hand, if real science turns round and tells them they're spouting nonsense, they tend to retreat into a kind

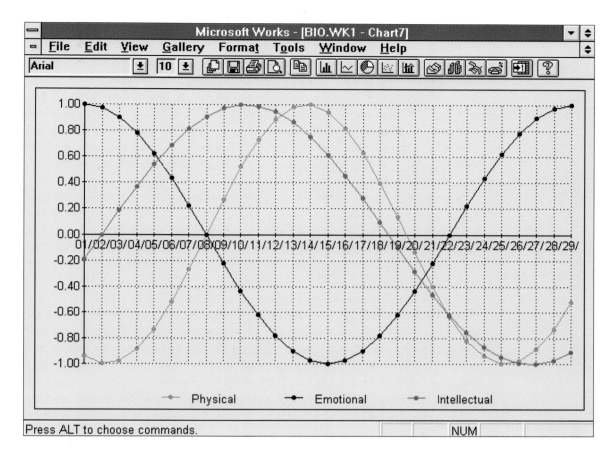

A computerised biorhythm chart calculated for the first twenty-nine days of 1996 for someone born on 8 October 1945. Derived from 'PC Answers' on a Microsoft spreadsheet.

of semi-religious mimsy, claiming that scientists are blinkered by their conventional habits of mind, and that a higher truth is there for those who will but see.

You might imagine that a theory which suggests that our lives are precisely controlled for decades by fixed, unvarying cycles would sound too improbable and bizarre to attract serious attention. But when the biorhythm theory first became popular, it did get taken up by some companies, especially those whose employees had to drive or to operate heavy machinery. It seemed a useful way of reducing accidents.

Which in some cases, it did. But the samples were small and other factors were probably involved. For instance, Tarek Khalil and Charles Kurucz, who are professors of industrial engineering at the University of Miami report a study in which a group of workers at one company was split into three. The first group was given the 'correct' biorhythmic information about critical days, and their foremen were asked to caution them on those days. The second was given inaccurate information, so foremen cautioned them on the 'wrong' days. The third group was given no information and no warnings.

Accident rates 'remained unchanged' for the first group, 'rose slightly' for the second, and 'climbed a lot' for the third. This could be interpreted as meaning that the biorhythm theory had scored a palpable hit. Or it could just as easily show that workers who are warned to take extra care, and given an apparently good reason for doing so, are less likely to have accidents. Certainly in 1976 T Hirsh reported in *National Safety News* that while many American companies did tell their staff about biorhythms, it was more to promote the general idea of safety than to suggest that the theory itself was valid.

Many reputable tests have been run on biorhythms and almost all suggest there is no truth in the theory at all. Even apparent correspondences between what the system claims and what reality produces are generally within the predictable range of chance.

For example, Khalil and Kurucz did two sets of different tests. One concerned single-occurrence type events, in this case aircraft accidents in which pilot error was deemed to be the cause, and traffic accidents in which the driver was at fault. They then plotted the biorhythms for the people involved, and discovered that the total number of events – deaths and accidents – were divided evenly between positive and negative portions of the various cycles. Only a small and statistically insignificant number occurred on the 'critical' days.

They also got data for repetitive events, in this case the records of twenty-three members of a university swimming team, and twenty-five members of the same university's bowling league. Again, the results offered no support to the biorhythm theory – though intriguingly, thirteen of the swimmers performed best when their physical cycle was low, and only eight when it was high. This might be thought that the opposite of the theory was true, which would be useful to know, though again the sample is too small to indicate that either. What it does seem to prove is that biorhythms just aren't any use.

Again, like all pseudo-science fans, the supporters of biorhythms airily move the goal posts whenever it suits them. For example, the 1994 *PC Answers* article suggests that you 'fine tune' the theory, tailoring it to your personal experience. 'Your chart may be just a fraction out...or perhaps your cycle is just fractionally longer or shorter than the norm...perhaps your biorhythms interact with those of a family member or partner', advice which breezily ignores the fact that the theory states as fact that all biorhythms are identical for everyone and cannot be changed by circumstance.

Perhaps this answers the great Arnold Palmer paradox. The celebrated golfer is often cited in biorhythm literature as near proof of the theory. Palmer won the British Open in July 1962, when he was high in all three rhythms, then lost the American PGA two weeks later when he was low in all three. Sports are useful for testing biorhythm theory because it's easy to measure comparative performances. Run through the computer all 243 days from 1955 to 1971 in which Palmer was playing in tournaments which he won, and you have a fascinating statistic: Palmer won far less often on his physical high days than chance would have predicted. In fact, the selective nature of the material means that this figure isn't significant either, but it's a great deal more suggestive than the two isolated events chosen by the biorhythm buffs.

However, the most exhaustive attempt ever to confirm or disprove biorhythms was undertaken by Britain's official Transport and Road Research Laboratory. This used insurance reports to cover the cases of no fewer than 112,560 drivers who were involved in crashes, much the largest sample ever used in an investigation of biorhythms. The reports included their birth dates, which made it easy to set up a computer program which analysed every incident.

The lengthy report shows that the Lab crunched the numbers every way they could think of, analysing drivers according to sex, according to whether they were to blame for each crash and according to their position on all three cycles. In the dry words of the abstract:

'Convincing evidence was not found to support the biorhythm theory. Accidents occurring when three 'critical' days coincide have not been fully studied, but one example indicates that these occur very rarely.'

Ironically there is much evidence that rhythms do affect our lives. A company called Biocron Systems in California maintains that people do have variations in their physical, mental and emotional states – as we all know. But BSC claims that our cycles are all different, and their research shows that rhythms can vary from two days to fifty-four days. They also showed that the rhythms vary from cycle to cycle in the same individual and are of different strengths. In other words, it would be almost impossible to measure the cycles reliably or to base future plans on them.

Which merely goes to show that real science, as opposed to pseudo-science, involves a great deal of hard work, and a lot of hacking through the statistics – frequently without any neatly packaged conclusion being available at the end. In short, real science tends to be complicated, difficult and boring, unlike pseudo-science, which is simple, fun and almost invariably wrong.

Hypnosis

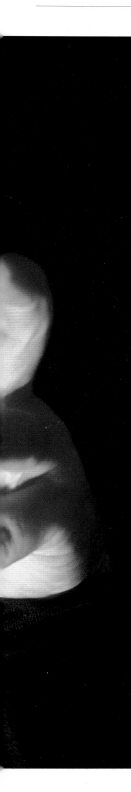

DOES SUCH A THING AS A HYPNOTIC TRANCE EVEN EXIST? Probably not. This seems an extraordinary allegation to make. We've all seen the performances, on stage and TV, in which apparently normal members of the public strut around pretending to be chickens, singing nonsense songs, or even taking their clothes off. As so often with the paranormal, because we don't know of any prosaic explanation, we assume that there must be *something* in it. No one would behave like this without being under some powerful, irresistible influence.

Yet a quick look at what really goes on is enough to make anyone ponder. In many stage performances (and on television, though you don't always see every detail of those shows) a large number of people are called up to join the hypnotist. They're all volunteers, which implies that they're excited and eager to join in the experience.

The performer then starts the process of finding the most co-operative volunteers from an already co-operative pool. He asks everyone to interlock their fingers and hold tight for a minute. Then he suggests that not all of them will be able to unclasp their hands. The ones who agree and say they can't are clearly excellent subjects. A few more small tests of the same kind keep the audience amused and also weed out subjects who are less inclined to go along with the whole farrago. The hypnotist is finally left with a small group of subjects, all preselected as the most helpful and willing in the audience.

He then claims to put them into a 'trance', whatever that might mean. They may be a trifle puzzled about their feelings. It doesn't really seem any different from being wide awake and aware of what's going on in the world outside. On the other hand, we have all been told about the wonders of hypnotism. How is an ordinary member of the public to know what the hypnotic experience is like? And it would be sensible to co-operate with the hypnotist. After all, he might not be able to take you out of the trance, and then where would you be? It's hardly amazing that the great majority of people who take part in these sessions are more than willing to go along with the performance, whatever their feelings at the time about what is actually happening.

But hypnotism, like many other paranormal phenomena, may be one of those instances where both sides believe, and both parties co-operate to create the expected effect. The hypnotist, after all, is doing what he's been taught to do, and there, on stage, is someone apparently in a trance.

Preceding page
A professional hypnotist
said to be making ritual
gestures. The value of
such gestures, however,
during the process of
hypnosis is questionable.

There are two important questions in hypnosis: does the hypnotic trance state exist in the first place, and can unhypnotised subjects perform in the same way as those who are supposedly in the trance?

The answer to the first question is, almost certainly, no. The word 'trance' is much favoured by supporters of the paranormal. Fire walkers are said to be in a 'trance', though as we well know, there's no need for any mental change other than that obtained – by some – through an invigorating slug of Dutch courage. Spiritualist mediums say they are in a trance, though this is apparently a means of allowing them to claim they've been 'taken over' by the spirits of the departed. The word 'trance' is really psychobabble used to account for behaviour which can be explained quite normally.

Nor is it good enough to say that some people go into a 'trance' while watching TV, or reading a book. All this means is that they are concentrating to the exclusion of everything around them. But they can easily be interrupted. They might ignore the phone ringing, or a pestering child, but they would certainly hear the word 'Fire!' being shouted. Nor do people who are concentrating hard on their book or television show generally display alleged hypnotic phenomena, such as pretending to be a chicken, or Elvis Presley.

One of the leading stage hypnotists in the United States goes by the name of Kreskin. In the past, Kreskin has claimed some paranormal powers for himself, so his assertions have to be considered with care. However, he is quite certain that hypnosis does *not* exist, and has offered a $100,000 reward to anyone who can prove him wrong. His money is probably quite safe. As *The Nursing Mirror* in Britain reported in 1982, the brainwaves of hypnotised subjects show the same activity as people who are awake in the normal way.

It is conceivable that, even if it is impossible to prove the existence of a hypnotic trance, the effects of hypnotic induction might nevertheless be real. But then you would need to prove that people do things under hypnosis which they would be quite incapable of doing while in a normal state. It's no good saying, well, this is a very shy woman who would never sit on all fours and bark like a dog in public. The whole point of the hypnotist's act is that it allows people to suspend the normal rules which govern their behaviour. By suggesting to his subjects that they are under his control and not responsible for their actions, he provides them with a perfect excuse for behaving in a manner which would strike them as outrageous if they were walking down a street or in a friend's living room. It's no more surprising than a shy clerk letting himself go at the office Christmas party.

Kreskin himself used hypnosis as the basis of his entertainment for many years, until he discovered that he didn't need it. People could just as easily be persuaded to do what he told them without putting them through hypnotic induction. Now he simply tells them about the power of suggestion, and how everyone can be influenced by it, without going into any kind of trance-like state. The act works just as well. As Kreskin said in his book *They Call It Hypnosis*:

'I practised what I believe to be so-called 'hypnosis' and ardently fostered the trance concept. I now tell my audiences that my references to 'hypno-

Stage hypnotist and magician Martin S Taylor telling Davinder (left) and Alice that their spectacles will enable them to see the audience naked. Said Davinder later:'I didn't see the audience naked, but the thought of doing so made me laugh.'

sis', both historically and as I practised it, are in the framework of the past. This is also why I use quotation marks when dealing with the subject.'

Stage hypnosis is obviously very different to one-on-one hypnotherapy, and it's clear many entertainers who perform it genuinely believe that it works. However, unlike Kreskin, they have never tried doing the same act without it.

One who has is the British magician Martin S Taylor, who experimented with what he called 'hypnosis with your eyes open'. His results were good, but not quite as good as they had been when subjects appeared to be hypnotised. One possible reason is that the members of the public on stage could see the reaction of the audience to what they were doing, and found it inhibiting. On the other hand, Taylor knows that if he asks subjects to keep their eyes closed, the audience will probably assume that they really are hypnotised, whatever he claims. (The best magicians have often been accused of having paranormal powers by believers, even when they point out as clearly as they can that they're just using skilful, non-supernatural devices. For example, Sir Arthur Conan Doyle believed that Harry Houdini had mysterious powers, even after Houdini assured him that all his tricks were performed by natural means.)

Martin Taylor's act came in useful in 1994. He was booked to appear in Bolton, Lancashire, which had banned hypnotism when a woman, a member of the audi-

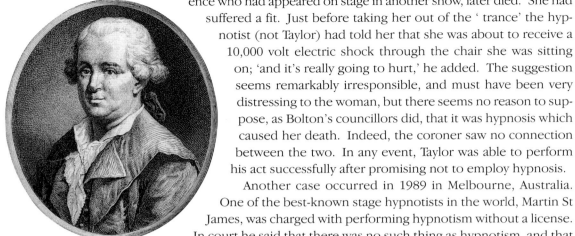

Franz Anton Mesmer (1733-1815), inventor of 'animal magnetism' which later developed into modern hypnotism.

ence who had appeared on stage in another show, later died. She had suffered a fit. Just before taking her out of the ' trance' the hypnotist (not Taylor) had told her that she was about to receive a 10,000 volt electric shock through the chair she was sitting on; 'and it's really going to hurt,' he added. The suggestion seems remarkably irresponsible, and must have been very distressing to the woman, but there seems no reason to suppose, as Bolton's councillors did, that it was hypnosis which caused her death. Indeed, the coroner saw no connection between the two. In any event, Taylor was able to perform his act successfully after promising not to employ hypnosis.

Another case occurred in 1989 in Melbourne, Australia. One of the best-known stage hypnotists in the world, Martin St James, was charged with performing hypnotism without a license. In court he said that there was no such thing as hypnotism, and that he was a 'mind magician'. He directed people's imagination on stage, and they took part in the fantasy. Professor Graham Burrows, president-elect of the International Society of Hypnosis, gave evidence for the prosecution, saying that hypnotism was 'an altered state of consciousness brought about by indirect or direct suggestion.' The magistrate, Linda Dessau, in an admirable display of judicial scepticism dismissed the case, saying that she did not wish to waste any more of the court's time.

Another stage hypnotist is the Las Vegas entertainer Peter J Reveen, who appears as 'Reveen the Impossiblist'. He too scorns the idea of hypnotism as a real phenomenon, preferring the term 'superconsciousness' in order to avoid any Svengali-like implications. Reveen believes that many people have an urge to 'please the operator': 'Where no adverse real-world consequences can be detected, the subject feels a strong inner compulsion to go through the motions of obeying, even when the only way he can do so is by simulating whatever effect he thinks the operator expects.'

In Reveen's act he tells people that they are going to relive their past lives. 'I carefully avoid giving the impression that I have any doubts about the reality of reincarnation, for then a sizable number of volunteers would pick up on my disbelief and fail to fantasise at all – and I am, after all, in the business of entertaining an audience.'

His participants are more than willing to join in.
'The same "pleasing the operator" syndrome helps to explain why a suggestible subject, when hypnotised by a person known to be associated with flying-saucer cults, often tells of being kidnapped and taken aboard a spacecraft by funny looking aliens.'

The effects of suggestion were probably known in China as long ago as 2600 BC, but the modern notion of hypnosis derives from the work begun in the 1770s with Franz Anton Mesmer, a celebrated if highly eccentric Austrian doctor. Mesmer invented what he called 'animal magnetism', a somewhat jumbled notion which postulated a universal magnetic fluid present in all objects. This produced disease when it was out of balance in the human body. This idea developed from his interest in astrology, since he also believed that perfect health depended on the individual having the correct relationship with the heavenly bodies. Mesmer treated patients using iron magnets and hypnosis, which he originated.

It was at first a huge success and greatly impressed Marie Antoinette. Her husband, Louis XVI was less inclined to take Mesmer on trust. He appointed two commissions, headed by senior scientific figures, Benjamin Franklin and Lavoisier, to investigate it. After seven years, they came to the practical conclusion that it was imagination rather than magnetism which accounted for the trance-like rigidity of Mesmer's subjects.

Nonetheless, some doctors continue to believe in hypnosis – or at least don't rule it out as a form of treatment. They are often encouraged by anecdotal evidence. One of the best-known stories of medical hypnosis was a case which occurred in 1951 when an unnamed patient suffering from a rare and extremely unpleasant skin complaint (congenital ichthyosiform erythrodermia of Brocq) was treated by hypnosis. He had 'large warty excrescences' 5 millimetres wide on

Counsellors and psychotherapists use many therapeutic methods including hypnotherapy as seen being paractised here.

his legs and feet, his hands were covered in a rigid horny casing, and he emitted an unpleasant smell.

Dr Albert Mason of the Queen Victoria Hospital in East Grinstead agreed to take over the case. The patient was hypnotised and was told that the warts would begin to disappear. According to Mason 'about five days later the horny layer was softened, became friable, and fell off'. After five days the left arm was entirely clear, though the right arm was unchanged. Later hypnotic treatment is recorded as having improved the patient's condition by 95 per cent.

All very impressive, though surgery had been tried on the patient, and it could be that its delayed effect caused the improvement. What medicine requires, however, is repeatability – the ability to cause the same improvement in different patients, time and again. Dr Mason tried hypnosis in another eight cases, but in 1961 he reported in The *British Medical Journal* that all had been failures. Proper tests of hypnosis have shown that there is little difference between subjects who are supposedly in a trance, and those who are merely given a suggestion. People often describe how hypnosis helped them, or their acquaintances, to give up smoking when all else had failed. But people who want to give up smoking usually have a strong motivation, and have come to realise that they need outside help. There have been several tests in which subjects are divided into three groups: some are 'hypnotised' and told that they will give up smoking, some are not hypnotised but merely have the suggestion put to them, and the remaining third make up the control group who receive no suggestions but are expected to do their best. All these tests show that the first two groups do roughly as well as each other, and better than the control group. In other words, the 'induction' process is not needed; it is the authority and the moral persuasion of the person making the suggestion which appears to count.

Hypnotists often claim that many different effects can be demonstrated by people under their influence. These included a reduced sensitivity to pain, hearing loss, sight changes, effects on the skin, age regression and amnesia – among many others. One of the easiest of these to check is deafness, and here hypnosis falls down every time.

- When a subject is fed two different tones into his ears, and told he is deaf in one of them, he still hears the combined tone which any normally awake person would hear.
- People under 'hypnosis' still blink at loud noises.
- When we read aloud and have a delayed echo of our voice fed into our ears moments afterwards, we slur our words and begin stammering and stumbling. It's a common problem for radio performers when their equipment has not been set up properly. 'Hypnotised' people who are supposed to be deaf do just the same when they get the feedback.
- The opposite is also true. 'Hypnotised' people told to imagine they are receiving the same feedback, do not slur or stammer.
- Many subjects, told by the hypnotist: 'You are now deaf. Can you hear me?' reply 'No, I cannot hear you.'

People often claim that hypnosis is a successful pain-killer and enables people to undergo simple surgery without anaesthetics. In April 1994 one man underwent a vasectomy operation under what was described as 'self-hypnosis'. This may well be true, but of course a cut with a very sharp knife is not too painful – at first. Often we don't even notice it until the blood appears; the agony comes later. There is a lot of evidence to show that surgical pain can be greatly reduced without hypnosis, by giving patients instructions that reduce their anxiety, distract the mind's attention from the pain, and create relaxation. If the man was confident and not fearful of the pain, and was good at making himself relaxed, then his heart would beat more slowly and would pump less blood.

The surgeon in this case, who reported that the patient did flinch once, remarked that there was less blood than usual. The surgeon may well have made a smaller cut than usual, being fearful of causing the man pain. All in all, as evidence that a hypnotic trance can create an altered mental state, this event suggests very little and proves nothing.

In 1993 there was a weird case in London which attracted a lot of publicity. A nineteen-year-old woman complained to police that she had been assaulted by a hypnotherapist in East London who had fondled her breasts when she had gone for treatment for her kidneys. Police found at the man's house forty videos which showed that he had plied the women with drink and drugs before assaulting them. The story seemed even more excitingly bizarre when it was reported that the hypnotist tried to control the detectives. One detective reported migraine and nausea after interviewing the suspect. Another described his 'amazingly hypnotic eyes'.

Mike Hutchinson called the police to reassure them that there was no reason to believe the man had any such powers over the detectives, and that the suggestion the women might have been assaulted and then forgotten the event was nonsense. (It's a myth that people forget what's happened to them under hypnosis, even if, encouraged by the hypnotist, they might claim that they do. They are perfectly well aware of what's going on around them while 'hypnotised', and these women would have known what the man was doing to them. It's also worth asking why, if hypnosis is so successful at making women submit to men's desires, he needed to ply them with drink and drugs first.)

In the end, the hypnotherapist was convicted of only one assault, and the forty videos turned out to show a total of only three other women. A detective reported to Hutchinson that one of these had admitted to enjoying the experience. In short, the absurd public expectations aroused by the word 'hypnotist' had turned a sorry but minor assault case into a huge and painful scandal for the women involved.

Dowsing

UNLIKE SOME OF THEIR FELLOW TOILERS in the laboratories of pseudo-science, nearly all the people who practise dowsing are sincere. They genuinely believe they can do it. And many folk are happy to accept their claims. Dowsing, or 'divining', is best known as a means of finding water, but there are dowsers who reckon they can find almost any kind of desired object underground.

There is something pleasingly old-fashioned and bucolic about the idea of an honest rustic, armed only with a long twig, discovering the water which all farmers need. Most of these dowsers are not in it for the money and offer their skills as a service to friends and neighbours. The whole idea seems somehow right to us; we're reminded of the old countryman who can predict rain when his bunions ache, or can sense a change in the weather by the way the cows behave. Dowsing takes us back to a warmer, less complicated time, when man was still at one with nature instead of busily destroying it with technology.

What's more, dowsing has been used since antiquity. The ancient Egyptians used divining rods, though to foretell the future rather than find underground objects. The technique was controversial, but widely used, as a means of detecting valuable metals in central Europe around the sixteenth century. In 1518, Martin Luther claimed that it violated the First Commandment. However, dowsers still used their techniques to find veins of metal for at least another hundred years without being punished by the Church. In the reign of Queen Elizabeth I, German miners, imported to work the mines in Cornwall, used birch rods. So dowsing has a long pedigree, which also adds to the vague feeling that there must be something in it.

Except that, sadly, there is almost certainly nothing in it at all. Every controlled test – that is, every test that is rigorously controlled, and not left as an easy-going free-for-all – has failed to come up with any evidence for the phenomenon. Even where dowsers have been offered massive sums as prizes, they have generally scored only according to chance. Even the occasional test which has produced a better result than chance would predict has fallen well short of indicating that dowsing is reliable, and has not been repeated.

Yet dowsing results can look terrific. This is not perhaps very startling. In Britain, for example, it is pretty well impossible not to find water. Dig down almost anywhere in the rain-sodden island, and you will come to water at some point. An experienced country dweller with some knowledge of the landscape might easily recognise – perhaps subconsciously – where the chances of finding it quickly and easily are best.

And dowsing looks good. The dowsing rod is traditionally a long switch of hazel, but it can be almost anything at all. Some dowsers use different kinds of wood, some prefer one or a pair of metal rods, others use whalebone. Some others favour a pendulum made of string, with a heavy weight, such as a stone or piece of jewellery, tied to the bottom. This swings or rotates violently whenever the desired object is thought to be located underground. What they all have in common is that they are extremely light and fairly long, so that the slightest muscular twitch can cause a reaction which seems out of all proportion. The effect is certainly striking. The dowsing tool appears to have a mind of its own, waving or swinging violently without any visible cause.

Add to this the fact that most dowsers genuinely believe in their own powers, and you have an effect which appears honest, natural – and extremely useful. As with all pseudo-sciences, only successes are allowed to count. Any frequent dowser can quickly build up an impressive portfolio of 'hits'; misses are either explained away or just ignored.

It's also very hard to prove a negative. The fact that numerous properly controlled dowsing tests have come up with nothing doesn't mean that, at some future time, a test might confirm the phenomenon. What we can say, however, is that a large number of people who believed – or at least claimed – that they had the power to locate water, minerals, oil or metal underground could not manage to do it under test conditions.

Take, for example, Paul Sevigny, President of the American Association of Dowsers. He was tested in 1981 by Michael Martin, a professor of philosophy at Boston University, who initiated a course in the 'Philosophy of Science and the Occult'. He obliged each of his students to do a project which would bring critical scrutiny to some aspect of the paranormal. Mr Sevigny agreed to come and give an informal talk to the students first, during which he made some spectacular claims for dowsers. They could not only detect underground water on the spot but could do it at a distance by studying a map of the area. Equipped with his rod, he could locate missing persons and even detect the position of US nuclear submarines in the world's oceans, merely by studying a chart. How fortunate for the Free World that the former Soviet Union, whose government was notoriously superstitious, did not kidnap him, or 'turn' him with huge sums of money.

Mr Sevigny also claimed that he could predict the sex of babies in the womb. Any parent knows of friends, or friends of friends, who make the same claim, often involving the use of a pendulum held over the belly of the pregnant mother. A circular motion means a boy, back and forth a girl – or just as often, the other way round. The classic scam is the soothsayer who charges, say, £10 to do the same job, guaranteeing her good faith by offering money back if she's wrong. That way she gets a steady £5 per guess, plus enthusiastic endorsements from roughly half her clients. Offering to pay back £15 for a wrong prediction would look even more impressive and clear an average of £2.50 per client. Like many such claims, this one has been overtaken by science; scans and new tests make it possible for parents to know in advance if they wish.

Michael Martin's students had set up a straightforward test. Four hose-pipes ran across a room from one plastic dustbin to another. At one end there was a water pump which could be attached to any of the four hoses. Both ends of the experiment were screened off, and the hoses covered by a piece of carpet. A student behind the curtain decided, at random, which hose to connect to the pump, and wrote down its number. After Mr Sevigny had tried to determine, with the help of his divining rod, which hose had the water flowing through it, the student would reveal the correct answer. There were forty tests, and naturally chance expectation would be roughly ten correct. Mr Sevigny scored nine out of forty.

Usually at this point dowsers look bewildered by their failure and start seeking explanations. In fact, according to Michael Martin, Mr Sevigny

Bohemian, Georg Agricola (1490-1555) was the first to include a detailed description of dowsing in 'De Re Metallica'. published in 1556. This woodcut, showing sixteenth-century dowsers looking for metal, is taken from his book.

laughed and joked, saying that the test was only a game, and that in a serious search for water he would have been successful. He probably believed it, too.

The problem with testing dowsers is that it can be wildly expensive. A water diviner says that he's detected water underground. A hole is dug. If water is found, it's deemed a hit. If it isn't, the dowser can easily say that it would have been found if the hole had been deeper.

Few people have the time or the money to test the claim to destruction. Except perhaps in Australia, a country with vast tracts of arid land, where water is often far more valuable than it is in more temperate countries. Dowsing has long been part of rural culture there, and it's commonplace for farmers to consult dowsers before sinking bores. Most are local people who have been trained by other dowsers. Inevitably their suggestions do sometimes lead to water being found, and this encourages everyone – not least the dowser himself – to believe that he must have the powers.

Consequently, some of the most useful tests on dowsing have been conducted in Australia. For example, there was the Vaisey case near Sydney, which took place in 1992. Vic Vaisey was an Australian water diviner who claimed never to

have had a failure. He was hired, for 100 Australian dollars, to search for water under a 5-acre suburban spread owned by a Mr Malcolm McDowell, who badly needed water for his stock. According to Dick Smith, an Australian sceptic who attended the event, Mr McDowell had written first to the New South Wales Water Commission, who had asked for a map of his property. After studying the details – presumably by normal, technical means rather than with a rod – the Commission told him that water might be found at a minimum depth of 50 feet, most probably at 200 feet, and without doubt by 330 feet.

Mr Vaisey arrived at the property, where he divined two streams which he said were 'definitely' present – one running east-west at a depth of 35 feet and the other running north-south, 5 feet deeper. He pointed to a precise location where the two streams crossed and suggested boring there.

The drilling rig arrived and was put into place at a spot marked by Mr Vaisey to the exact inch. The drill passed down through the 35-foot and 40-foot levels. Then it hit dry shale down to 80 feet. Water was eventually struck at 210 feet – the figure 'divined' by the Water Resources Commission, which had not visited the property, but merely used, old-fashioned scientific know-how. According to Dick Smith, Mr Viasey offered no explanation for his – apparently unique – failure, but neither did he offer to return the $100.

Those were just two tests however, and while they are highly suggestive, they do not prove anything. A more thorough test of dowsing was carried out in 1989, also in Australia. James Randi had conducted an earlier test there in 1980, involving the use of underground pipes (the dowsers had scored no better than chance), but since then the Australian Skeptics had offered a $20,000 challenge for the demonstration of any psychic, paranormal or pseudo-scientific phenomenon. Many dowsers had put themselves forward for this handsome prize, and it was decided to mount a whole new set of tests. The results were reported by Ian Bryce, an aeronautical engineer who is project co-ordinator for the Australian Skeptics.

One interesting applicant was Dr Baden Williams, of the Division of Water Resources in Canberra. Dr Williams is a scientist who uses both technical instruments and dowsing rods to find water. He found that both techniques often agreed with each other, and suggested that dowsing rods might be responding to the different electrical conductivity in strata where water was flowing, or even that humans might have an unconscious magnetic sense, similar to the one which is thought to help homing pigeons find their way.

The 1989 tests, held on a farm near the suburbs of Sydney, were extremely rigorous and very carefully controlled. It is a measure not only of the generous prize but of how convinced many dowsers are by their own skills that some of the nine who were tested came from vast distances. One chartered a plane to Sydney from Townsville, another flew from South Australia. All said that they never asked for nor accepted a fee, except for an occasional donation to charity.

The diviners were offered a choice of targets: water in plastic containers, gold ingots or coins, and electric cable – with or without current passing through it.

The various objects were then buried in a series of rows, each covered by a strip of carpet 2 meters by 8 meters (6 feet x 26 feet). Each row contained five 'locations', each 1.3 meters (4 feet) apart.

The two 'concealers' worked inside temporary cloth-covered wooden frames so that nobody at all could see where they were burying the objects. This meant that onlookers could not even signal subconsciously to the dowsers. The location of each buried object was decided by throwing a die in a bottle, making it impossible for one of the concealers to have been in league with a dowser. And just to make absolutely certain, the concealers left the site as soon as their job was done, so that nobody remaining at the test had a clue to the hiding places. This is the 'double blind' control, which makes it impossible for there to be any – even unwitting – collusion between testers and examinees.

All the important possible areas of dispute had to be settled before the tests began. For example, it was necessary to use carpeting so that the people being tested could not get clues from marks left in the grass by the digging. Every dowser was asked to test his powers through carpeting before he came, and a few ruled themselves out beforehand.

Once on site the diviners were asked to confirm that there were no people or things present which might affect their powers. Before the various objects were buried, they were asked to go over the area to make sure that there was no water, nor cables, minerals or other subterranean distractions. Finally they were shown the target objects – water in bottles, cable, and 100 grams of gold ingot – and asked to make sure that they were getting the right reaction. All of them did.

The dowsers used a wide variety of methods and tools. One used a forked stick made of custard-apple wood. Another's whalebone broke, so he used fibreglass instead. Some used wire rods. One Swiss dowser used his bare hands, which shook and flew apart when he thought he was near the object.

Each dowser was allowed five minutes in each row and asked to pick which of the five locations the object was in. Usually their rod – or hands – responded positively to one location straightaway. Often they would walk about, then return to the location, and find that the reaction was stronger than ever.

The end result were statistically complex, but the fact is that not one of the dowsers got remotely near a winning score. For example, one of the cable diviners did manage to get four locations right out of ten (chance would be two right) but another scored zero on the same test. Put at its crudest, the total success rate for all the participants was twelve out of forty-eight – marginally better than chance, which was one in five, but comfortably within the bounds of statistical significance.

Many of the dowsers appeared genuinely astonished when the carpets were rolled back and their failures were apparent. One, in the grand tradition, claimed a paranormal explanation for a wholly predictable failure: the influence, he said, must have travelled along the carpet. Dr Baden Williams, the scientist, said that he would now have to reconsider his views on divining.

We've described this test at length because it does seem to be the most thorough and careful ever carried out on dowsers. What was obviously baffling to the people involved was their own failure. They truly believed in the reaction which they felt and saw. The rod swings up, or the twin rods clash dramatically and noisily into each other, when water is visibly present; what makes the same thing happen when none can be seen?

One likely explanation comes from the fact that dowsing rods are extremely long and light. A tiny muscular twitch, even one which is imperceptible to the dowser and invisible to anyone else, can cause the rods to swing sharply and unexpectedly. The same applies to pendulums. None of us can hold our hands entirely still. One slight movement starts the weight swinging or spinning; almost unconsciously the holder reinforces this, attributing the start of the motion to whatever strange force is operating.

(The same principle applies to the ouija board. It is easy to exert the most minute, imperceptible pressure on the rim of the glass, or whatever is being used as a 'pointer'. Once it is clear that a particular message is being spelled out, such as the start of someone's name, or the beginning of a word such as D-E-A-, the glass starts skidding wildly and even frighteningly across the board, unknowingly pushed by everyone present. No one can quite believe that such force can be generated by muscular movements which cannot be felt, never mind seen.)

However, dowsers and diviners do not always search for water or precious metals. Some claim to find missing bodies. As always, their occasional successes are trumpeted; their more frequent failures ignored. One 'psychic' who claims he can find bodies is Brian Terris. In 1987 he joined in the search for a fifty-five-year-old woman called Lorraine Vaudin who had vanished on Guernsey. Her car had been found parked near some cliffs at Le Prevote, but the police were unable to find her after searching for two days. Mr Terris dowsed over a map of the island, and sensed he was being influenced to go to Le Prevote. There he felt drawn to a particular spot at the edge of the cliffs, which he reached by pushing his way through dense bracken.

Looking over the cliff, he saw the woman's body 200 feet below, hidden by boulders. He told reporters later that he hadn't told the police earlier because 'I haven't always been right. I didn't want to alert the police until I was certain.' The police said that they had missed the body because it had been hidden by the boulders, and couldn't be spotted from the clifftops or the seashore. The only spot from which it was visible was the one to which Mr Terris had scrambled.

Impressive, certainly, at least at first sight. Yet Mr Terris freely admitted that he was not always right, and it doesn't seem particularly astonishing that anyone should find a body of a dead person near to the place where they disappeared. One has to wonder just how thorough the original police search was.

Still, if Mr Terris's dowsing hadn't caused him to visit the spot and climb through the bracken, the body might never have been found, so dowsing can claim that much credit. And in this case nobody was any the poorer for Mr Terris's claim. For the most part, dowsers are among the mildest and least hysterical of all paranormal proponents.

Ghosts and Hauntings

DURING 1994 A SERIES OF WEIRD and inexplicable events happened in an ordinary suburban house in west London. Strange creaking noises occurred at night and in the early morning, as if some restless person were walking about in the attic. More than once, the couple who owned the house were woken by a persistent, rhythmic thumping, like a tortured spirit trying to get inside. A voice yelled out for no reason, again as if an anguished soul was trying to communicate with the inhabitants of the house. A dreadful smell filled one of the rooms; on another occasion the bathroom went inexplicably cold. A bottle of wine was dashed from the husband's hands and crashed on the floor. Once, the cat bolted in terror from the garden, as if it had seen some hideous, terrifying apparition.

In fact, the house belonged to Simon Hoggart and his wife, and the scary events were easily explained at the time. All houses creak at night as the temperature cools and the timbers strain. The thumping was their little boy kicking the wall as he slept through a disturbing dream. The voice came from a radio, switched on by a visiting infant who, frightened by the noise, switched it straight off. The smell was from a blocked drain and the cold bathroom due to a broken radiator. The wine fell by accident; Hoggart was trying to carry too many things at once. As for the cat, who knows what grisly manifestation it had seen? A dog?

This is ludicrous of course, yet full-scale hauntings, with their excitable newspaper coverage, films, TV specials and massive investigations by psychic 'experts' have been based on very little more. As soon as people start to believe that their house is haunted, they will attribute almost any strange event to the ghost, even when a humdrum explanation is available. If you have come to sense that your house is haunted, clearly you imagine that the desperate scrabbling noises above your head are a soul in torment, rather than mice. The belief feeds on itself. Why bother searching for a normal reason when the incident is clearly part of an all too terrible pattern?

Human beings have probably believed in ghosts, or at least in the spirits of the dead, since *homo sapiens* first appeared. Ghosts have taken different forms in different eras and societies. Some have religious overtones, such as the Tonton Macoute of Haiti, originally 'Uncle Knapsack', who carried off young children from their homes and gave his name to the vicious – and all too corporeal – private militia. In classical Greece ghosts were skittish and harmless. In mediaeval Europe, they were vengeful, returning to earth to extract justice from those who had wronged them in life. In our less religious times, ghosts tend to be fairly harmless, sad or eccentric figures wandering the earth to no particular purpose.

Many people think they've seen a ghost, and it's conceivable that they have. However, it seems far more likely that they mistook a curtain billowing in the wind, or a reflection in an unexpected place, or an animal, or – most likely of all – a real person. If you see a ghostly nun walking between the yew trees near the old churchyard, can you be certain it isn't a real nun? Or a woman in a caped coat? Or someone going to amateur dramatics? Did she really disappear in front of your eyes, or just turn into a passageway you couldn't see? And was she actually headless, or was her head covered against the rain? It's no wonder that ghosts are more commonly seen at night, when we are most tired and suggestible, most inclined to suspect something threatening in our surroundings.

Hallucination may be the most common cause of ghost sightings. This is a very well established phenomenon. People who are tired and stressed may well 'see' things which aren't there; the weaker the body, the weaker the mind's defences, and it is easy to confuse a particularly vivid dream with reality. It's not uncommon for us to mistake the most ordinary dream for something which actually happened. Did you really send a birthday card to your nephew, or did you just dream you had? People who feel they are being haunted are often under great stress from some other cause, and the 'haunting' is a symptom of that. Hallucinations can be symptoms of the same thing, and the two can easily combine in one person's mind to unsettling, even frightening, effect. People whose sleep is frequently disturbed, or are recovering from illness or trauma, sometimes suffer from 'night terrors', a fairly common condition which makes them wake up certain that some dreadful – but unspecific – thing has just happened. This is usually curable, but is extremely distressing for all concerned. To someone who felt they were already the victim of demons, it must seem yet more horrible proof.

Once fears and dreads are established, they can also affect other people living with the victim of the 'haunting'. Indeed, whole families can convince each other that the house they live in is infested with ghosts. This seems to be especially true if the family is very religious or inclined to believe in the supernatural. Sometimes it's because the family is dysfunctional in another way, and the idea of being haunted is, in a peculiar fashion, rather gratifying. For people who have lived their life in obscurity, the fame a good haunting brings can be very pleasing.

Robert A Baker, a psychology professor in the University of Kentucky, has won himself a substantial reputation as a real-life 'ghostbuster', finding the reason for hauntings, and curing people who believe they are victims. One of his cases concerned a young woman who was being haunted by her uncle, who had died at the age of thirty-five when she was eleven. She had been close to him. As she grew up he appeared to her when she was alone in bed, then began to bother her when she was out with young men. His spectral visits grew more and more frequent as she got engaged, and came virtually every night during her honeymoon.

The ghostly uncle started to time his visits for when the couple were making love, and on one of these occasions, the wife suddenly shouted: 'Oh no, he's here

'The Hammersmith Ghost' from Kirby's 'Wonderful & Eccentric Museum' published in 1820. From October 1803 Hammersmith was alive with rumours about ghosts. On the night of 3 January 1804 exciseman Francis Smith and a friend set-out with a gun in quest of the ghosts. Seeing the figure of Thomas Millwood, dressed in white trousers and jacket, coming towards him Smith fired, killing Millwood. Smith was tried for murder, found guilty and sentenced to death. He was subsequently pardoned.

It later transpired that one of the Hammersmith ghosts (illustrated here) was really John Graham, a shoemaker, dressed in a sheet to scare his apprentice who had teased Graham's children 'upon the subject of ghosts and apparitions'. Another 'ghost', at first believed to be a madwoman turned out to be a youth who frequently appeared in the churchyard and other places dressed in a maid's clothes. A third, which was challenged with a quaint 'Ghost, or whatever you may be, pray be civil' was a young lady with her companion.

again!' The husband turned his head and thought he caught a glimpse of a man in a green jacket, the uncle's favourite haunting apparel. The wraith was ruining their married life and the husband sought help from Dr Baker, who – while noting the obvious implications about the wife's sense of sexual guilt – got rid of the ghost speedily and inexpensively by shouting loud imprecations at it. He advised the couple to do the same if the uncle returned. He didn't. As Dr Baker says, 'places aren't haunted, only people are haunted. If a person is convinced that the ghost has been scared away, the visitations frequently end.'

This is one reason why exorcisms often appear to work. Since the haunting has generally been a delusion in the mind of someone – or a group of people – living in a house, the manifestations end as soon as they expect them to end. (This would not necessarily work in the case of a haunted highway. The Revd Donald Omand, a British clergyman, exorcises roads which have particularly bad accident rates. Mr Omand claims that he was successful with a stretch of road which had had eight accidents in two years. After his work it was accident free for six years, until another crash did happen. It had to be exorcised again.)

Many ghosts are simply legends that have been passed on down the years. Urban myths – the 'granny in the roofrack' type of tale, passed on as true ('it happened to this friend of a friend of mine...') – frequently concern ghosts and hauntings. One common tale is told with numerous variations: a man picks up a young woman hitchhiker. It turns out she lives on his route home, so he drops her off at her house. When he gets back he finds that she has left her pullover in his car, so the next day he stops by to return it. He meets her parents, who tell him that their daughter died exactly a year before, at the spot where he picked her up. And, yes, that was her pullover...

Because such stories are passed on as true, people may well be inclined to believe them, especially if the teller is trusted. But of course the fact that someone is honest, doesn't mean that they are right.

Completely fictitious ghost stories sometimes acquire a patina of factual detail which makes people believe them. Take the terrifying story of the Russian ship *Ivan Vassilli*. As the story is generally told, the ship sailed in 1903 from the Baltic Sea to Vladivostok. The crew sensed an evil presence on board, as though the whole ship had become saturated with evil. They panicked, and one crewman hurled himself overboard. This death caused the evil presence to depart.

Three days later it was back. The crew tried to desert but were forced back on board and made to set sail for Hong Kong. Some members of the crew saw the ghost through the mist, looking almost human. Two more men jumped overboard and another died of fright. The ship made only two more voyages, to Australia and to San Francisco, and there were more deaths on each trip. Finally, after it had returned to Russia, no sailor could be persuaded to get on board, and the ship was destroyed.

We have a bizarre and inexplicable tale. How could all those deaths have occurred? What phantom is so terrifying that it can literally scare a hardened mariner to death?

Actually, it would be a lot more inexplicable if it were true. The investigator Robert Sheaffer (he found that the alien 'abductee' Betty Hill had actually perceived the planet Jupiter as a UFO) went to every imaginable record, and could not find any mention of the ship *Ivan Vassilli*. He combed *Lloyd's Register, Jane's All The World's Ships*, the American *Register of Shipping* and newspaper lists of sailings in the cities where the boat was supposed to have berthed. Nobody has any sign that the Ivan Vassilli ever existed, yet the story still crops up now and again in allegedly authoritative accounts of famous hauntings.

A much-loved ghost in Alabama was that of Abigail Lylia Burns, an actress who appeared in the first show at a new auditorium at Athens State College in 1914. After receiving tremendous acclaim for her performance in *La Traviata*, she promised that she would return 'if it is the last thing I do'. That night she left by carriage for her next engagement, in Huntsville, Alabama. On the way the carriage plunged over a bridge, wounding her fatally. But before she died she was heard to say: 'I have a promise to keep; I must return.'

And return she did, haunting the auditorium, her gold hair glinting in the moonlight, a bouquet of red roses in her arms. Many people claim to have seen her, and even some who haven't say they have sensed her presence.

Even those who don't believe in ghosts might have found such a story affecting. However, Mark W Durm, a professor of psychology at Athens State College, had students in his class investigate the legend. They could find no evidence anywhere that someone called Abigail Lylia Burns had ever performed at the college, and certainly not at the opening of the new auditorium. Nobody of that name had died in the area any time between 1908 and 1922. There was no record of anyone with the name being booked to play in Huntsville. Old alumni of the college were contacted and asked if they had heard the story; none had. It appears to have been concocted at some point (possibly after an ouija board or table-tapping session) and had taken on a life of its own. And if people expect to see ghosts, then many will. Young blonde women carrying flowers have been known to walk around universities, though very few of them are ghosts. Practical jokers are also not exactly rare on campuses.

Many victims of ghosts are perfectly honest. One of the most celebrated cases in Britain was the Dieppe raid haunting of 1951. This was an unusual example of the genre, since it involved only noises. Two women, a Mrs Dorothy Norton and her sister-in-law Miss Agnes Norton (the surname was a pseudonym) were staying at Puys, near Dieppe, in a hotel overlooking the sea during August 1951. One night both were woken by loud noises from the beach. When they went out on the balcony they could hear the sounds of a battle. There were men shouting, gunfire, dive bombers, landing craft crashing onto the beach, and so on. The noises continued until seven in the morning.

The two women took extensive notes at the time they heard the sounds. Later they made enquiries and discovered that other guests in the hotel had not heard the noises. This made them suspect that they must be psychic in origin. They decided that what they had heard matched to a large extent the sounds of the

Dieppe raid, which had taken place in August 1942. The women seemed entirely normal and completely honest – indeed there's no reason to suppose they were not. The notion that an event with dreadful loss of life could be psychically re-enacted, but only 'received' by certain sensitive people, was extremely exciting, and the case attracted a great deal of publicity.

It was solved by chance, seventeen years later. A Mr R A Eades reported that he had been camping with his family just east of Dieppe in August 1951. During the night they had been woken by an 'indescribable' noise which continued for several hours. When they asked in the town what might have caused it, they discovered that it was a dredger. This would account for most of the noise and, presumably, for the sounds of men shouting. There were no dive-bombers in action during the Dieppe raid, but Puys itself was located underneath a civilian flight path in 1951, and so planes could no doubt be heard overhead.

Mr Eades said that the clatter of the dredger was frequently dimmed when the wind changed and sometimes sounded quite soft – which might well account for other people not being woken in the Puys hotel. The ladies were no doubt perfectly sincere in believing they had heard a psychic event, but if they had made local inquiries at the time they wouldn't have been misled.

Robert Baker and investigator Joe Nickell – who is also a private detective – describe in their book *Missing Pieces* a haunting they researched in Lexington, Kentucky. A middle-aged woman described a series of strange domestic events. Her son had bought a car whose original owner had died in it. She saw her son in the car, working on it; when she got upstairs, seconds later, he was sitting in the living room. Another time the son had put a head gasket on a shelf attached to the garage wall; it was suddenly flung violently onto the car. The woman and her mother heard people playing on a pool table; when they went to see who it was, the room was empty. A vacuum cleaner started of its own accord. A telephone flew off its own table and landed on the kitchen table. A pan of melted butter left the stove and landed on the kitchen floor without a drop being spilled.

This might have been an example of a poltergeist, a German word which means 'noisy spirit', and refers to a type of malevolent ghost which creates havoc in houses by wrecking things, hurling objects about and generally creating mayhem. Poltergeists are usually associated with disturbed teenage girls. Believers argue that they need a human being to focus their energies; sceptics suspect that it is the teenage girl who is covertly flinging objects around the place in order to get the attention and excitement she craves.

When Baker came to the house he was able quickly to set the woman's mind at rest. Every incident had a different, separate, cause; it was the combination of strange events which gave the appearance of ghostly activity.

The car had tinted windows. What the woman saw was her own reflection, but she assumed it was her son because she had seen him working on the car earlier. The gasket was covered in oil and the shelf was sloping; as it fell off it gathered speed and crashed into the car. The pool balls were in a rack. When lorries rumbled by on a nearby road, they rattled and clicked together, as if someone was playing on the table. The vacuum cleaner could be started with a kick or a thump, and it turned out that the woman's dog had been playing nearby at the time. The phone incident was easily duplicated when a chair leg tugged at the phone wire, which had got caught behind it. And the pan of butter had been resting in another pan of turbulently boiling water which had forced it out and onto the floor. Good luck had kept it upright. As with the non-haunting at the start of this chapter, it was only the idea that a poltergeist was at work which gave significance to these unusual, but hardly surprising, incidents.

The best-known British haunting was at Borley Rectory in Essex, which became known as *The Most Haunted House in England*, the title of a book by Harry Price

Borley Rectory, Essex - 'The Most Haunted House in England' photographed the day after it was destroyed by fire on 27 February 1939.

The celebrated ghostwatcher Harry Price (left), with Marianne Foyster, the Revd Lionel Foyster, and researcher Mrs Goldney with two foster children at Borley Rectory in October 1931.

published in 1940. (Price was the man who conducted the fire walking test of Kuda Bux in 1935 – see the chapter on Fire Walking p137.) Borley was celebrated as the home of almost all the psychic phenomena then known, including mysterious noises, voices, bells ringing, masonry flying, and a ghostly nun. The various clerics who lived there soon found their lives made unpleasant by the crowds of sightseers flocking to see the wonders. In fact, Price had invented much of the story up out of whole cloth, and wildly exaggerated other events, ignoring perfectly obvious explanations.

Price's work, a blend of gullibility, stupidity and mendacity, has been amply demolished, most notably by Trevor H Hall. The chief victim of the alleged events, Marianne Foyster, wife of the Revd Lionel Foyster, was supposed to be the most psychic person of all those who lived there, and sensitive to the weirdest events. In fact, she said later, she had never seen any apparitions, and that most of the ghostly noises were caused by wind in the crumbling building and by boys from the village who had climbed in to play. Mysterious fires had been started by tramps, who could easily get into the Rectory. She had become the lover of a man who tenanted the Rectory cottage, and who played practical jokes on her sick, cuckolded husband by pretending to have seen the apparitions. (To be fair, she wrote to Trevor Hall in 1956 saying that 'things' had continued to happen while she was away from the house '...it was not me. I got the blame for it, but that doesn't matter, people saying a thing is so cannot make it so, and I've found that out.' She also said that her husband was not popular and that had led to much of the mischief. 'But there were a great many things which he and I went through which no one can explain away as mischief.')

However, many legends about the rectory were simply invented. For instance, the children of the Revd Harry Bull, who had the living but one before Lionel Foyster, said they were astonished to find they had been inhabiting England's most haunted house; all the years they had lived there, they had seen nothing. *Picture Post* magazine reported in 1955, fifteen years after Price's book was published:

'The Bulls had several more comments to make about statements by Price; their father did *not* have the dining–room window bricked up to prevent the nun staring in, but to stop the view of ordinary nosey passers-by; that he did not build the summer-house as a grandstand for the nun's perambulations, but for use during tennis parties; and the title the Nun's Walk, must have been given by Price, because they never knew it as that.'

The most grotesque recent example of fraud was the Amityville Horror, which led to a best-selling book and two hugely successful films, *The Amityville Horror* and *Amityvile II – The Possession*. In November 1974, a youth called Ronald DeFoe shot dead six members of his family in their house in Amityville, New York. He was sentenced to six terms of life imprisonment, though his lawyer insisted he was insane and claimed to have heard voices in the house telling him what to do.

A year later George and Kathy Lutz bought the house in spite of its gory history, because the price was low. They moved in with their three children on 18 December, and a family friend, Father Frank Mancuso (the book used an alias for Father Ralph Pecararo) blessed the new home. While he did this he heard a strong masculine voice saying 'Get out!'

The family moved out four weeks later after a succession of terrifying events had happened to them. A heavy door was ripped open, dangling on a hinge; hundreds of flies infested a room in the middle of winter; the telephone mysteriously went wrong, especially when 'Mancuso' was on the line; a 4-foot statue moved about the house, Mrs Lutz levitated while asleep, her face wrinkled like an old woman, mysterious green slime oozed from the hall ceiling, the daughter acquired a piglike playmate, the family dog (and the two sons) misbehaved.

Margot Kidder and James Brolin in a scene from the 1979- film 'The Amityville Horror' which was publicised as 'A true story'. This film was followed by 'Amityville II - The Possession' and several television films based on the same theme.

Just how many of these events, if any, actually happened is hard to work out, since it has long been established that the story was a hoax. Some investigators, such as Robert L Morris, now Professor of Parapsychology at Edinburgh University, but then a Lecturer in Parapsychology at the University of California, had their suspicions from the start. The book, *The Amityville Horror* by Jay Anson, was too full of impossibilities and contradictions to be taken seriously by anyone who was not disposed to believe in the first place. As Morris pointed out at the time, some of the incidents may have happened but for perfectly ordinary reasons: for example, the flies might have hatched out in a room which was being centrally heated for the first time in a year. Many events were demonstrably untrue. For example, a tremendous twelve-hour storm which allegedly lashed the house and the town did not occur.

William Weber, Ronald DeFoe's lawyer who had suggested his client had heard voices telling him to murder his family, admitted that he and the Lutzes had 'created this horror story over many bottles of wine' in order to make money. He added: 'We were really creating something the public would want to hear about. If the public is gullible enough to believe the story, so be it.' The Lutzes sold the house to another family, who noticed nothing strange at all, except for hordes of curious sightseers pestering them. They successfully sued the Lutzes, Anson and the publishers 'to enjoin them from characterising their story as true'. Father Pecararo also sued the Lutzes for distorting his role, and settled out of court. There are, of course, no books, films or TV blockbusters called 'Amityville – the Real Story'.

One couple who involved themselves with this case were Ed and Lorraine Warren. They also turned up at the West Pittston haunting, which also attracted a great deal of publicity – if not as much as Amityville. The demons which haunted the house in Chase Street, West Pittston (a mining town near Scranton) were first reported in 1986. The Smurl family, who lived there, had four daughters and were all devout Roman Catholics. They claimed to have been terrorised by demons, subjected to foul smells, objects disappearing and moving around, physical attacks and rappings. The eight-year-old twins said they had been hurled out of bed and dashed down the stairs. Most dramatically the father, Jack Smurl, said that: 'at least a dozen times it, or whatever you want to call this grotesque woman, has had intercourse with me in bed. I was awake, but I was immobile.'

As often happens with these cases, the psychics – in this case the Warrens – made sure that sceptical investigators were kept well clear of the house. However, two scientific consultants of CSICOP (the Committee for the Scientific Investigation of Claims of the Paranormal) were able to find out a great deal from neighbours and local people. The house was built over disused mine workings, and subsistence was a serious problem in the area. This would certainly account for many of the ghostly noises. (Or, the empty workings would provide passages for demons to rise to the surface; take your pick.) Teenage girls – the Smurls's elder daughters were seventeen and fourteen – are frequently found in poltergeist cases, and could have been responsible for some of the incidents. In particular the oldest child, Dawn, then seventeen, changed her story several times.

As for the hideous ghost-lover who climbed between the sheets with Jack Smurl – it emerged that three years before he had been treated for hydrocephalus, or water on the brain. This is a highly dangerous condition which can cause mental impairment, paralysis, loss of hearing and sight. Mr Smurl insisted that his doctor had ruled the illness out as a possible cause of his experiences, but that doesn't mean we have to.

In Britain there was great excitement in 1978 about the Enfield haunting. This involved a divorced mother with four children (adolescents in poltergeist cases tend to be disturbed for one reason or another. Tina Resch, centre of the fraudulent haunting in Columbus, Ohio, was adopted and at loggerheads with her adoptive parents over finding her natural ones.) In the Enfield case, psychic researchers logged 1,500 'paranormal' happenings. They also acquired film of the twelve-year-old daughter producing words with her mouth tightly shut.

"Bloody hell, Alice – the poltergeist has been dialling Adelaide again."

In April 1978 there was a rare example of a popular newspaper printing the sceptical side as well as the mysterious claims. *The News of the World* printed quotes from a researcher from the Society for Psychical Research, who was unimpressed by the little girl's noises which they could easily produce with their mouths shut.

'I was only able to visit the house once, but it looked to me like kids mucking about. Furniture only moved when investigators were out of the room. The kitchen table went over while colleagues and I were taking things to our cars. The children were in the kitchen at the time...

'Later I filled two balloons with water and placed them in a pot beneath the children's beds. When the children woke, I showed them the balloons and joked that the poltergeist couldn't be very clever because he had left them alone. I went out of the room and was barely halfway down the stairs when the children shouted to me that the poltergeist had burst the balloons. Sure enough, we had water coming through the downstairs ceiling.'

The SPR researchers thought that it might have started as a genuine poltergeist case, and that the children had kept it going. But that is a typical example of paranormal straw-clutching. If they were satisfied that all the phenomena they witnessed were caused by the children, why invent another explanation? Because, presumably, that would be to admit the terrible truth – there are no ghosts, no poltergeists and no hauntings. They are all mistaken, imaginary or fakes. For true believers, that is the spookiest news of all.

The Curse of Tutankhamun

BY THE AUTUMN OF 1922, archeologists had already spent sixteen years searching for the tomb of Tutankhamun in the Valley of the Kings, near Thebes in Egypt. The patron of the current expedition, Lord Carnarvon, had decided that further work was pointless; the whole team would pack up and go home. However, as they prepared to leave, a group of Egyptian workmen were prodding around some boulders near the tomb of Rameses VI which had already been opened. Here they found a flight of steps covered by sand. After a week of digging down through the 60 feet of desert, the expedition's chief excavator, Howard Carter, discovered at the bottom the prize they had been seeking for so long: the tomb of the fourteenth-century-BC boy-pharoah, marked by the inscription 'Lo, I am here'.

For three years they worked through the antechamber and then the 5,000 breathtaking and priceless treasures in the burial chamber itself. These were finer than anything which had been discovered in any other Egyptian tomb. Finally, in October of 1925, they opened the coffin and found a death mask of beaten gold. This was the face of Tutankhamun, an image which gripped the world immediately and which still holds an immensely powerful resonance for millions of people.

What the archeologists and their servants could not know was that a terrible curse would now settle upon all those who had defiled the tomb: a curse so vengeful that it not only killed many people on the original expedition, often in bizarre and unexpected circumstances, but persisted to the end of the century – even causing havoc among the makers of a TV film about the discovery, nearly sixty years later.

The first example of the curse's awesome power came just five months after the tomb was entered, when Lord Carnarvon died in Cairo. The moment he breathed his last, all the lights in the city went out. Simultaneously, at his home in England, his favourite fox-terrier threw back its head, howled, and dropped dead.

Since then there have been many other deaths and weird goings-on associated with the tomb and the pharaoh. Howard Carter's assistant, Richard Bethell, died suddenly of a circulatory illness six years after the opening. Grief stricken by his son's death, his father, Lord Westbury, committed suicide by jumping from a block of flats. George Jay Gould, the son of the wealthy financier Jay Gould, died in 1923 within days of being one of the early visitors to the tomb.

But the curse can affect anyone who comes in contact even indirectly with the

Preceding page

The awesome, haunting and powerful gold-inlaid mummy mask of Tutankhamun dating from between 1580 and 1314 BC is still associated with many curses since it was first discovered in 1922 near Luxor by a British archaeological expedition led by Lord Carnarvon.

desecrators. In 1980 a British TV company made a film based on the story. One actor, Raymond Burr, collapsed on the set and another, Ian McShane, broke his leg in a car crash. In 1992, Christopher Frayling made a series called 'The Face of Tutankhamun' for the BBC. During the filming, the crew shot a sequence in the Cairo Museum, but found the tape blank when they played it back. While they were working in the tomb, the TV lights went out for twenty minutes, at the very moment Frayling mentioned the curse. Soon afterwards he suddenly stopped breathing and believes only prompt action by his wife saved his life. And a hotel lift he was travelling in fell twenty-one floors when the cable snapped.

In spite of all these mysteries and terrors, those involved remained sceptical about the curse. The actress Angharad Rees, who played Carnarvon's daughter, Lady Evelyn Herbert, in the 1980 film, said afterwards: 'It's all nonsense. Film sets can be dangerous and full of problems – this location was no worse than others I've worked at.' Nor was Christopher Frayling a believer: 'I am sure there are rational explanations,' he said afterwards.

And he is perfectly right. This is a good example of a paranormal event, or series of events, in which we don't need to surmise that there's a perfectly rational explanation – we are virtually certain there is.

But first, the curse. It does seem to have been a remarkably selective one. Though Lord Carnarvon died shortly afterwards, his daughter, who was also present at the opening, went on to live to the age of seventy-nine, dying fifty-seven years after the event. Indeed, the average survival rate for the twenty-two main participants was 20.9 years, and at least three lived for more than forty years after the event. As the table opposite shows, out of the people it's been possible to track down, only two had the misfortune to die when they were younger than sixty-five. These include Carnarvon himself, who was in Egypt partly because he

Lord Carnarvon and his daughter Lady Evelyn Herbert supervising the packing of artifacts from Tutankhamun's tomb in 1923.

was ill already and his doctor had recommended the climate. He went to hospital after a mosquito bite he received in the Valley of the Kings turned septic.

The story about the lights of Cairo going out at the moment of his death is dramatic but hardly improbable. The power supply frequently failed in Cairo in the early part of the century; it was an event scarcely more surprising than rain in England. As for the faithful dog which died at the same instant as its master, first-hand information about the timing is hard to come by, but one believer in the curse quotes Carnavon's son as saying it was 4 am British time. His father died at 1.55 am in Egypt. Since these time zones are two hours apart, the dog must have died within five minutes of the doomed desecrator.

A good story, except that Britain is not ahead of, but two hours *behind* Egypt. Therefore even if the timing is accurate, the dog died four hours later. Nevertheless, it is an interesting coincidence that the two deaths occurred in the same night – except that for true believers any domestic mishap, from a death in the family to a grandfather clock stopping, would have served the purpose of making the event look spookier.

The real explanation of this non-existent curse is probably much simpler. In 1980 *The Daily Mail* printed an interview with Richard Adamson, a former soldier,

A table showing the people most associated with the discovery and excavation of Tutankhamun's tomb and how long they survived the 'Curse'.

NAME	DIED	AGE	YRS AFTER TOMB OPENING	FUNCTION	COMMENTS
Richard Adamson	1980+	81+	57+	Guard who slept in tomb	
Georges Benedite	1926	69	3	Louvre representative	Died of heat stroke
Richard Bethell	1929	-	6	Carter's personal secretary	No connection with tomb
Prof James H Breasted	1935	70	12	University of Chicago archaeologist	
Bernard Bruyere	1965+	80+	42+		
Harry Burton	1939+	-	16+	Official photographer	Intimately involved in all operations
A R Callender	1939	-	16	Assistant to Carter	Present at all tomb procedures
Jean Capart	1947	70	24	Belgian Archaeologist	
Herbert Carnarvon	1923	57	4 months	Patron of excavation	Died before mummy was uncovered
Howard Carter	1939	66	16	Chief of operations	Most involved
Dr Douglas Derry	1969	87	46	Cairo University anatomist	Analysed body of Tut in detail
Reginald Engelbach	1946	58	23	Cairo Museum	
Sir Alan Gardiner	1963	84	40	Philologist	Handled all written material in tomb
Lindsley F Hall	1939+	-	16+	Draftsman	Present at all tomb operations
Walter Hauser	1939+	-	16+	Draftsman	Present at all tomb operations
Lady Evelyn Herbert	1980	78	57	Daughter of Carnarvon	One of 3 at tomb opening
Charles Kuentz	1939+	-	16+		
Pierre Lacau	1965	92	42	Egyptologist	Intimately involved in all operations
Gustave Lefebvre	1957	78	34	Cairo Museum	
Alfred Lucas	1950+	79+	27+	Chemist for government of Egypt	
A M Lythgoe	1934	66	11	Metropolitan Museum, NYC	
Arthur C Mace	1928	-	5	NYC Museum Archaeologist	Very ill when signed on. Left project
Herbert E Winlock	1950	66	27	Metropolitan Museum, NYC	
AVERAGE		73+	24+		

- information not available   + minimum information available

BANX

"Well, what kind of curse did you expect? He was nine."

who had mysteriously avoided the effects of the curse in spite of having slept in the tomb to protect its contents for seven years. His head was a few inches away from the mummy in its solid gold coffin, and his feet were recklessly pointed at the two Ka statues, which had guarded the remains for 3,300 years. He told the newspaper that his main defence against grave robbers had been a wind-up gramophone and three records. He would play them – one was the triumphal march from *Aida* – so that the sound wafted eerily through the valley, enough to deter anyone remotely superstitious.

He had been sent to Egypt in 1921 as a military policeman during the British military occupation. The following year he was detailed to help Lord Carnarvon pack up the expedition, which at that stage had appeared to end in failure.

When the discovery was first made in 1922, crowds of people descended on the site. They had begun to hamper the digging work, and there seemed a real danger that thieves would break in and ransack the burial chamber before the archeologists could get there. Mr Adamson told *The Daily Mail*:

'We realised we need something to keep the armies of curious people away. Many items down there were so fragile, they would have crumbled in the hands of people trying to carry them off.

'Quite suddenly we thought about a curse. Inscriptions laying curses on intruders had been found on the walls of tombs nearer Cairo, and it so happened that a reporter had been hanging around asking about curses there. We saw no such inscriptions laying curses in Tut's tomb, but, let's say, we didn't discourage him from thinking there was. With a wink and nod from us he was quite happy to make up the tale of a curse over King Tut's tomb.'

The story grew in fertile ground. The Victorian novelist Maria Corelli had already written: 'No good will come of disturbing Pharaoh's bones.' One Egyptologist from the British Museum, Carol Andrews, says that in fact curses were not found in tombs, and archeologists wouldn't expect to find them – though they might find curses inveighing against anyone who disturbed the funery offerings of food and drink which were commonly left in chapels for the spirits to consume. Speaking more than fifty-five years after the event, Mr Adamson might easily have got some details wrong, but there seems no reason to doubt his statement that the curse was an *ad hoc* invention to serve a pressing purpose.

An air of dark mystery already hung over Egyptian tombs. For instance, in the early part of the century there were popular stories, among the 'urban legends' of their day, about a coffin lid which had belonged to a Princess from Thebes and had ended up in the British Museum. The lid, which carried the face of an unhappy woman, was said to represent a soul in torment. This lid was supposed to have created numerous mishaps, so it was sold secretly to an American, who took it home on the *Titanic*... None of this elaborate story was true, and the lid is still safely in the British Museum.

But the Curse of Tut is a classic example of a paranormal myth. (Even Prince Charles asked Mr Adamson if the fact that both his legs were amputated was the result of the curse. Mr Adamson pointed out that this was the late result of injuries he'd suffered in the First World War long before the tomb was opened.) As with so many similar yarns, the story has gathered 'facts', which are passed from one account to another without ever being checked. For example, Sir Lee Stack, the Governor-General of the Sudan from 1917, is often quoted as a victim of the curse. He was assassinated in Cairo in November 1924 – but there is no apparent evidence that he ever visited the tomb.

But the curse is a beguiling story. It implies, excitingly, that the dead live on and can still influence those still on earth. It has mystery and history, romance and colour. Any event which seems to bear out the story can be drafted in its support. Anything which doesn't, such as the long healthy life passed by Lord Carnavon's daughter, is simply ignored.

A glance at the the real facts shows how nonsensical the curse is; but it's also nice to have Mr Adamson's testimony to show how the story probably started.

Howard Carter, the archaeologist who accompanied Lord Carnarvon in 1922, chipping unguents from the third and innermost gold coffin which contained the mummy and portrait mask of Tutankhamun. At the time his findings were described as 'the most sensational discovery of the century'.

The Loch Ness Monster and other Elusive Beasts

THE LOCH NESS MONSTER INDUSTRY was struck a harsh and cruel blow in March of 1994, when *The Sunday Telegraph* printed a front-page article with the headline 'Revealed: the Loch Ness picture hoax'. Under this was the dark, blotchy shape (see illustration) which for millions of people around the world is the Loch Ness Monster: a long, serpentine neck and a prehistoric head apparently gliding through the peat-stained waters of this most mysterious of all lakes.

The article described how and why this hoax picture was created. To be fair, very few people who have examined the Loch Ness legend, with the exception of the most dedicated believers, ever doubted that this picture was a hoax – or at least that it showed something other than a monster. There were many possible explanations: the shape of the head and neck had been cut out and stuck to a bottle which had been floated on the loch; perhaps it could have been a log, a bird or an otter's tail. In any event, though there was nothing else in the picture to judge how big the object was, it was clear that the size of the ripples around the neck didn't match the bulk of a full-size monster. These ripples were also consistent with something which had been dropped into the water rather than one which had risen up from underneath. It was pretty clear to reasonable observers that if there was a monster, its most famous portrait was of something else.

For some sixty years this picture was known as the Surgeon's photograph. It was thought to have been taken by a Harley Street gynaecologist called Robert Wilson. He said he had been driving along the side of the loch, when his companion had seen a commotion in the water and yelled: 'My God, it's the monster!' Wilson had taken four pictures with a plate camera. Two turned out to be blank, one showed a meaningless blob, and the other was the celebrated image. It created an immediate sensation when it was published in *The Daily Mail* .

Monster sightings had began in 1933 (one curiosity of many paranormal phenomena is that they tend to be remarkably recent). These sightings followed the improvement of a road along the north side of the loch which had made it easier for travellers to view the whole 22-mile length. One sighting was by John Mackay, a businessman who told *The Inverness Courier* in May 1933 that he and his wife had watched a strange creature while it 'disported itself, rolling and plunging for fully a minute'. Mr Mackay owned a hotel near the loch, which did seem faintly suspicious. However, Alex Campbell, the water bailiff of the loch, who wrote the newspaper article, said that he firmly believed in the creature because he had seen it several times. He described it as a 'monster' not because it was frightening, but because he couldn't think what else to call it. These sightings were mentioned in the local press but attracted little attention south of the border.

Then in December 1933, *The Daily Mail* hired a so-called 'big-game hunter', a flamboyant figure called Marmaduke Wetherell, to track the monster down. He succeeded, with amazing speed. Three days after his arrival at the loch side, *The Daily Mail* revealed that he had discovered proof of the monster's existence. He had found two recent footprints in the soft mud on the south shore of the loch. It was of a 'four-toed...very powerful, soft-footed animal about 20 feet long'.

Sadly, casts of the prints sent to the Natural History Museum in London turned out to be those of a young hippo, and had probably been made by an umbrella stand. *The Daily Mail*, and 'Duke' Wetherell, were humiliated.

What happened next might never have emerged if it hadn't been for the dedication of two Loch Ness researchers, David Martin and Alastair Boyd. They had spotted a 1975 newspaper item in which Wetherell's son Ian had said his father had once fabricated a monster picture. Years later Martin and Boyd discovered that Ian was dead, but his stepbrother Christian Spurling was living in southern England at the age of ninety. He told them the story.

Wetherell had returned to his home in Twickenham, still stinging from the angry rebuff he'd received from *The Daily Mail*. 'All right,' he had told Ian, 'if they want a monster, we'll give them a monster.' He had set Ian and Christian, a keen modeller, to make him one. Christian thought that a monster would have a long neck, like a sea serpent. Ian was dispatched to buy a toy submarine to put it on. The neck was made of plastic wood built up in layers, and the submarine was fitted with a lead ballast strip to keep it stable. Finally, in February or March 1934, Duke and Ian returned to Loch Ness. They put the submarine in a shallow bay and took the pictures. (The dark patch in front of the neck, often described as a 'flipper', was in fact the deck of the submarine.)

Wetherell knew that if the pictures came directly from him, they would be immediately discredited. He asked a friend, Maurice Chambers, if he knew of anyone whose name would not be linked to his own, but might be prepared to join in the jape. Chambers came up with Robert Wilson. Wilson agreed, and was given the four plates to take to a chemist's shop in Inverness for developing. The monster was born and the world has never quite got over the excitement.

In later years, Wilson became evasive, saying he had never believed he had photographed the monster; he had merely 'seen something in the water'. He had been warned by the British Medical Association that all the publicity was bringing the profession into disrepute. He hinted darkly that his companion had been a married woman, which was why he could not be more forthcoming. As for the submarine, Spurling said that his stepbrother and father had heard a water bailiff approaching. Duke put out his foot and sunk the model, meaning that for a while at least there was at least one monster in Loch Ness.

Some other monster experts claim that this story cannot be true. The toy submarine would not have been able to carry so much weight. Yet given an explana-

tion which fits virtually all the facts, and meshes in so neatly with what we know of Duke Wetherell (and the gullibility of tabloid newspaper editors) it seems positively perverse not to accept the Spurling account.

Of course, the fact that one picture – even the most famous – is a hoax doesn't prove that the monster doesn't exist, any more than a fake Picasso means that Picasso never lived. But this picture is important because if it had not appeared, the monster legend might never have gathered its mad momentum.

With the generous *post hoc* recasting of the evidence typical of paranormal fans, it's sometimes suggested that there has been a long and ancient tradition of monster-sighting in the loch. Not so. It's certainly true that people have often thought they saw monsters on lakes around the world. The Scottish 'kelpie' or water monster was believed by Highlanders to live in many lakes. Possibly they had observed the same kind of thing which has accounted for many Loch Ness sight-

A photograph often reproduced in books and articles on the Loch Ness Monster even though it looks somewhat confusing. It has been suggested that it is a dog with a stick as can be seen (inset) in this artist's impression.

Loch Ness

photographed in 1982 by Canadian Jennifer Bruce. She hadn't noticed anything unusual at the time. Is this the monster? Or is it something common, like a large bird or floating debris, disregarded at the time, and forgotten later?

ings: logs, boats, fish, animals swimming, optical illusions. Or it might have simply been a popular myth. Admittedly the first written account of the monster came in a legend about Saint Columba, a sixth-century missionary, who saved someone from the beast in the River Ness (not the Loch), though there is no reason to imagine this was anything other than a traditional miracle story.

In their book, *The Loch Ness Mystery Solved*, Ronald Binns and R J Bell manage to kill the suggestion that people had been spotting the monster for centuries. Urquart Castle, sited on the loch side, was occupied from 1297 if not earlier; no sighting was ever reported there, or none that has survived. Road builders working from 1732 never mentioned it, nor did the men who built the Caledonian Canal, whose work was centred on the loch. Victorian tourists visited Loch Ness

by the thousand, but none mentioned a gigantic beastie. Nor did staff from the Royal Geographical Society, who investigated the loch's geography and natural history during 1903 and 1904.

True believers often repeat the claim that it was the construction of the new road in 1933 which enabled people to get close to the loch and so see the monster more often; in fact, the road had been there for a long time, and was merely improved in 1933. In short, the sightings only really began when people were told that there was a monster in the lake's cold and murky depths. And they believed it was there because there was a – faked – picture to prove it.

But the search for the monster has been astonishingly persistent. Millions of pounds have been sunk, in some cases literally, in its pursuit. Amazing quantities

of technological equipment have been shipped to this remote lake, including gyrocopters, blimps, underwater cameras, sonar scanners and submarines – real ones, too. Sensible and reputable people have become convinced that there is something in the legend of a giant sea monster, including Sir Peter Scott, the distinguished naturalist, who was so certain that he even gave the monster a zoological classification, *Nessiteras Rhombopteryx*, meaning 'Ness beast with diamond-shaped fin'. No doubt his confidence was only slightly shaken by the discovery that the Latin name was a, presumably unwitting, anagram of the phrase 'Monster hoax by Sir Peter S'.

The monster has, like hemlines, had its ups and downs over the years. Interest tended to flag for a while, but in 1960 an aeronautical engineer called Tim Dinsdale took a short and largely indecipherable film of what he said was the monster moving along near the opposite shore of the loch. An RAF reconnaissance team analysed the film and said that it probably showed an animate object, possibly 90 feet long. Other people thought it was more likely to be a boat. One of these was Dr Maurice Burton, formerly of the Natural History Museum in London, who noticed that the apparent creature was moving at the same speed as motor boats on the loch, was much the same size, leaving the same kind of wake and following a route frequently employed by boatmen. The point at which Dinsdale said the monster suddenly submerged is the 'the spot where the boats I watched crossing over, in 1960, shut off their motor, turned hard towards the beach, and disappeared suddenly under the overhanging branches of trees,' Burton reported. Perhaps the 'monster' was a boat.

Whatever it really was, interest in the monster intensified again and hunters returned to the loch. More pictures of the beast appeared, sporadically. Some were obvious fakes, one appearing to be nothing more than a plastic sack with a stick put inside to make the shape of a neck. In 1972 a monster hunter called Frank Searle, who had moved to live by the lake, produced a set of impressive-looking photos, showing a sinuous object with a bulky body and a long neck, a mouth open as if feeding, apparently moving about in the water. However, a

Tim Dinsdale, the Loch Ness Monster hunter, who died in 1987. In 1960 he made a short film of the Loch Ness Monster.

leading monster sceptic, Steuart Campbell, discovered from a local garage owner who lives by Urquhart Bay – said to be a favoured locale for the monster – that on the day the pictures were taken a large and distinctive tree trunk had been washed into the bay by heavy rains. He thought – admittedly nine years after the event – that the 'monster' in the pictures clearly resembled the log he had seen. The 'mouth' appeared to be the point where the trunk had been broken.

This view was backed up by Charles Cazeau, a geology professor at the State University of New York in Buffalo, and the author of the book *Exploring the Unknown*. He said about the Searle pictures: 'Most damning of their authenticity as "monster" photos is, upon close examination, the lack of any indication of water disturbance around the "monster"...this "creature" is hanging dead in the water, like a tree trunk." '

Each sighting, and especially each picture, stimulates more interest, though in sixty-odd years nobody has yet come up with a picture which is remotely con-

Dr Robert Rhines at Loch Ness with the Academy of Applied Science team during a search for the monster in 1973.

vincing. Many sightings are without doubt honest, even if mistaken. It is notoriously hard to judge distances over long stretches of water since there are no objects of known size to compare things with. Otters can grow to surprising lengths and might easily be confused; indeed some of the sightings of the monster on land are certainly otters, since the behaviour matches. Groups of otters playing in the water could easily look like a monster on the move, especially in poor light. Boats can be confusing, and their wake can create a silhouette of ripples looking remarkably like serpentine coils. Dr Burton's theory was that some of the sightings were masses of rotting vegetation that had been forced up by their own gases, and appeared on the surface with an impressive amount of noise, heaving and commotion.

Quite the most ambitious attempt to find the monster was made by the Academy of Applied Science, an American body whose members spent several years exploring the loch, chiefly with sonar equipment. Sonar searches had been made of the loch at least twice before, in 1960 and 1962, but all these indicated what most people expected: because Loch Ness is short of nutrients, animal life there is scarce. However, in August 1972 the leader of the expedition, Bob Rines, produced what was the first picture of the monster to receive serious attention from serious scientists. The sonar equipment seemed to have detected a large moving object and the underwater camera took the picture. The simultaneous sonar traces would in turn help the team to interpret the pictures.

The results were somewhat disappointing to the layman's eye, showing little more than a large indeterminate shape. However, when these were enhanced by computer at the Jet Propulsion Laboratory in California – the high-tech equivalent of the Inverness chemist who handled the first monster photos – they appeared to show the fin of a prehistoric animal. It was this single image which led Sir Peter Scott to announce the discovery of Nessiteras and to produce a rather beautiful portrait of the whole monster, looking somewhat like a plesiosaur, frolicking with young ones. Necessarily this picture was based more on supposition than on established fact.

The original photos soon came under attack. Rikki Razdan and Alan Kielar, two American engineers specialising in underwater sonar work, made two important accusations. (Later they set up their own sonar array of 144 transducers, fixed to the surface, covering nearly 7,000 square feet in Urquhart Bay. Over seven weeks it recorded nothing more than a single $3\frac{1}{4}$ foot-long fish.)

Razdan and Kielar said that the sonar transducer used by the Rines team had, unlike theirs, not been fixed, but had been swinging freely around behind the boat – making the data it produced useless for constructing a 3D image of whatever was in the photograph. And, they said, the pictures had been enhanced twice – once in the Jet Propulsion Lab, and a second time before they were published. Rines denied these allegations. The argument between the two engineers and Rines swiftly became hostile and very technical. But the fact remains that since the flipper photograph, nothing remotely similar has been detected. What at one time looked like proof of the monster turned out to be yet another dead end.

The debate about the monster has become as predictable as so many others in the world of the paranormal. Believers argue that because there have been so many sightings, at least some must be valid. Non-believers point out that virtually every piece of evidence crumbles when it's examined closely. Negative evidence can never *prove* anything, at least not beyond the shadow of a doubt. But we are entitled to ask why no one has ever found any trace – of skin, of bone, or anything – to indicate the presence of a monster. It may be very nimble at avoiding humans when it's alive, but it could hardly pull the same trick when dead. Is it immortal? If not there must be a large breeding colony of monsters with many descendants. If it breeds and dies, then it must leave something of itself behind.

Finally there is the coelacanth argument. This is a fish, 5 to 6 feet long, which had been thought to be extinct for millions of years, until in 1938 one was caught off southern Africa. Several

SIR HUNT :
- Les sherpas
  ont vu
L'HOMME
DES NEIGES
VOIR SUITE PAGE 2

An artist's version of a Yeti waking sherpas with a Japanese Everest expedition, from 'Radar' magazine.

more specimens have since turned up. Which leaves us with the question, if the coelacanth can be found in the vastness of the oceans, how is it that a monster many times larger has evaded discovery in a 22-mile-long lake?

It is technically possible that, one day, a hitherto unknown beast will appear in Loch Ness. It is also technically possible that the authors of this book will play football for England. In neither case would it be wise to hold your breath waiting.

All this applies to almost all the world's other favourite monsters. The most famous, and most eagerly sought by cryptozoologists – people who look for evidence of animals unknown to science – are the Yeti of the Himalayas, and the Sasquatch of North America, often known as Bigfoot. But there are many others. Water monsters are supposed to dwell in Lake Baikal and the 'Ogipogo' is said to inhabit a lake in British Columbia. Australia has the Binyip, New Jersey the Jersey Devil, and giant pumas may or may not prowl the southern counties of England. Some may exist, though the evidence for most is very slight.

As Daniel Cohen shows in his chapter on monsters in *Science and the Paranormal*, it is a myth among fans of the Yeti that the people of the Himalayas believe in this hairy giant, half man and half animal. Such of their folklore as has been studied shows that the references are either to bears or entirely mythical figures.

References to people seeing the Yeti are almost all second- or third-hand. The first, and still by a long chalk the best, was by N A Tombazi, a Greek photographer who accompanied the 1925 Royal Geographical Photographical Expedition. He was camping at 15,000 feet in the mountains of Sikkim when his porters pointed something out. After peering through the glare, Tomabazi saw the creature, which he estimated was around 300 yards away.

'Unquestionably, the figure in outline was exactly like a human being, walking upright and stopping occasionally to uproot or pull at some dwarf rhododendron bushes,' he wrote later. 'It showed up dark against the snow and, as far as I could make out, wore no clothes. Within the next minute or so it had moved into some thick scrub and was lost to view.' He found the footprints, which were 'similar in shape to those of a man, but only 6 to 7 inches long by 4 inches wide at the broadest part of the foot. The marks of five distinct toes and of the instep were perfectly clear...' The porters thought they had seen a demon.

Since it looked like a man, walked like a man, and had the footprints of a man (if somewhat small) it would take quite a feat of the imagination to conclude that it was anything except a man. There is of course the problem of why it was apparently naked, and what it was doing tugging at the rhododendron bushes, but that part of the world contains many hermits and ascetics who might well walk around naked seeking unusual sources of food. Strange, certainly, but no stranger than a weird beast undiscovered by anyone else before or since.

In 1960 Sir Edmund Hillary, the first man to conquer Everest, led a commercially sponsored expedition to find the Yeti. He returned saying he had found no evidence for its existence and thought the whole idea was nonsense. He brought back with him a 'sacred Yeti scalp' claimed by Yeti fans to be revered by lamas in the local monasteries. It turned out to be a goatskin cap.

So the Yeti seems to be even more improbable than the Loch Ness Monster. However, North Americans have turned their attention to their own man-beast, the gigantic Bigfoot. This got its name from the first 'evidence' to turn up, when a road crew working in an isolated area of northern California in 1958 found huge footprints around their camp. One of them made a plaster cast and took it to a local paper. The Yeti was a subject of great interest then, and the idea of an American equivalent had huge appeal.

Then in 1967 the first film of Bigfoot was taken by two men, Roger Patterson and Bob Gimlin, who had been hunting for the monster, also in northern California. The film looks like a man in a monkey suit. On the other hand, one could argue, Bigfoot would *look* like a man in a monkey suit. At least this film has the virtue that – unlike in some of the other photographic evidence – you can't actually see the seams on the outfit.

Since then there have been plenty of sightings and no hard evidence. If we rule out a single immortal Bigfoot, there ought to be signs of a few dead ones, unless there is a secret Bigfoot Graveyard somewhere. No one has ever found the bones

Part of a frame from the movie taken by Roger Patterson in 1967 showing a Bigfoot.

Rene Dahinden (left) with a cast of a footprint said to have been found after the filming of Bigfoot by Roger Patterson who is shown here with the cast of a footprint found several years earlier.

or skin of a specimen. Much of the north-western United States is fairly sparsely populated, but thousands of people go hunting there, so that it seems almost miraculous that nobody has got close enough to get a really convincing photograph. The original footprints were probably hoaxes by somebody; if the creature is in the habit of leaving footprints around the place, why haven't we seen more since?

As it happens, some were found in 1982, and they turned out to be the most exciting yet. The prints were discovered in the Blue Mountains of Oregon at a place called the Mill Creek Watershed, which is generally off limits to the public because local streams provide drinking water for nearby communities. What was remarkable about these 15-inch long prints was that they showed dermal ridges, the foot equivalent of fingerprints. Dermatologists agreed that the ridges were worn in exactly the right places for an individual who walked barefoot for most of the time. Benny Kling, an expert on skin, said: 'Such highly specialised knowledge of primate dermal wear patterns would probably not be known to a potential hoaxer.' He also noted a pattern of dermal-ridge failure which occurred 'in the correct places, an almost impossible fact for even a sophisticated hoaxer to predict'.

The casts of the prints quickly became cryptozoological celebrities, turning up on TV, in newspapers and in magazines, helping to rekindle national excitement about Bigfoot. However, the story soon began to fall to pieces. It emerged that the day after the prints had been discovered, the US Forest Service – concerned that unknown primates might be stomping around its land – sent Rodney Johnson, a wildlife biologist, to investigate. He found that the forest litter, such as pine needles, had been brushed aside before the track was made. It also looked to Johnson as if the foot had been rocked from side to side to make the track. Even more damaging was the fact that the stride did not appear to change even when the creature was climbing uphill. Neither its toes or heels showed any signs of slipping on the steep slope.

Next the Forest Service sent a Border Patrol officer, Joel Hardin, to investigate. Hardin is an accomplished tracker who searches for fugitives and lost hikers by picking up tiny traces of their passing, such as bent grass, and scrape marks. He could not find any sign of the creature either before the tracks began or after they finished. Since the thing did not presumably dematerialise, the tracks must have been a hoax.

That conclusion seemed inescapable after more was discovered about the man who found the tracks, a Forest Service patrolman called Paul Freeman. Mr Freeman had had a long history of discovering dubious Sasquatch bits and pieces, such as hair and dung. He has admitted faking footprints in the past. And earlier in his life he worked for an orthopaedic shoe company. Writing in The *Skeptical Inquirer*, Michael Dennett described how he had found a cobbler in Portland who was willing and able to make a cast of a real person's foot which would show the dermal patterns perfectly clearly. Men with feet as big as the Mill Creek prints are uncommon, but they do exist, and would need to go to a specialist company to get their shoes.

With such painstaking research positive evidence is turned into yet more negative evidence, though of course the believers will still keep the faith come what may. But cryptozoologists are in many ways nicer people than some of the characters in this book. Most are motivated by the genuinely romantic notion of finding a great unknown creature. Some want the satisfaction of demonstrating that so-called experts don't know everything. A few try to take money off sensationalist newspaper editors, but they don't relieve desperate people of their savings by claiming to predict their future or give meaning to their lives.

As Daniel Cohen put it:

'In the main, monster hunting is a harmless, even charming activity. There are, after all, far worse ways to spend a summer than sitting on the shores of Loch Ness looking for the monster, even if you don't find it.'

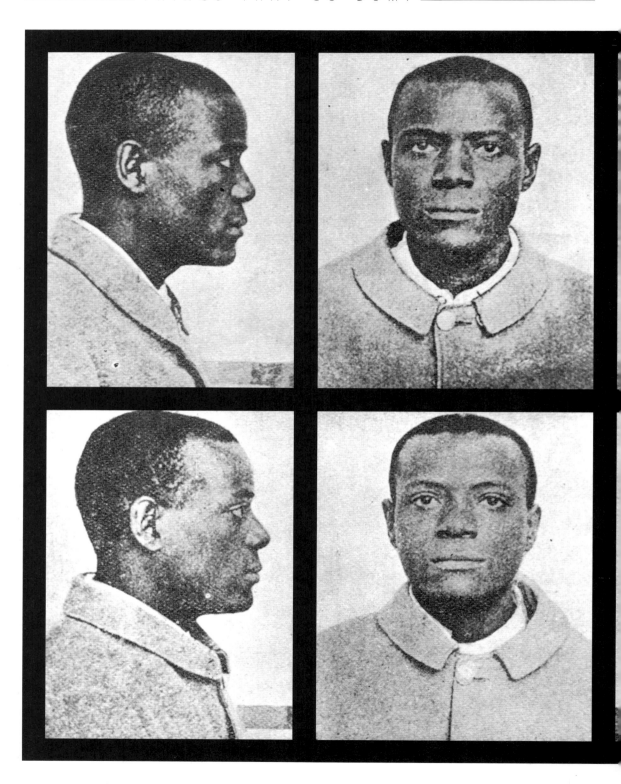

Coincidence

IN 1980, SIMON HOGGART WAS WRITING a travel article about Texas. As he walked past the Alamo in the city of San Antonio, he saw a familiar figure – Peter Riddell, the political analyst, a friend from London. Neither had had the faintest idea the other was in the United States. Over a drink, they discussed the odds against the two of them, in that whole vast continent, walking down exactly the same street at exactly the same time.

A few months later Mike Hutchinson was reading a paragraph which mentioned grain alcohol, C_2H_5OH, in the first line. His wife was watching TV in the same room. At that very instant a trailer was shown for a play later that evening. Its title was 'C_2H_5OH'.

In 1994, Simon Hoggart's wife was travelling with a friend on a tube train. They were to visit an exhibition in central London. She was talking about the actor, Richard E Grant, who she did not know, but who lived in her neighbourhood. The friend said she could not place him; what did he look like? At that moment, Richard E Grant got onto the train, and sat opposite them. He was holding a ticket for the same exhibition they were going to.

Few of us cannot recall similar coincidences. We think, for the first time in years, of a long-lost friend who emigrated to Canada. That moment the phone rings, and it's them on the line. How often has it happened that you decide to ring someone, and, just as you are about to dial, they call you? You badly need to find an out-of-print book and mention this problem to a colleague, who says that the author was their uncle and can get you a copy immediately. You tell a friend that you dreamed about them last night: they were in danger while swimming in the sea. Astonished, your friend says that at the same time you were dreaming about him swimming he was dreaming that he was drowning.

In his book *Coincidence*, the late Brian Inglis recounted what is sometimes called the *ne plus ultra* of coincidences. As a schoolboy in Orleans, the poet Emile Deschamps was given a taste of plum pudding – then hardly known in France – by a M de Fontgibu. Ten years later, strolling in Paris, he noticed a plum pudding in a restaurant window, and went in to ask for a slice. The woman behind the counter called out to another customer: 'M de Fontgibu, would you have the goodness to share your plum pudding with this gentleman?'

Many years after that, he was invited to dine in a Paris apartment, and his hostess told him he would be having plum pudding. Jokingly, he said he was sure M de Fontgibu would be one of the party. When the pudding was served, the door opened and a servant announced 'M de Fontgibu'. At first Deschamps thought this was a joke, but it wasn't: M de Fontgibu, by now an old man, had been invited to dinner in the same house but had come to the wrong apartment.

Such events seem astonishing to us. (Especially to *us*; research shows that people are far more impressed by coincidences which happen to them rather than similar events in the lives of other people.) Naturally we sometimes imagine that they cannot be the work of chance alone. Yet the fact is that there is no reason to suppose that they are the result of anything except chance, however powerfully we must feel that this is not enough of an explanation.

Look at the three true incidents at the start of this chapter. They seemed amazing at the time, but appear slightly less so after a moment's thought. If Hoggart or Riddell had asked themselves that morning what were their chances of meeting the other at 3.55 pm in the street opposite the Alamo, they would have concluded that they were infinitesimal. Try putting it another way, though: 'What are the chances that I, who travel quite a lot, will one day run unexpectedly into somebody I know well?' The answer must be: 'very great'.

Similarly, the chemical formula appeared on TV in front of millions of people. Of those, dozens, perhaps even hundreds, might have encountered it in another context for the first time that day. That would bring them up short for a moment. But it's not surprising that *someone* might actually be reading about the same subject at the same time – startling for Hutchinson, of course, but not for anyone who considers *all* the people who were watching that channel at that moment.

The sighting of Richard E Grant seemed astounding for the two women involved, enhanced by the fact that he is a well-known celebrity. But again, put it another way: 'Two friends were going to an exhibition. A neighbour who planned to go to the same show got on the same train, at a time they were talking about him.' A coincidence, to be sure, but hardly earth-shattering, and likely to be repeated in different ways thousands of times all over the country.

The story of M de Fontgibu and the plum pudding is remarkable, and unlike many other experiences recounted here, something so extraordinary will not happen to most of us. Even so, the middle part of the story is a weak link: it boils down to 'two people who both like a particular dessert meet in a restaurant which advertises it in the window'. As a whole the story can be summarised: 'By chance, a man bumps into an old acquaintance just as he is eating the dish the acquaintance introduced him to.' Fascinating and surprising, yes; so astonishing that we must seek an explanation from beyond the known world, perhaps not.

Though people do seek such an explanation. We can hardly blame them. Extraordinary events occur in the world, and newspapers say something like: 'Statisticians say that the chances against this happening are fourteen million to one.' We are duly amazed. Yet the chances of anyone winning the British National Lottery are fourteen million to one, and someone – occasionally several people – wins most weeks. (The odds against one particular person winning the jackpot in two particular successive weeks are 196 billion to one, which would be truly remarkable.) We can hardly blame the winners for imagining that they have been singled out in some way by Fate, rather than by chance. If they chose six numbers from, say, the birthdays in their family, they might well believe that these were blessed in some magical way. But as Martin Gardner put it:

'It is easy to understand how anyone personally involved in a remarkable coincidence will believe that occult forces are at work. You can hardly blame the winner of the Irish Sweepstakes for thinking that Providence has smiled on him, even though he knows it is absolutely certain that someone will win.'

More examples of the same principle can be seen whenever there is an air crash. It usually turns out that several people missed the flight: they took a wrong route on the way to the airport, they decided to cancel their trip for no particular reason, they had a flat tyre. The plane goes down and, of course, it would be almost superhuman not to imagine that Fate had decided to spare you. Yet the fact is that numerous people booked on every flight fail to get on board; airlines use this knowledge to 'oversell' seats and keep their profits up. There is nothing extraordinary in the fact that this also happens with flights which crash, however miraculous it must seem to those whose lives are spared.

The difference is between the *union* of events, and the *intersection* of all the components. The Israeli psychologist Ruma Falk describes something which happened to her during a stay in New York. One New Year's Eve she met an old friend from Jerusalem, at the very crossroads where she was staying.

'The first question we asked each other was: " What is the probability that this would happen?" However, we did not stop to analyse what we meant by "this". What precisely was the event, the probability of which we wished to ascertain?

'I might have asked about the probability, while spending a whole year in New York, of meeting, at any time, in any part of the city, anyone from my large circle of friends and acquaintances...the number of such combinations is immeasurably large; therefore, the probability that at least one of them will actually occur is close to certainty.'

Since we are dealing with a virtually limitless multitude of events, it's almost impossible to measure the chance that any one coincidence will occur – still harder to judge what particular coincidence might happen out of all the millions and billion which could take place. However, the physicist Luis Alvarez tried just that in 1965. He told the journal *Science* that he had been reading a newspaper, and one phrase in it had reminded him of a long-forgotten figure from his youth, someone he hadn't thought about for thirty years. Less than five minutes later, leafing through the same newspaper, he came upon the man's obituary.

Parapsychologists often assume that some kind of thought transference must be at work; Alvarez was caused to think about the old acquaintance by an outside force or agency. He reckoned otherwise, and using fairly cautious assumptions, worked out that the probability of a coincidental recollection of a known person in a five-minute period just before learning of that person's death is 3×10^{-5} per year. Less technically, this works out at around 3,000 occurrences per year in the US alone, or about fifty-eight a week. Alvarez was no doubt surprised that it happened to *him*, though, as he points out, *we* should not be surprised that it happened at all.

Ruma Falk devised a test to find out just how unlikely people thought particular coincidences were. By presenting them in different ways, it would be possible to demonstrate that the an event which might seem near miraculous when described in one style, could appear far more probable in another – even though both versions were entirely accurate.

She gave seventy-nine adults a true story and asked them to rate it for perceived likelihood in four different versions. The first she terms 'past intersection', or PI. A female soldier in the Israeli army had told her that on the previous day, her nineteenth birthday, she had been hitchhiking from the outskirts of Jerusalem, towards a small and little-known settlement in the Western Negev called Mivtahim, where she worked as a teacher. The first driver who stopped for her was going to exactly that settlement.

The 'past union', or PU, version told the same story, but adding the facts that the young woman often hitchhiked and that Mivtahim is on a major highway, making it more likely that someone would be driving through there.

The 'future union', FU, version cast the same story into the future while describing the same general union of events. The soldier is about to start work as a teacher and will be hitchhiking to her job. She wants to know what the chances are that sometime during the coming year she will be offered a lift to the settlement – which is on a major highway.

The last version was the 'future intersection', or FI. This was a much more specific question. The young woman wanted to know what were the chances that precisely on her nineteenth birthday, the first car which stopped would be going directly to the town of Mivtahim where she works.

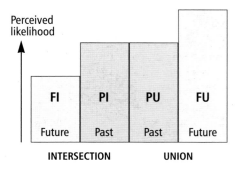

A diagram produced by psychologist Ruma Falk showing how people perceive coincidences depending on whether the event is in the past (P) or the future (F), and whether it is specific (I) or less specific (U).

Perceived likelihood

FI	PI	PU	FU
Future	Past	Past	Future
INTERSECTION		**UNION**	

Falk repeated the experiment in the United States, changing some details to make the stories more American. But the results were much the same: people thought the 'future intersection', i.e. that all those particular events would happen at the same time, the least likely of all. They rated the 'past intersection' and the 'past union' events roughly 50 per cent more likely (perhaps because of their knowledge that the past intersection had actually happened already). The subjects thought that the most probable version – twice as likely as the future intersection – was the 'future union' (see chart). As we mentioned in describing Simon Hoggart's encounter in San Antonio, the FU version: 'What are the chances that during your travels that somewhere unexpected you will run into a friend?' seems far more likely than 'What are the chances that you will bump into a particular person, at a particular time, in a particular place?'

Then there is the selection fallacy. By isolating the surprising events from all the teeming circumstances of our lives, we make them appear more astonishing. A comparison would be shooting an arrow into a door and then drawing the target around it. The classic instance of this misleading technique is the Lincoln/Kennedy spooky parallels list. This list of similarities between the famous assassinated presidents, is constantly printed in American newspapers and has become

The assassination of President Abraham Lincoln shot by John Wilkes Booth at a theatre in Washington, DC, in April 1865. From a lithograph by Nathaniel Currier (1813-1888) and James Merrit Ives (1824-1895).

Frame from a film showing the moment the first bullet struck President John Kennedy at Dallas, Texas, on 21 November 1963.

part of the national sub-culture. As usually told, it goes:

1 Lincoln was elected president in 1860, Kennedy in 1960.

2 Both were concerned with civil rights.

3 Each has seven letters in his surname.

4 Lincoln had a secretary named Kennedy and Kennedy had a secretary named Lincoln.

5 Both were succeeded by southerners named Johnson.

6 Both were assassinated by men with three names, John Wilkes Booth and Lee Harvey Oswald.

7 Booth and Oswald both espoused unpopular political ideas.

8 Booth shot Lincoln in a theatre and hid in a warehouse; Oswald shot Kennedy from a warehouse and hid in a (movie) theatre.

Some lists are longer, but the general idea is clear from this one. Even on the

short list, many of the comparisons are pretty feeble (3, 6) and some are just vague (2). Johnson happens to be the second most common name in America (5). Both 7 and 8 are inaccurate: Booth fled to a barn, not a warehouse, and his ideas were extremely popular in large parts of the US, unlike Oswald's communism. What's more, the list is quite arbitrary. You could find thousands of aspects of each man's life, and by picking and could find plenty of similarities. (Naturally, the list of dissimilarities would be much longer.)

Nevertheless, many people do find the list surprising and even eerie – maybe there is some mysterious link between the two presidents; perhaps destiny is doomed to repeat itself in the lives of great men.

John Leavy, a computer programmer at the University of Texas, got so fed up with seeing this list repeated that he decided to see if he could match up other pairs of American presidents. It proved very easy. He even found six pairings from the lives of Thomas Jefferson, one of the most highly esteemed presidents, and Richard Nixon, one of the most reviled. (Both had vice-presidents who left after scandals, both lost an election to a Harvard graduate named John from a wealthy Massachusetts family before finally winning the presidency, both were succeeded by southerners named James...) In a subsequent competition in *The Skeptical Inquirer*, a reader in Mexico won by finding no fewer than sixteen equally spooky parallels in the lives of JFK and assassinated Mexican president Alvaro Obregón.

The fact is that most people read thousands of words every day: in newspapers, magazines, books, letters and adverts. We hear tens of thousands more spoken, on radio, TV or in conversation. Innumerable thoughts pass through our minds. Hundreds of events happen to us from the minor and commonplace, such as stepping in a puddle, to the unusual and dramatic, such as being mugged or meeting the love of one's life. It would be quite astounding if coincidences didn't occur. If someone lived to be seventy-five and never, ever experienced some strange conjunction of thought and word, or deed and memory, then their lives would perhaps be worthy of study.

However, the psychologist Carl Jung believed that chance was not an adequate explanation of some coincidences. A few were so incredible that 'chance' occurrence could only be expressed by astronomical figures. (Of course, that is what we are dealing with. As Stephen Jay Gould says: 'Give me a million years, and I'll flip a hundred heads in a row more than once.' We are luckier than Gould; we are dipping into a reservoir provided by billions of people to whom thousands of things are happening every day.)

Swiss psychologist
Carl Gustav Jung (1876-1961), who believed that some coincidences must be caused by 'another principle, namely the contingencies of events'.

Jung believed that some coincidences must be caused by 'another principle, namely the contingency of events'. He coined the term 'synchronicity' for this, as distinct from synchronism, which meant things occurring at the same time.

His often-quoted first instance was the story of a young woman patient who had dreamed she was given a golden scarab. As she spoke to Jung, he heard a gentle tapping on the window behind him. It was a common rose-chafer, the nearest equivalent to a scarab in Europe. Contrary to its usual habits, it was trying to get into a darkened room.

Jung saw this as much more than a surprising chance. The scarab was an ancient symbol of rebirth, which fitted in with his belief in messengers from the collective unconscious. Jung's patient had been a strictly rational person and the course of treatment had been going badly; this event broke through her mental armour and 'the process of transformation could at last begin to move'.

It seems an awful lot of weight to place on a very small incident. A woman is talking about a beetle; a not dissimilar beetle – possibly disoriented – is in the meantime banging against the window. Still, if it helped the woman's treatment we can at least say it was fortunate.

Brian Inglis described another event which he suggests indicates synchronicity. He called it 'the most remarkable case' of its kind. It happened just after the Second World War. A publisher, Jeffrey Simmons, found that a sexy thriller had been bound in covers meant for a children's book. It was cheaper to pulp the lot, but he hadn't the name of a firm which could do the job. An office boy said he did know of one.

'I asked our switchboard operator to look up their number and telephone them for me. "Their representative is here," was her reply...in fact he had walked in literally seconds before I spoke to the operator. He told me the office was on his beat...he had passed the office almost every weekday for years, but had never called in.' When Simmons asked him why he called now, 'he said he did not know: something just told him to do so.'

If that's the most remarkable example, one can, charitably, say that the theory of synchronicity remains unproven. 'Man who works for a pulping firm calls, on impulse, at a company which might well need some pulping done,' is hardly an astounding event. Much rests on the man saying that 'something just told him' to call in. But we all do umpteen things for no particular reason – calling at a shop we've never been in before, phoning a friend we've lost touch with, taking a different route to work. This impulse only seems strange and remarkable if your long-lost brother happens to be in the shop, the friend turns out to have died that morning, or the different route to work means you avoided a runaway petrol tanker. The alternative is to believe that there is some unknown force in Nature which protects and looks after publishers with a pulping problem.

Nor does synchronicity always work in people's favour. In July 1944, as Inglis points out, Count Stauffenberg left the bomb in the briefcase under the table where Hitler would be standing. One of the generals in the room noticed it, and moved it out of the way, so that the wooden plinth on which the table was standing diverted the blast, saving Hitler's life. Tens of thousands of people died between then and the end of the War, as a direct result of this chance.

We can add all the people who had called on impulse into Northern Ireland pubs just before the assassination squad arrived with their machine guns. Or the people whose business ended sooner than expected, so that they could catch the earlier flight, which crashed...

Undeterred, believers in synchronicity continue to spin their theories. Arthur Koestler wrote in *The Roots of Coincidence* in 1972:

'We thus arrive at the image of a world mosaic or cosmic kaleidoscope, which in spite of constant shufflings and rearrangements also takes care of bringing like and like together.'

As Ruma Falk puts it, he imagined a prolonged process of random mixing, and decided that the clusters – or coincidences – which he saw could not be random. If they were random, they could not appear in clusters, so that an explanation must be required.

This is the gambler's fallacy, or clustering illusion – the belief that if red has come up five times in a row, black must almost certainly come up on the sixth turn of the wheel. It's nonsense; if the wheel is not crooked, and so produces completely random results, then red has just as much of a chance on the sixth turn and on every one that follows. (Suppose you stood by a spinning roulette wheel and noted which colour slot the ball fell in. What are the odds that the same colour will come up in all of the next six spins? The answer is one in sixty-four, which means that event happens before the wondering gaze of gamblers thousands of times every day throughout the casinos of the world.) According to Thomas Gilovich in his book *How We Know What Isn't So*:

'Random distribution seems to us to have too many clusters, or streaks of consecutive outcomes of the same type, and so we have difficulty in accepting their true origins. The term illusion is well-chosen because, like a perceptual illusion, it is not eliminated by repeated examination.'

As is so often the case with belief in the paranormal, it is much less a matter of logic than of emotion. Some of us feel the need to believe that our lives are being guided by some outside power; some don't. As Koestler himself agreed in *The Challenge of Chance*:

'Whether one believes that some highly improbable meaningful coincidences are manifestations of some such unknown principle operating beyond physical causality, or are produced by that immortal monkey at the typewriter, is ultimately a matter of inclination and temperament.'

Bibliography

BOOKS

Abell, George O and Singer, Barry: *Science and the Paranormal,* Junction Books, London, 1981

Baker, Robert A and Nickell, Joe: *Missing Pieces: How to Investigate Ghosts, UFOs, Psychics and Other Mysteries,* Prometheus Books, New York, 1992

Baker, Robert A: *They Call It Hypnosis,* Prometheus Books, New York, 1990

Beattie, John: *The Yorkshire Ripper Story,* Quartet Books, London, 1981

Beyerstein, Barry L and Beyerstein, Dale F (ed): 1992 *The Write Stuff: Evaluations of Graphology, the Study of Handwriting Analysis,* Prometheus Books, New York, 1992

Binns, Ronald: *The Loch Ness Mystery – Solved,* Prometheus Books, New York, 1984

Brandon, Ruth: *The Spiritualists: The Passion for the Occult in the Nineteenth and Twentieth Centuries*, Prometheus Books, New York, 1984

Christopher, Milbourne: *Seers, Psychics, and ESP Cassell,* London, 1970

Coleman, Michael H (ed.): *The Ghosts of the Trianon,* Aquarian Press, Wellingborough, 1988

Culver Roger B and Ianna, Philip A: *Astrology: True or False: A Critical Examination of the Evidence,* Prometheus Books, New York, 1988

Edmunds, Simeon: *Spiritualism; A Critical Survey,* Aquarian Press, Wellingborough, 1966

Eysenck, H J and Nias, D K B: *Astrology: Science or Superstition,* Temple Smith, London, 1982

Fairley, John and Welfare, Simon: *Arthur C Clarke's World of Strange Powers,* Collins, London, 1984

Harris, Melvin: *Investigating the Unexplained ,* Prometheus Books, New York, 1986.

Hendry, Allan: *The UFO Handbook: A Guide to Investigating, Evaluating and Reporting UFO Sightings,* Doubleday, New York, 1979

Hines, Terence: *Pseudoscience and the Paranormal: A Critical Examination of the Evidence,* Prometheus Books, New York, 1988

Hyman, Ray: *The Elusive Quarry: A Scientific Appraisal of Psychical Research,* Prometheus Books, New York, 1989

Jones, Nella with Davenport, Shirley: *Ghost of a Chance,* Pan Books, London, 1982

Klass, Philip J:
UFOs:The Public Deceived, Prometheus Books, New York, 1983

UFO-Abductions: A Dangerous Game, Prometheus Books, New York, 1988

Korff, Kal K: *Spaceships of the Pleiades: The Billy Meier Story,* Prometheus Books, New York, 1995

Kurtz, Paul (ed.): *A Skeptic's Handbook of Parapsychology,* Prometheus Books, New York, 1985

Kusche; Larry: *The Bermuda Triangle Mystery Solved,* Prometheus Books, New York, 1995

Loftus, Elizabeth F: 'The Reality of Repressed Memories', *American Psychologist* Vol. 48, pp518-537, 1993

Nickell, Joe (ed.): *Psychic Sleuths: ESP and Sensational Cases,* Prometheus Books, New York, 1994

Pearsall, Ronald: *The Table Rappers,* Michael Joseph: London, 1972

Playfair, Guy Lyon: *If This Be Magic,* Jonathan Cape: London, 1985

Randi, James:

Flim-Flam!: The Truth About Unicorns, Parapsychology and Other Delusions, Prometheus Books, New York, 1982

James Randi: Psychic Investigator, Boxtree, London, 1991

The Mask of Nostradamus: The Prophecies of the World's Most Famous Seer, Prometheus Books, New York, 1993

The Supernatural A-Z , Headline, London, 1995

Schnabel, Jim: *Round in Circles: Poltergeists, Pranksters, and the Secret History of Cropwatchers,* Hamish Hamilton, London, 1983

Sheaffer, Robert: *The UFO Verdict: Examining the Evidence,* Prometheus Books, New York, 1981

Stein, Gordon: *The Sorcerer of Kings: The Case of Daniel Dunglas Home and William Crookes,* Prometheus Books, New York, 1993

Vogt, Evan Z and Ray Hyman: *Water Witching USA,* University of Chicago Press, Chicago, 1979.

Wilson, Ian: *The After Death Experience,* Sidgwick & Jackson, London, 1987

MAGAZINES

The Skeptical Inquirer, Buffalo, New York

Index

Figures in **bold** refer to illustrations

Picture Credits